TRAILS SOUTH

TRAILS SOUTH

The Wagon-Road Economy
in the Dodge City–Panhandle Region

By C. Robert Haywood

UNIVERSITY OF OKLAHOMA PRESS : NORMAN AND LONDON

Library of Congress Cataloging-in-Publication Data

Haywood, C. Robert (Clarence Robert), 1921–
  Trails South.

  Bibliography: p.
  Includes index.
  1. Trails—Kansas—History. 2. Trails—Oklahoma—
History. 3. Trails—Texas—History. 4. Kansas—
History. 5. Oklahoma—History. 6. Texas—History—
1846–1950. I. Title.
F681.H38 1986   978.1′031   85-40946
ISBN 0-8061-1987-X (alk. paper)

TO

Marie, my wife—who was not only patient, sympathetic, and self-sacrificing as we explored the trails, but also survived the jolting ruts of the rough drafts

Louis Haywood, my cousin—who read the maps and pointed the way as he rode shotgun while we sorted out the true from the mythical trails

Contents

Illustrations

Maps

Preface

As a child, I was aware of the old ruts of the Jones and Plummer Trail, which cut across my great-grandfather's homestead in Meade County, Kansas. There are advantages and handicaps to being indigenous to the locale of a historical study. In my case, my grandmother's tales of the Blizzard of '86 made that a fearsome and personal adventure. On the other hand, I have a hard time visualizing the dry draw that we called the Mulberry as a flowing stream with whitecaps, dangerous in its crossing to cowboy and freighter alike or romantic enough to be a rendezvous for the flamboyant General George A. Custer. Nothing in my immediate vicinity as a child seemed important or unusual enough to be historical. Even today I need to remind myself that familiarity breeds historical contempt.

The great advantage I had was that I knew there was a Jones and Plummer Trail. Both the professional and popular histories I have read over the years concerning Dodge City and environs gave much space to trails leading north into Kansas. But these were cattle trails headed for the stockyards of the Cowboy Capital of the World. The dusty business of freighting was largely ignored. All trails in Kansas seemed crowded with Texas cattle, and even the one ballad alluding to the Jones and Plummer Trail I knew lamented the passing of "the last cattle trail."

Only the old-timers in their reminiscences, oral histories, and tall tales remembered the old ruts, the creaking wagons, and the sod way stations. To them the trails were once their anchor of safety and compass as they came onto the lonely prairie. Old settlers remembered the visit to an isolated road ranch with the same excitement and thrill as a contemporary child would recall a weekend visit to Kansas City or New York. If the trails south were so important to these little people, the undocumented first settlers, they must have been significant in the larger development of Kansas. I was to discover a new region extending into the Texas Panhandle, larger than many eastern states, held together by the freighting trails with Dodge City as an unofficial capital.

During the summers of 1982 and 1983, my cousin, whose father had run cattle in southwestern Kansas and the Oklahoma Panhandle as a young man, and I traveled south, tracing the freighting trails. We were aided by the descendants of pioneers who recalled what those who remembered it firsthand had to say and by the town historians who had followed fact, gossip, myth, and old maps. The trails were not forgotten; their history simply had not been recorded systematically. The wealth of documents in major libraries of four states served as a check on tradition and secondhand remembrances. But to walk the old ruts and visit the sites of old road ranches, the town and county historians were invaluable.

Published local histories tend to be designed for two readerships: the professional historian, who requires careful, documented analyses that reflect case studies or unusual insights into the larger historical mosaic, and the general reader who is interested in personalities, the flavor of lifestyles, or tales of adventure, tragedy, humor, and successes of recognizable common folk. A growing number of social historians do not see these as incompatible objectives. The settlement and early nurturing of the Dodge City–Panhandle Region seemed uniquely fitted for a happy blending of the two approaches.

Indispensable aids to research were the many librarians, known and unknown, who recovered elusive materials and made helpful suggestions. To Wilma Rife, Readers' Service Librarian, Washburn University, who turned the cranks and cogs of the magical machine known as Interlibrary Loan, go special thanks. Others who assisted include Claire Kuehn and T. Lindsay Baker of the Panhandle-Plains Historical Museum; Joseph Snell and staff at the Kansas

State Historical Society; J. Evetts Haley, who gave of his rich files and facilities with a generous hand; Richard Welch, Boot Hill Museum; Betty Braddock, Kansas Heritage Center of Dodge City; and the staff of the Barker Library, University of Texas-Austin, where I was received graciously as a Visiting Scholar.

Descendants of old-timers and local historians are too numerous to mention. A few, however, who gave unusual assistance were Rex Reynolds of Niles, Michigan; Bill Jones of Anaheim, California; Berenice Jackson of Gage, Oklahoma; and Fred Squyres of Dumas, Texas.

Robert Richmond of the Kansas State Historical Society and Mary Rowland and Tom Averill of Washburn University, who read with a critical and helpful eye the semirough drafts, greatly enhanced the quality of the final production. Donna Carter, who restores order out of chaos on the word processor, and Anne Fund, who maintains order in the History Department, were of much assistance. Naturally, I take, and deserve, all credit for errors.

A sincere word of appreciation goes to Washburn University for time release and financial aid and to the Washburn College Trustees for the Mary B. Sweet Sabbatical grant.

C. ROBERT HAYWOOD

Topeka, Kansas

TRAILS SOUTH

1. The Dodge City–Panhandle Region

We, and all others who took land, came south from Dodge City. We kept as near the beaten trails as we could because they were the anchor of safety. The trail was the only compass we had on these lonely prairies. —Mrs. E. May Novinger, Meade County, Kansas pioneer[1]

AT ONE POINT in the historiography of the United States, the study of regionalism took on the dimensions of faddish popularity. The proper use of such terms as *area, regional, sectional,* and *localism* were the sources of heated debates. *The South, Prairie Provinces,* and *Trans-Mississippi West* were expressions given nuances of meaning that were understood to help explain why certain areas in certain times developed as they did. Professor Howard W. Odum of the University of North Carolina found the concept "a highly useful instrument of analysis, understanding, and synthesis in the social science." As a frame of reference, the concept was useful but, unfortunately, overrefined and frayed to tatters. If the problems of precise definitions can be set aside, however, the study of a geographical area, reflecting its cultural and economic similarities, can contribute to the clarification of that region's development and its place in history.[2]

In the 1870s and 1880s there was such a region—localized area or subdivision, if you will—in what was to become the panhandle of Texas and Oklahoma and in southwestern Kansas. For those few

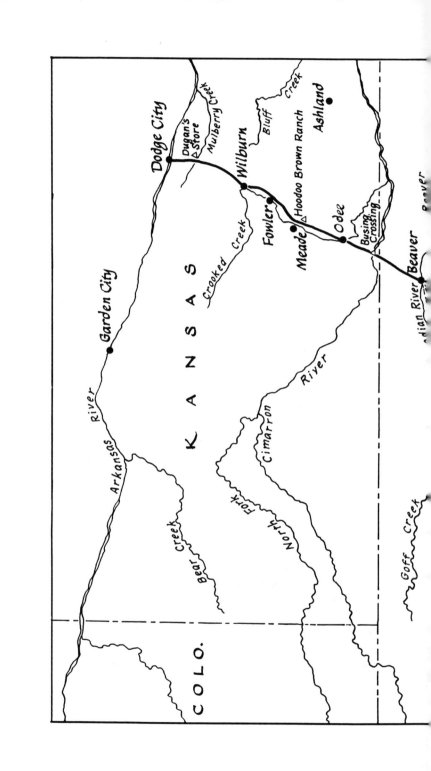

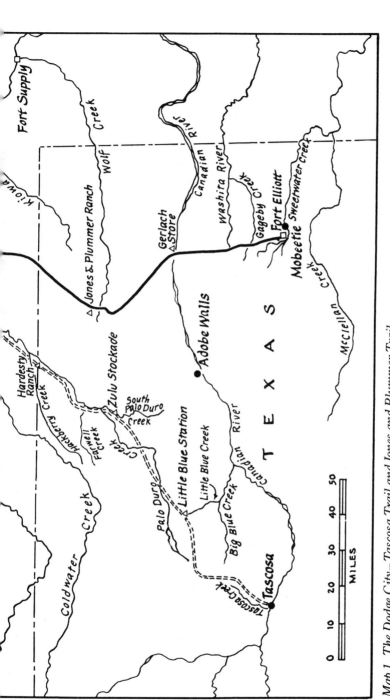

Map 1. *The Dodge City–Tascosa Trail and Jones and Plummer Trail*

years, that section of the West appears to have had enough distinctly identifiable and significantly interdependent characteristics to warrant a separate designation. The area met most of the agreed-upon criteria of a region. There was cultural consistency, which uniformly changed as the economic base was altered; there were common physiographical and demographical characteristics, such as rainfall and population density; there were shared attitudes relating to the land, the natives, dress, and acceptable social behavior; there was interdependence of trade area, market, and transportation lines; and, finally, there was a recognition of this commonality by those who lived there.

The region at hand can best be described as a ragged, imprecise triangle encompassing the upper panhandle of Texas, the northwestern tier of counties plus the panhandle of Oklahoma, and the major portion of half a dozen counties in southwestern Kansas. Irregular fingers of related territory extended from the triangle at some points, as they did in the south while Clarendon flourished in Donley County, Texas. What held the region together were the north-south lines of communications connected at their base by an east-west route, forming a tenuous interior skeleton. These freighting trails with their north-south orientation to Dodge City did much to maintain the region. Other trails and roads, including railroads, exerted varying degrees of pressure on the continuity of the region, but such pressures were successfully resisted until near the close of the 1880s; continuity remained intact for at least two decades. In order to have a shorthand designation for the area, it will be referred to as the Dodge City–Panhandle Region or, simply, the Region. It is at best an awkward term. However, political divisions have so firmly labeled the geographical areas today that the triangle symbol and the Dodge City–Panhandle designation is as clear as any that can be found.

At the apex of the Region stood Dodge City, with the three trails—the Dodge City–Fort Supply Trail, or Military Road, the Tascosa–Dodge City Trail, and the Jones and Plummer Trail—converging on the railhead that gave the town its preeminence. For a quarter of a century Dodge City was to be the marketplace for and the purveyor of goods to the Region. Whether the economy was fueled by buffalo hunters, cattlemen, or grangers, the town remained the essential hub as long as the wagon-road economy existed. Dodge City's astute journalist Nicholas ("Nick") Klaine explained in an editorial titled "Our Southern Tributary":

The topographical position of a country has much to do with its destiny. History points to great centers of trade that have grown up through their superior commercial advantages endowed by nature. . . . Dodge City lies in a favorable position . . . at the gateway of a great country that leads south and southwest . . . in a direct line with the eastern boundary of the Panhandle of Texas. That vast extent of country is a tributary to this by reason of the advantages nature has given.

With a town booster's myopia, Klaine must have assumed that the Santa Fe Railroad was a localized natural phenomenon on the order of the Arkansas River or the hills of Dodge City. He implied that geography and railroad construction had combined to give Dodge City a kind of manifest destiny to dominate the region. These conditions did, in fact, make Dodge City the center, if not the capital, of the Region in all but governmental matters.[3]

As the unofficial capital, Dodge City was an amicable host, and the arrangement was mutually satisfying. Cattlemen from Potter County, Texas walked the streets with as much easy familiarity as those from Ford or Clark counties in Kansas. The citizens of Beaver, Oklahoma tended to describe their town's amenities in terms of comparison with Dodge City. When a Dodge City merchant, such as Charles Rath, thought of expansion, the new opportunities at Adobe Walls, Texas seemed as natural as adding a new warehouse on Front Street. The Dodge papers carried social items from Clarendon, "jottings from the Panhandle," and the reports of the Tascosa market as regular features. The salty comments of Old Cactus and Young Cactus, the Fort Supply correspondents, were as familiar to the readers of the *Dodge City Times* as Nick Klaine's editorials. Gamblers, such as Johnson Gallagher, floated between Mobeetie and Dodge with the seasonal trade or as their luck changed. J. Wright Mooar reported a similar pattern for the soiled doves, who "just made a grand circuit down there. Any number of those women at Tascosa were Dodge City women." The common interest of all the Region was accepted without question.[4]

There was, in fact, little competition for the merchants of Dodge

Dodge City in 1874, a widely distributed postcard view of the town at the opening of the wagon-road era.

City. The editor of the *Ford County Globe* hoped this fact would not be lost on prospective settlers and businessmen:

As a commercial emporium, Dodge City has no equal, in proportion to size, in the west; being situated only fifty-two miles from the north line of Indian Territory, and being the nearest rail road point to that vast country contained in the western half of the Territory, the Pan-Handle of Texas, and all of Kansas situated south of the Arkansas River and west of Dodge City, and to which she is the commercial key, her business assumes proportions that are truly enormous. Millions of pounds of supplies are here transferred from the rail road trains to the mule and cattle trains, which permeate this vast country in all directions. To Fort Elliott, to Camp Supply, to the cattlemen who are located upon every creek and river, and last, but not least, to the immense number of men, who are constantly engaged in buffalo hunting. For a verification of the above, we ask the skeptical to look at the map of the Western States, and see the immense tract of country which is compelled to draw its supplies, either from or through Dodge City.

Although some goods and services did trickle into the Region from the south, Dodge was the uncontested center of trade. Buffalo hunters did use other markets sparingly, and even loads of Panhandle bones were sold at Texas railheads, but never in the quantity offered to the Dodge merchants. In 1883, Nick Klaine editorialized that in seeking business at Wichita Falls, Mobeetie no doubt would "benefit from a healthy competition." The seriousness of the threat, however, was noted in reporting a mule train that had reached Mobeetie from the Texas rival carrying three thousand pounds of goods on the same day an ox train from Dodge delivered one hundred thirty-seven thousand pounds of supplies. Texans tried repeatedly to divert mail routes to the south but generally were thwarted by the more competitive bids from Dodge. Fort Bascom also had trade and military connections with the Panhandle Region, since it was supplied by the northern town; however, it remained an isolated appendage to the Region. In spite of these minor intrusions, Dodge City remained the main source of trade and contact with the outside world. Dodge City merchants in turn were totally dependent upon the Atchison, Topeka and Santa Fe Railroad to bring the goods of the world to their point of dispersal.[5]

Through three economic phases that beneficial relationship between the Kansas town and the inland Region did not change; not until new railheads emerged was there a major shift of business. What had been a natural region was then split into three distinct political units with new east-west configurations. Like Charles Goodnight's drift fence, the state lines seemed to cut off historical relationships that had developed from the earliest settlements. Today, as far as parochial historians are concerned, the history of the Oklahoma Panhandle is unique; the Texas Panhandle has its own bibliography; Kansans see little connection between the Canadian River and the Cowboy Capital of the World. The existence of the once clearly defined Region has been forgotten. Unfortunately, acceptance of the Region is not all that has been lost in this transition. The slicing of the Region's history into present-day political units has lessened our ability to see the significance of the agencies and institutions that created the Region's unique character and fit it logically into the flow of frontier history. Oklahoma-based agents were not the exclusive molders of Oklahoma's development. The Texas Panhandle did not always look south for support. Southwestern Kansas has not always been oriented toward Topeka. The wagon roads and those who used them in servicing the Region in the 1870s and 1880s were not restricted by arbitrary state lines, and it is this apolitical condition that was fundamental to the success of the transitional period in the Region.

One of the most perceptive of the explorers the United States government dispatched to the Region was Lieutenant James H. Simpson of the Corps of Topographical Engineers. In 1848 he was assigned to accompany a large expeditionary force seeking to find and charter a more southerly route to the gold fields of California. His instructions were to make a "report and plan . . . in which you will include all circumstances bearing upon the facilities in grass, wood, and water." On his return, Simpson's official response reflected not only a keen awareness of the natural attributes of the region, but his own philosophical bent as well. He speculated on the effects of the "Noahic deluge" on land formations, gave advice to future travelers, and made recommendations on dealing with the Plains Indians. His most cogent remarks, however, were those related to the transcontinental railroad and the settlement of the area. He wrote of the railroad: "That this work will some day be accomplished, I would not be so presumptuous as to say that it will not; but that it can be commenced now, and be brought to successful period within ten or twenty years I do not believe." The reason for his hesitancy obviously was not the formidable nature of the terrain. With the exception of some erratic river crossings, the level topography was to make, at a later date, some of the easiest track laying in transcontinental railway construction. The difficulty, as Lieutenant Simpson saw it, was in building through and maintaining a line in sparsely populated country. There was not, as he insisted, "a good, producing population," developing the resources of the land, that would sustain the railroad. On the surface, this seemed a convoluting dilemma. Railroads could not be supported without a productive population; a productive population could not be developed without adequate transportation. But Simpson saw a solution. As an alternative to railroads, he advocated military roads, that is, wagon roads, and the construction of forts along their routes to support migration and around which centers of population could develop.

In a word, to my mind the order of means in respect to the establishment of this railroad is, first the creation of centres of population wherever along this route they can be created; second, the development of the resources of these several points by this population; and, third, the taking advantage of these resources to aid in the prosecution of the road.[6]

History was to follow Simpson's scenario with remarkable precision. There were to be forts and military roads, and there was to be a period of wagon-road economy. For twenty years between 1868, when the Camp Supply military route was laid out, and 1888, when the stagecoach era in the Region generally ended, there occurred the kind of transitional phase Simpson had suggested. The existence of the wagon roads connecting the chain of military forts made life possible for the folk who were to become "a good, producing population." As in the cardiovascular system of a living body, a network branched out from the main arterial roads to a myriad of barely discernible capillary ruts carrying the essentials of settled life into the remotest areas of the Region. As soon as the rail magnates felt the permanency of the surging strength of these pulsing arteries, that is, the transportation of large quantities of goods, tracks were pushed into the area. The Fort Worth and Denver City reached the lower Panhandle in the summer of 1887 (Clarendon in July), and the Rock Island set off celebrations in Clark and Meade counties as it passed through the center of the upper Kansas area a few months later (Minneola in Clark County, December 1888; Fowler in Meade County, January 1888).

In a brief, two-decade span the wagon-road economy had altered Simpson's suggestion to the status of prediction. Although the population of the Region was thinly scattered, it was clear to more than just the railroad builders that the resources of the land were beginning to be used and growth would be assured. The transitory flashes of prosperity brought by the trail drivers' cattle and the buffalo hunter's slaughter, with its separate meat, hide, and bone phases, were replaced by more substantial and durable granger and ranching enterprises. The trails south played a major role in this transition.

It was an essential phase, an exciting, tough, and vigorous time. Those who held the locomotive power, that is, the freighters and wagoners, were expected to meet the personal and commercial needs of a rapidly changing and expanding population. Freight, supplies, and mail had to move with some certainty, regardless of weather or road conditions. Millions of tons of goods to forts, towns, ranches, farms, and troops in the field were dependent upon ox, mule, and horse power. Business and military communications had to be relatively swift and very sure, expressed in the phrase coined by the Post Office Department: "with celerity, certainty, and security." The wagoners responded to the challenge. How well they responded can best be judged by the rapidity and eagerness with which the railroads claimed the Region for their own.

In other sections of the West the federal government played a direct role in developing the wagon-road network. W. Turrentine Jackson has effectively demonstrated the federal government's contribution in determining and maintaining wagon roads. In the Dodge City–Panhandle Region, however, direct federal assistance was quite limited. The United States Army did stake one of the major trails and did maintain another in passable condition, if not always in good repair. The indirect aid was, on the other hand, highly significant. The contracts for carrying freight to the forts in the early years and the mail contracts throughout the period accounted for much of the traffic on the trails. Furthermore, the protection the army gave, first to the buffalo hunter, who cleared the last natural impediment to ranching and farming from the Region, and then to the ranchers and farmers, who filled the void, was essential if permanent settlers were to be attracted to develop the land.[7]

For all his rugged independence, the buffalo hunter left a record of dismal failures in protecting himself in confrontations with the Indians. Rancher-Indian relations on the surface appeared more favorable, considering the kinds of uneasy accommodations made by such men as Charles Goodnight. However, rancher-cowboy attempts to use force to settle the issue, as in Dull Knife's raid or the aftermath of the Adobe Walls fight, were no more effective than that of their sharpshooting, buffalo-hunting compatriots. If the plains were to be cleared of hostile tribes, what was needed was the dogged persistence of a Ranald S. Mackenzie leading a military expedition supported by the full military resources of the nation. Only by such force and courage were the equally courageous and resourceful Indians subdued and restrained, an essential, albeit tragic, historical epoch. Still, it was not the military accomplishments that made the period between 1868 and 1888 a successful transitional one of population and economic growth. The army's exploits did not prove the Region's worth and potential. The reports of the official government explorers, such as Stephen H. Long, J. W. Abert, Randolph Marcy, and Simpson, even when their findings were widely published, only hinted of the possibilities to be found in the Dodge City–Panhandle Region. The potential could be realized only by individuals who were brought to the Region and were supported by outside markets and contacts once there. Mackenzie's remarkable trek across a desolate area like the Staked Plains might demonstrate that life could be sustained there, but it was the extension of the wagon trails into remote regions that proved "good, producing populations" could prosper there.

It is also true that the extension of cattle trails through the Region had few lasting effects or, for that matter, little immediate impact on the territory through which they passed. The cattle trail was intended only to convey a commodity, cattle, from one terminus to another as quickly and with as little contact with people along the way as possible. Wagon roads, on the other hand, required local involvement and were designed to serve as many people in an area as possible. Where the freighting trails made direct and continuous contribution, cattle trails had little more to do with the territory through which they passed than do the flight patterns of today's airliners as they fly over small western Kansas towns at forty thousand feet. Way stations, road ranches, and towns dotted the wagon trails; few posts on the order of Doane's Store on the Red River and no towns developed along the Great Western Cattle Trail. Once the business transactions were complete in Dodge City, the trail driver attempted an even more rapid passage back to his home base. Where a cattle trail avoided people, especially the permanent settlers, a wagon trail lured, encouraged, and sustained the come-to-stay citizen. The wagon trail was indeed the settlers' compass and anchor of safety. Throughout the transitional period when the prairie was changed to a settled community, the trails gave orientation and direction to settlement.

Therefore, the emphasis of this study will be on the trails: the motivation for their establishment, the restraints and opportunities they afforded, the personalities that shaped them and were in turn changed by the experience. To that extent, this book may appear on the surface to be an examination of a failure, since none of the trails existed for any great length of time. Today only a hazy memory, a few sod-covered depressions in the soil, and an occasional highway marker note their passing. Of the towns founded to take advantage of the trails—all conceived of ninety parts of euphoria to every ten parts of reality—only those remain whose location coincided with the new, more serviceable rail lines. With the ruts obliterated, few concrete reminders of the trails are in evidence today: the community museum at Beaver, Oklahoma for the Jones and Plummer; a few street names, such as Military Avenue in Dodge City; and a rare preservation, such as the stage drivers' bunkhouse at Fort Supply.

If the focus of this history is on the trails, it is to be remembered that roads were only the means, not the substance, of commerce. The men who drove the wagons and stages and manned the way stations are the active cast in the drama. Their backgrounds were as diverse as those of any pioneer population on the cutting edge of the frontier. They came off the farms of Kentucky and Wisconsin, from the Maine woods, and from the industrial towns of Ohio and New England. Not a settled state, eastern or southern, went unrepresented. A few people could claim educational accomplishments and important family connections, but most could not. In the main, they were young adventurers looking to improve their lot. Once their brief stint on the wagon roads was over, many remained in the Region to become homesteaders, ranchers, and storekeepers in the new towns. Others moved on, following the will-o'-the-wisp of new and grander opportunities offered by the untamed and unsettled frontier. Contributions of both types, although minor and brief in their trail days, when considered as a group and as a lifetime venture, become crucial to the evolution of the Region. If there is validity in Wilbur Zelinsky's concept of "The Doctrine of First Effective Settlement," the men and women who developed the wagon-road economy and remained as permanent settlers were an important element in placing the first, strong imprint on the culture of the Region.[8]

Standing somewhat apart from the drivers and way-station keepers, who invested little more than their time and courage, were the entrepreneurs, the owners of freighting and mercantile firms, such men as W. M. D. Lee, Charles Rath, Robert Wright, and Casimiro Romero, the organizers of commerce, who operated with different motives and made substantially larger commitments to the Region. They filled a role similar to that of the cattle kings. Like the large ranchers, they "tried to dominate their environment, and at least succeeded in modifying it." The hired drivers and independent road ranchers, as was true of the cattle kings' cowboys, tended to compromise "with their environment at relatively low levels," accepting the conditions of their hire and the hardships of the frontier as they did the inevitable weather. Both classes must be dealt with. The entrepreneurs will be much in evidence but will be specifically and more thoroughly represented by one mail contractor who built a modest but successful network of stage lines in the Region. The career of Philander Gillette (usually referred to as P. G.) Reynolds roughly approximated the life of the Dodge City–Panhandle Region. He came to Dodge City in 1875 when the trails were beginning to take form and died in 1888 as the wagon-road era was closing down. Toward the end, he, too, began stretching his holdings beyond the Dodge City–Panhandle network, absorbing other lines that were experiencing the disintegration of regional unity and the advancement of a new economy and settlement. Reynolds' life can be used as a case study of the entrepreneurial venture that preserved the short-lived but essential unity of the Region.[9]

The hired and independent drivers, freighters, and way-station keepers also will be discussed. Buffalo hunters–turned–trail blazers, farm boys who matured quickly into manhood as freighters, lumbermen from timber states converted to prairie stage drivers—all play small but significant roles. The lives and backgrounds of certain of these pioneers are treated in some depth, revealing something of the character and courage of these men and women who changed forever the nature of the prairie and left the imprint of their lives and convictions upon the Region. When possible, their own words are used to describe conditions as they found them.

The transformation of the raw prairie of the buffalo to the settled communities of ranchers and grangers passed with the certainty of time. The men who used the trails south in their enterprise were instrumental in transforming the Region from what it had always been to what they believed would be a better place to live and die.

2. The Dodge City–Fort Supply Trail: From Military Road to Commercial Highway

THE October 1867 Treaty of Medicine Lodge was a dazzling show-piece for both the Indians and the army. Satanta, Little Raven, and Black Kettle were never more eloquent. They spoke of their desire to grow old in peace on the prairie, of their disappointment with their white brother and the sorrow in their hearts at the killing of the buffalo. Now they had come willing to "listen to the good word" so that the chiefs could lay down lance and bow. All five of the major Plains Indian tribes were there, thousands of them, with the two hundred fifty Cheyenne lodges prominently in sight. And the soldiers came. As one Indian eyewitness reported, "they came and came and came, in part of the evening and all night. I did not know when they stopped coming in." Commissioner Nathaniel Taylor welcomed each tribe and spoke as forcefully as the chiefs of a troubled Great Father and the white brothers' desire for peace. The sixty wagons of presents were distributed, papers signed, promises made. The red man and the white smoked and drank whiskey together and pledged lasting friendship.[1]

Despite the pageantry and dramatic oratory, both forces at the council knew that Medicine Lodge was little more than an interruption in the continuing conquest of Indian lands as the frontier moved west. The Cheyennes and Arapahos broke camp at the end of the council and moved south as they had agreed to do. Other tribes and other individuals were not impressed with the sincerity

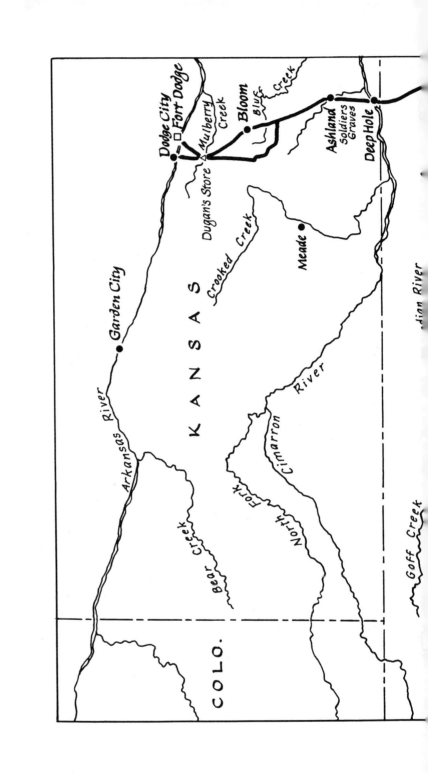

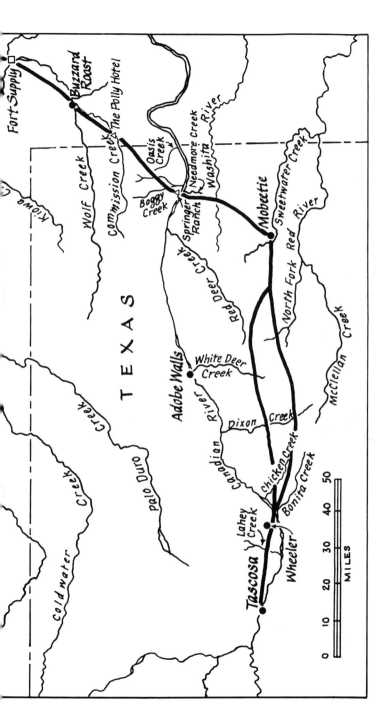

Map 2. The Military Road (Dodge City–Fort Supply Trail) and the Fort Elliott and Tascosa Extension

of the white man. Roman Nose did not sign. And before the main body of lodges were struck, some four hundred Indians already were heading north from the Cimarron, their lives committed to a warrior who would not surrender. By June 1868 the Cheyennes had raided the Council Grove countryside and the Kaw Reservation, and Major General Philip H. Sheridan had been placed in command of the Department of Missouri with orders to control Indian depredations by driving them south of the Kansas border, "pursuing to kill if necessary."[2]

It was a difficult assignment, although not a disagreeable one for the general. The summer of 1868 saw brief skirmishes, but the army was for the most part helpless in the face of the scattered, free-ranging tribes, who used an attack-and-run strategy. Winter was another matter. If Sheridan could maintain his troops in the field—better fed, better clothed, better mounted and better armed than his adversary—he was certain he could force his will on the Indians. The key to his strategy, the absolute necessity, was supplies. At this point the concept of Camp Supply and a protected trail to it from Fort Dodge turned into reality.

Brigadier General Alfred Sully had noted a likely site for a base camp on his extended scouting expedition in the Panhandle during the fall. He was now put in command of a force consisting of elements of the Nineteenth Kansas Volunteer Cavalry and the Seventh U.S. Cavalry with orders to march south and establish a temporary "camp for supplies." On November 12 the forces assigned to the expedition were joined at Mulberry Creek just south of Fort Dodge by an immense train of approximately four hundred wagons guarded by a few companies of infantry. Heading south, the troops proceeded to Cavalry Creek, then on to Bear Creek, the Cimarron, and the Beaver, a distance of one hundred thirteen miles. On November 18 they reached Wolf Creek at its confluence with the North Canadian, the site Sully had noted in his earlier tour. The spot was identified as Camp Supply. For the moment it was assumed that Camp Supply would be a temporary base, lasting only until General Sheridan had completed his winter campaign. It was a shortsighted view of the tenacity of the Indian and the difficulty of the terrain in which they were to find refuge.[3]

The first passage down what was to be known as the Military

Camp Supply, Indian Territory, as seen in Harper's Weekly Magazine, *February 27, 1869. Courtesy Western History Collections, University of Oklahoma Library.*

Road was one of the most impressive expeditions in the West. Among the officers of this force of more than one thousand one hundred men and four hundred wagons was Lieutenant Colonel George A. Custer, who described in detail the line of march:

> Everything being in readiness, the cavalry moved from its camp on the north bank of the Arkansas on the morning of the 12th of November and after fording the river began its march toward the Indian Territory. That night we encamped on Mulberry Creek, where we were joined by the infantry and the supply train. General Sully, commanding the district, here took active command of the combined forces. Much anxiety existed in the minds of some of the officers, remembering no doubt their late experience, lest the Indians should attack us while on the march, when, hampered as we should be in the protection of so large a train of wagons, we might fare badly. The country over which we were to march was favorable to us, as we were able to move our wagons in four parallel columns formed close together. . . . The infantry on beginning the march in the morning were distributed throughout the train in such a manner that should the enemy attack, their services could be rendered most effective. Unaccustomed, however, to field service, particularly marching, the infantry apparently were only able to march for a few hours in the early part of the day, when, becoming weary, they would straggle from their companies and climb into covered wagons, from which there was no determined effort to rout them. In the afternoon there would be little evidence perceptible to the eye that infantry formed any portion of the expedition, save here and there the butt of a musket or point of a bayonet peeping out from under the canvas wagon-covers, or perhaps an officer of infantry "treading alone his native heath," or better still mounted on an Indian pony, the result of some barter with the Indians when times were a little more peaceable, and neither wars nor rumors of wars disturbed the monotony of garrison life. [4]

From the first excursion in November 1868 until near the time Camp Supply was abandoned and turned over to the Department of Interior on February 26, 1895, a safe and convenient road was to be a key link in the military and economic development of the Dodge City–Panhandle Region. For the next quarter of a century, the road that followed the route marked by the Nineteenth Kansas Cavalry was to carry supplies to two forts, to the troops in the field during three winter campaigns, to a growing number of reservation Indians, to the new, isolated towns, ranchers, and settlers. As the major military supply line it remained, until the Jones and Plummer

Trail took over part of the burden, one of the most heavily traveled roads south and one of the most familiar in the Western Plains. Within days of the arrival of the first caravan—in fact, as soon as Sheridan felt it safe enough to do so—a train of 250 empty wagons was sent north for supplies, followed on December 8 by another 180 wagons, which reached Fort Dodge on December 14. Later in December, 270 additional wagons went up the trail to be refilled, and still the requirements of the winter campaign were not fully met. However, the troops and horses were rarely hungry, and supplies in sufficient quantity to complete the campaign successfully proved the wisdom of attacking the Indians in winter. As the first season drew to a close, the number of trips to and from Fort Dodge was greatly reduced, and for the wagoners there was to be a welcome, if short, respite. The Indians had not fared well in the cold and snows of the plains warfare and were now forced to go to one of the designated forts, where they could be kept under surveillance. Camp Supply was assigned as a temporary reservation. With a large number of defeated Indians assembled, more or less peacefully, around the camp, plus the soldiers garrisoned there, more than 1,500 rations had to be delivered every ten days. Wagons once again creaked and groaned their way between Forts Dodge and Supply in a near-endless procession.[5]

To compound logistics problems, the camp had become a permanent establishment. Since recent recruits had crowded the garrison to nearly six hundred men, much of the fall of 1869 was spent providing new living quarters. Five new barracks were added, constructed of upright logs nine feet high. The top of each ninety-foot-long building was covered with logs and a layer of earth a foot thick. The picket logs were chinked with wood strips or mud to keep out the wind. Married men's and officers' quarters were smaller and private, with the added advantage of an attached kitchen. Although the heavy log-and-earth construction kept out the cold and wind, it also shut out the sun and air. The quarters were damp, and "toadstools and mushrooms sprang up nightly, to be cut down each day."[6]

Up to this point, the military trains had followed Sully's first line of march, but during the winter of 1869, Lieutenant I. Wallace surveyed the territory between the two posts, and Ben Clark, the chief army scout, selected a more direct route that shortened the distance by some twenty miles. The old route was known after 1876 as the Mount Jesus Road because it passed near the hill bearing that name. The new route was to the west of the original trail, and with a few minor variations, including a terminus at Dodge City, it was to remain the principal road south into the Panhandle for many years; for the next two, it was used almost exclusively to accommodate military traffic. Mail, supplies, and troop movements were always under escort. Civilians might travel alone at their own risk or attach themselves to a military train. Frequently, military details were sent out to reinforce the escort of a train deemed to be lacking in sufficient supporting strength.

The early treks down the military trail revealed many of the difficulties that were to beset it as long as it existed. A firsthand account of some of the earliest passages was recorded by young Alfred Lee Runyon, who had been employed briefly by two newspapers in Manhattan before he joined the Nineteenth Kansas Volunteers. His letters back to his old boss, published in the *Manhattan Standard*, recorded the passage of his regiment from Topeka to Camp Supply and his service there. He and others in his company were assigned escort duty accompanying supply trains over the Military Road. His first trip "opened very cold and disagreeable," and others failed to improve much. At one point he thought "the elements were trying which could out do the other. It rained, snowed, blew, and hailed tremendously." Even the easy crossing at Mulberry Creek proved disastrous. "The first day out," Runyon reported, "we camped on Mulberry Creek. In crossing the train over the creek, two mule teams tangled, and one of the drivers was knocked down and run over, the wagon passing over his breast. He was taken up and sent back to Fort Dodge. He was severely, if not fatally, injured."[7]

Communication, both official and personal, was vital to the new outpost, and couriers and scouts brought official messages with reasonable dispatch. Routine business and personal mail, on the other hand, were served poorly, and the morale of the troops suffered. Until late 1870, mail came once a week to Camp Supply from Fort Hays via Fort Dodge. Post commander Colonel John Davidson, responding to the troops' complaints, allowed Captain Richard T.

Jacobs to seek more deliveries. With one enlisted man in a buckboard, Jacobs made a nervous trip to Fort Larned, traveling at night to avoid Indian attack. For his efforts he succeeded in getting a promise of one additional delivery each week. But even with an escort and using the camp's ambulance, mail call was erratic and uncertain, totally dependent on irregular delivery service as long as it remained in military hands. Although the natural hazards of weather and the trail made all communication difficult, the reason for the poor mail service was largely a matter of military priority. The Indian threat was more or less constant, and dealing with real and imagined incidents took precedence over troopers' morale.[8]

Satanta, who thought more of his old and continuing grievances than he did his hour of oratory at Medicine Lodge, continued to raid trail herds and threatened even greater destruction. The Kiowas also were restive, although a minor campaign drove them south for a while during the winter of 1869–70. To make the trail more secure and provide a point of refuge along the Dodge-Supply route, a temporary station was established in December 1869 just south of present-day Ashland. The first of a series of redoubts to be built, it was on the east bank of Bear Creek about halfway between the two forts. Known as Soldiers' Graves, the redoubt was named in honor of two soldiers, John Conniston and August Buck, who were killed and buried there May 1, 1870. As part of a detachment protecting supplies at the redoubt, they were shot while offering food to a small band of Indians who had ridden in professing peaceful intentions. All of the soldiers stationed there would have been killed but for the timely arrival of the cavalry. In the words of Fort Supply correspondent Old Cactus: "The Indians discovered them [approaching] and cried 'Washuchu sappa' and retreated without waiting to count their scalps." This incident was the first indication of renewed hostilities.[9]

Throughout the spring of 1870 both the Kiowas and Cheyennes became increasingly active in attacking mail detachments and supply trains. Patrols had to be sent out frequently to rescue beleaguered parties. In June the danger came home when Camp Supply itself was attacked. Cheyennes and Kiowas boldly fired into camp, attacked individuals who wandered even a short distance afield, and made several attempts to drive off camp stock. Colonel Davidson decided that, for the safety of military traffic on the trail, two more redoubts should be added to the Bear Creek camp. He first proposed a new earthwork on Upper (East Branch) Bear Creek thirty-three miles south of Dodge, and later (February 12, 1871) Captain John H. Page was dispatched to build Cimarron Redoubt thirty-eight miles north of Camp Supply and about three miles from the Kansas–Indian Territory line. The latter fortification was just east of Redoubt (Big Sandy) Creek and became known as Deep Hole, a name it retained when it was designated a post office in May 1881. Captain Robert P. Hughes continued work on the redoubt at Deep Hole, but Lieutenant Faye W. Roe replaced him in command before the structure had been completed, with specific orders to halt the bootlegging of whiskey. [10]

Roe, a recent graduate of West Point, was accompanied by his wife, Frances. She left an unusually accurate and personal description of the new camp:

The redoubt is made of gunny sacks filled with sand, and is built on the principle of a permanent fortification in miniature, with bastions, flanks, curtains, and ditch, and has two pieces of artillery. The parapet is about ten feet high, upon the top of which a sentry walks all the time. This is technically correct, for Faye has just explained it all to me, so I could tell you about our castle on the plains. We have only two rooms for our own use. These are partitioned off with vertical logs in one corner of the fortification and our only roof is of canvas.

When we first got here the dirt floor was very much like the side of a mountain—so sloping that we had difficulty setting up the chairs. Faye had these made level at once, and dry, fresh sand sprinkled everywhere. [11]

With a few housewifely touches, Mrs. Roe soon brightened the place, but the extreme cold weather and danger of Indians did little to ease her mind:

Some of the men are working at the wood still, and others are making their quarters a little more decent. Every tiny opening in our own log walls has been chinked with pieces of blanket or anything that could be found, and the entire dirt floor has been covered with clean grain sacks that are held down smooth and tight by little pegs of wood, and over this rough carpet we have three rugs we brought with us. At the small window are turkey red curtains that make very good shades when let down at night. There are warm army blankets on the camp bed, and a folded red squaw blanket on the trunk. The stove is as bright and shining as the strong arm of a soldier could make it, and on it is a little brass tea kettle singing merrily.

Altogether, the little place looks clean and cheerful, quite unlike the "hole" we came to. Farrar has attended to his part in the kitchen also and things look neat and orderly there. . . .

At the first coming of the blizzard, the sentry was ordered from the parapet, and is still off, and I am positive that unless one goes on soon at night, I shall be wholly deaf, because I strain my ears the whole night through listening for Indians.[12]

Captain Richard T. Jacobs gave an equally good description of the northern redoubt on the East Branch of Bear Creek, which closely resembled Deep Hole in design:

The redoubt which we built was about fifty feet square. The interior wall was built of burlap bags, filled with earth. Loose earth was filled against this wall on the outside, sloping down to a trench which was about fifteen feet wide. The wall or embankment was about ten feet thick at the base. Bastions were built at diagonally opposite corners. There was a stable for the mules on the inside of the enclosure, built against the wall on the western side. On the eastern side there was a living room and kitchen for the men. Both of these structures were of "hackall" or stockade, the earthen embankment forming one wall of each. The roofs were covered with earth and were a foot or two lower than the walls, so that they could be occupied for defensive purposes in case of an attack. A well was dug on a high creek bank, or second bottom, [on] the outside of the enclosure, near the gate, which was at the northeast corner.[13]

The three earthen citadels were to stand in place of way stations, which served less-troubled trails, until the Indians finally were pacified by the Red River War of 1875. The redoubts' importance grew as the functions of Camp Supply changed, so that by 1878 the post was no longer considered a temporary base for supporting troops in the field but became another link in a chain of forts designed to ring the remaining hostile tribes on the Western Plains. A number of new assignments related to support of the campaign were carried out, but the old role of patrolling the military road remained and increased as the Indians became more aggressive. All mail, supply, and contractor trains were required to be under military guard. The policies were strict and spelled out in detail. Marches were cut to shorter stints twice a day, with substantial rest periods between them. Extra precautions were taken. Flankers were placed well out from the main body of troops, and posted pickets were warned to be on the alert.[14]

Even with the strictest escort requirement the trail was considered unsafe throughout the winter of 1872–73, although there were relatively few specific incidents. But an Indian raid was not the only, or even the gravest, danger a freighter faced. A sudden blizzard sweeping across the trail could be far more deadly than an attack by warriors who were generally not well armed. Robert M. Wright, one of the first Dodge Citians and an experienced freighter, describes one such December storm that required the aid of a relief party:

In the summer and fall of 1872 I was freighting supplies from Fort Dodge to Camp Supply, I.T. Up to the middle of December we had had no cold weather—plenty of grass all along the route. I loaded some twenty-mule wagons with corn, along about the twentieth of December, and the outfit crossed the river at Fort Dodge, and went into camp that night at Five-mile Hollow, about five miles from Fort Dodge. It had been a warm, pleasant day, and the sun disappeared in a clear sky. Along in the night the wind whipped around in the north, and a blizzard set in. By morning the draw that they were camped in was full of snow, and the air so full that one could not see from one wagon to the other. The men with the outfit were all old, experienced, plainsmen, but the suddenness and severity of the storm rendered them almost helpless. They had brought along only wood enough for breakfast, and that was soon exhausted. They then tried burning corn, but with poor success. As a last resort they began burning the wagons. They used economy in their fire, but the second day saw no prospect of a letting up of the storm, in fact, it was getting worse hourly. It was then that P. G. Cook, . . . and another whose name escapes me, volunteered to make an effort to reach Fort Dodge, only five miles distant, for succor. They bundled up in a way that it seemed impossible for them to suffer, and, each mounting a mule, started for the fort. The first few hours, Cook has told me, they guided the mules, and then recognizing that they were lost, they gave the animals a loose rein and trusted to their instinct. This was very hard for them to do, as they were almost convinced that they were going wrong all the time, but they soon got so numbed with the cold that they lost all sense of being. They reached the fort in this condition, after being out eight hours. They each had to be thawed out of their saddles. Cook, being a very strong, vigorous man, had suffered the least, and soon was in a condition to tell of the trouble of his comrades. Major E. B. Kirk, the quartermaster at the fort, immediately detailed a relief party, and, with Cook at their head, started for the camp. The storm by this time had spent itself, and the relief party, with an ample supply of wood, reached them without great hardship, and the entire outfit, minus the three wagons which had been burned for fuel, were brought back to the fort. Cook's companion was so badly frost-bitten that amputation of one of his limbs was necessary to save his life.[15]

During the next two years the trail was bloodied frequently. In June 1874 Dodge City experienced an authentic Indian scare, and the headlines of the local paper would have made any eastern yellow journal proud. Major E. E. Compton, with the mail escort, was attacked on June 19 just south of Dodge, and six Indians were killed in the fight that followed. One of the troopers later displayed the scalp he had taken in various saloons around town. In November the first white man was killed and scalped on the trail while bringing a wagonload of wild turkeys to Camp Supply. This was followed by an attack on the mail party on the way to Dodge, and two days later another escort had to fight off Indians on its trips to and from Camp Supply. Reports of other Indian depredations in the Panhandle began coming in with alarming frequency.[16]

The news of the Adobe Walls fight on June 27 put Camp Supply into a flurry of activity, and once again the Military Road was to serve as a supply line for a major campaign. The Red River War, which was to extend through the winter of 1874–75, had an enormous appetite. Thousands of pounds of goods, ammunition, ordnance, and supplies were required. By November nearly 300,000 rations, plus 100,000 pounds of grain and 107,000 pounds of ordnance, medical supplies, and clothing, were stockpiled at Camp Supply in readiness for the winter campaign. As was usual in such peak seasons, freighters were much in demand, and even old, experienced scouts, such as Bat Masterson and George Reighard, were converted to teamsters. Perhaps not as dangerous as scouting, the life of a freighter was not an easy one. The supply trains found travel throughout much of the winter impeded by frigid weather and heavy snows. Ox teams were stalled, animals froze, and teamsters suffered cruelly.[17]

The successful completion of the Red River War guaranteed the safety of buffalo hunters in the Panhandle and in turn doomed the Indian-buffalo culture to extinction. The Military Road was to be free of Indian harassment after the spring of 1875; although there were Indian scares, there were no major incidents related specifically to the trail. With the threat of Indian depredations removed, the country south of Kansas opened for settlement, and civilian travel increased dramatically. New status was given to the old temporary camp when it was designated Fort Supply in December 1878.

Ironically, just as the camp was officially recognized as a significant and permanent military base, the military importance of the old road declined. The exclusive military character had begun to wane when the buffalo and hide hunters turned to it as a major route to the eastern Panhandle herds. By 1875, travel was considered safe enough to relax escort service and to turn the mail contracts over to civilians. The nature of the traffic was much altered by then, and the trail became more of an artery of commerce than a military supply line. Way stations and road ranches replaced redoubts, and even the name changed in common parlance from the Military Road to the Dodge-Supply Trail or the Fort Supply Trail.

Up to that point the trail had followed the traditional pattern of federal development of wagon roads described by W. Turrentine Jackson. The dominant role had been played by agents of the federal government, in this case the army, in locating, surveying, and protecting the road. The four years of army control had determined to a large extent the nature of the traffic, since both of the road's termini were federal military installations. But, as was true of the pre–Civil War trails, the demands of the army had not excluded either the entrepreneur or the settler. The result was that a new route of migration had been opened. The removal of hostile Indians from the area ended the necessity for military control, but until the close of the wagon-road era the army's presence was maintained. The first phase in the life of the Fort Supply Trail had ended.

The second phase of the Dodge City–Fort Supply Trail ushered in civilian dominance. Military operations in the eastern Panhandle continued for a time, but when the hide men began using the trail, military traffic became secondary. The northern terminus shifted from the military post at Fort Dodge to the commercial and shipping center of Dodge City. After 1874 a major inducement to use the Dodge City route was a new toll bridge, but even before it was completed the town, with growing commercial facilities and an Atchison, Topeka and Santa Fe rail connection, was far more attractive than the old fort.

For many a traveler down the trail, his trip started from the Dodge House when he was awakened by someone shouting outside his door. Mrs. Ethel Watkins' parents remember being aroused at an early hour by P. G. Reynolds' stage-line man calling through the halls at daybreak, "Stage for Touzalin, Camp Supply, Fort Elliott leaves at seven. Hurry. Hu-rr-y." P. G.'s stage or any freighter's wagon would have followed the same street and routes out of Dodge as the wagons headed for the Jones and Plummer Trail or the Tascosa Trail. Crossing a stretch of bottomland covered with sand washed in by the Arkansas River, the stage or wagon moved past shifting hillocks of sand, some covered with vegetation, others still drifting with the force of the wind. Much of this first plains was covered by bluestem grass, which gradually gave over to buffalo grass on the flat tableland that stretched all the way to Mulberry Creek. The common trunk of the three trails leading away from Dodge City divided about thirteen miles out after reaching the Mulberry.[18]

Mulberry Creek was a running stream in the 1870s, normally moving within deep banks but frequently overflowing and spreading over the adjacent bottomland. At such times the creek was reported to show "rolling white caps" and could be disruptive and dangerous. During a rain-swollen crest in 1883, a cowboy lost his life there when his foot became caught in a stirrup after his horse threw him and dragged him downstream. It was not unusual to have a stage held up for two days while the whitecaps swirled by. Usually, however, it was an easy crossing, with little water in the summer and no quicksand.[19]

A. H. Dugan's road ranch on the north bank was a profitable if somewhat untidy accommodation that made the most of a water well when the creek was low and provided accommodations, corrals, and feed for stock during the winter. As the point of division for the Fort Supply, Jones and Plummer, and Tascosa trails and near the Western and Tuttle Cattle trails, the Mulberry crossing became a landmark for freighters and cattlemen alike. As long as the trails remained open, a road-ranch soddy was maintained there.

The next water hazard, the Bluff Creek crossings, was some

fourteen miles south of the Mulberry, and it, too, was to be a landmark as long as the old wagon trail survived. It was an ideal campsite, sheltered well by a bluff, with an ample supply of grass, water,
and wood. Old Cactus described the setting in 1878 when he accompanied U.S. Paymaster A. H. Brodhead on one of his bimonthly
trips to Fort Supply:

> To strike Bluff Creek, after traveling twenty-five miles without crossing
> a stream, was something of a relief, and this was our camping place for the
> first night. You never heard anyone ask why the stream was named Bluff
> Creek. It would have been a libel to give it any other name, as the bluffs
> that rise on either side of its bank are as genuine an article as the Creator
> ever made, and predominate every other freak of nature. They may not be
> "towering" or as "gorgeous" as the Montana bluffs we read of in dime nov-
> els, but they are the pure, unvarnished Kansas bluffs, rising a hundred
> feet or more above the level of the stream. The camp was struck on a little
> plateau not far from Maley ranche, the most fashionable hotel in that vicin-
> ity, built a la stockade, and of cedar.[20]

The bluff overlooked a fertile valley covered with lush grass,
which gave it an advantage as a campsite and later as a way station. The Fort Supply correspondent was enthusiastic about the
valley's prospects:

> This valley, as well as the entire scope of country for miles around, is cov-
> ered with excellent blue stem and winter grass and the never-failing buf-
> falo grass is everywhere to be. Horses and cattle will find sustenance in
> buffalo grass, as its nature is to grow continually, and the part next to the
> ground—almost in it—being the most nutritious part and very sweet,
> horses and cattle of all kinds, and also sheep, will graze on buffalo grass in
> preference to places where the grass is more spontaneous. . . .
> In addition to being a good agricultural and grazing locality, Bluff Creek
> is an excellent place for sportsmen. Fish in large varieties are taken in
> abundance from the stream, and to those who are fond of the gun, they
> can practice their marksmanship on the buffalo, antelope, bear, jackrabbit,
> chicken, or quail which abound in the vicinity.[21]

The first road ranch at Bluff Creek, owned by Charles Kaufholz
and his partner, remembered only as Mr. Beauregard, was an
eighteen- by thirty-six-foot soddy that served as restaurant, bar,
and general store. The two had a good, even lively, business serving military personnel before the buffalo hunters began using the
trail as one of the main routes to the Panhandle herds. In 1872,

Kaufholz and Beauregard sold their holdings to a former customer, George Reighard, an old buffalo hunter looking for an easier and safer life. Reighard improved the road ranch and remained there five years. In March 1873 he and George Oakes entered into a freighting partnership with a limited number of wagons and stock. When Oakes left, Reighard continued both operations until 1877, when he traded the ranch for the Great Western Hotel in Dodge City.[22]

Old Cactus had high hopes for the Bluff Creek station when the former hotel proprietor acquired it from Reighard. "Silas Maley," he wrote, "has splendid qualifications in his new business." Later he added: "He knows just how to run a ranch and consequence is that he is always 'chuckful.'" Maley, on the other hand, wanted to be a farmer and not an innkeeper. He spent much of his time fencing some four hundred acres of pastureland and getting another forty under cultivation. The food at the road ranch did improve, even if the rest of the accommodations did not. The troopers on the trail particularly appreciated the new atmosphere and judged the way station a convenient and congenial place for "rusticating and fishing." They also found there what Old Cactus called "the spirits to warm the inner man" and, along with the convivial drinking, a certain amount of good-natured horseplay. Old Cactus faithfully reported it all:

> As the two companies were going down to Supply this week, they received a shock which only a brave soldier could have stood up under. They camped near the Bluff Creek Ranche. Some of them strolled out to reconnoiter the country, and had not gone far when lo and behold they discovered, hanging to the limbs of some trees, several unfortunate civilians. Without making a close examination of the dead men, they hurried back to Mr. Maley's ranche and informed him that they had found two or three men hanging by the neck on the limbs of trees. Mr. Maley, without fear or consternation at all, discovered a few pair of empty pants which the cowboys had hung up to dry.[23]

Maley quickly discovered what other operators were to find out: that road ranching was a full-time job and did not mix well with other time-consuming enterprises. The following summer he sold the road-ranch part of his holdings to Charles Trask for one thousand dollars; the Bluff Creek Ranch, as it was now familiarly known,

was once again in the hands of an old buffalo hunter. Trask had
resigned his job as policeman under Wyatt Earp a week before
completing the Bluff Creek deal. Charlie Bassett had appointed
Trask to office shortly after taking over as sheriff following Ed
Masterson's murder. He was one of several future lawmen who had
worked together in the winter of 1871–72 when they were on
the Salt Fork as members of various buffalo-hunting crews. With
his new ranch, Trask took on a partner, Ed Arit, and they hired
J. W. Dawson "to take charge of the culinary department." Trask
held the ranch for an even shorter time than Maley; before the
summer was out, he sold it to John Glenn and Pete Henderson.[24]

By the time Old Pete's Place, as it was now called, began serving
hard liquor and lamb stew to freighters, the station had been dou-
bled in size by a stockade addition on the north side as large as the
original sod building. Old Pete became the last of the Bluff Creek
Ranch owners when he and Glenn ended their partnership in 1883.
Finding the partner less than a welcome companion, slovenly of
habit, and somewhat dull-witted, John Glenn proposed a dissolution. He offered what was called in those days "a give or take, sell
or buy" proposition. Intending to buy from what he believed was a
near destitute partner, Glenn set the price far below actual worth.
Old Pete listened to Glenn's pitch and said, "Vell, I want to think it
over a vile." He walked down to the nearby creek and, after a brief
time, returned. Much to Glenn's chagrin, he said, "Shonnie, I think
I buy dot ranch," and paid off in gold on the spot. In later dealings
with Ham Bell at the Elephant Livery Stable in Dodge City, Old
Pete paid in gold for a complete rig, horses, and supplies. When he
settled with Bell, he said, "Shonnie didn't know I had this, Ham-
mie, but I still got some left yet." To prove his point, he showed
Bell a bag containing a small fortune in gold pieces. Of the two
partners, Bell doubted that Old Pete was the dull-witted one.[25]

Old Pete's Place served the stagecoach as one of three major
stops on the way to Fort Supply where horses were changed and
cowboys could pick up their mail. It had a bar and tables for food.
There was also opportunity for excitement and danger. Ike Berry's
quarrel with a Mexican freighter ended when Berry, a frequent
customer at the ranch, killed the man in an exchange of shots.
Berry sent word to the sheriff not to bother to come after him, he

had his freight to deliver to Fort Supply and on his return trip to Dodge he would give himself up. It seemed to be all in a day's work. Old Pete homesteaded some land near the ranch and ran sheep, as Maley had done before him. Over the years the bachelor's quarters gradually deteriorated, and rumors of Old Pete's dousing himself with kerosene to keep down the personal flea population made it a questionable stop for anything but a quick drink. As he grew older, Old Pete became more eccentric, and "the neighbors finally took him to an institution" for his last days. [26]

From Bluff Creek Ranch the trail ran fourteen miles over rolling prairie to Bear Creek Valley, where the early redoubt had stood. The road continued past the old redoubt, which had fallen into disrepair and after 1875 was not used as a station or road ranch, to John ("Red") Clarke's Boss Ranch on the Cimarron. Old Cactus describes the land between Bear Creek and the Cimarron as it appeared in 1877:

> Just beyond Old Bear Creek station is one of the most beautiful prairies that it has ever been my fortune to see. For a distance of four miles long by two wide the surface is almost as level as a floor and completely surrounded with isolated trees, which set forth the panorama in all its fascinating beauty. [27]

Before his brief and unhappy arrangement with Old Pete, John Glenn had converted the house he built in 1874 at Soldiers' Graves into a ranch house. P. G. Reynolds used the "small adobe roundlike shack" as a stage station, and Glenn also could accommodate overnight visitors. J. W. Driskill assumed ownership sometime before 1877 and improved accommodations for the traveling public by providing a frame structure that also served as headquarters for his cattle operations. Southwest of this ranch house was a range of bluffs extending four miles along the creek; they were even more spectacular than those at Reighard's station. Old Cactus found the outcroppings "a splendid field for a geologist to collect specimens" because the "different strata revealed feldspar, mica, talc, chlorite, hornblende, slate, clay, quartz, flint, opal, chalcedony, stilbite, epidote, and zealite, silex, and magnesia." Mrs. Alice Brown, a widow with two sons, took over the Soldiers' Graves station for a brief time in 1878, but she was unable to make a go of it. [28]

The trail from Bear Creek Station (Soldiers' Graves) crossed a flat plain with red, low-lying hills to the west until it came to the banks of the Cimarron. Four miles beyond the mineral marvels of the bluffs at Soldiers' Graves was another camping site known as Red Hole. Various attempts at road ranching were made there, including those of Mrs. Brown, W. C. Shinn, and "Messers Allen and Brady." In 1883, W. D. Baker came from Oxford, Kansas to build a store near there. It became a post office called Klaine, in honor of Dodge City's editor and postmaster. Five more miles brought the trail to the Cimarron crossing.[29]

The old redoubt on the Cimarron withstood the elements far better than the northern fortification, and Lon McCoy converted it into a cramped but serviceable way station. The mud walls of the old officers' quarters built into one corner of the enclosure were lined with McCoy's canned goods and supplies. A counter, table, and two chairs supplied the furniture needed, since the owners slept on one of the low shelves under the counter and the guests were welcome to any spot on the dirt floor. For a time, Clem Nichia (or Netche) ran the Cimarron Ranch, to Old Cactus' great satisfaction, and apparently acquired a partner named Andy Jard. The Fort Supply correspondent was even more pleased when a new owner took over. John Clarke, who followed Nichia at Deep Hole, moved out of the adobe fortification into a building framed with lumber hauled down from Dodge City. P. G. Reynolds eventually came to use this station for his second change of teams on the way down to Fort Supply from Dodge. It was a mail drop also, and after May 1881 it was designated a post office with the name Deep Hole, honoring the soldiers' favorite swimming spot where Clark (Big Sandy) Creek met the Cimarron River. Charles Kaufholz was the first postmaster, and Deep Hole was still postmarking letters six years later.[30]

As long as Red Clarke operated Boss Ranch, it was the most popular stop on the Fort Supply road. In spring the site was particularly attractive with fields covered with violets. Its only drawback was the swarm of mosquitoes attracted by the water and low marshy areas near the creek, which made it impossible to sleep without a mosquito bar. The frame buildings and corral constituting the station were located on the south side of the Cimarron. Clarke usually kept a decent cook, was always accommodating, and was willing to join any pleasurable enterprise.[31]

It was, in fact, Clarke's personality that made the ranch a major attraction. He was born in Illinois in 1847 and came to Kansas as a buffalo hunter about the time the good hunting ended. He continued a close connection with Dodge City, visiting the town frequently and joining in its rough social life. "A visit from Red Clarke of the Cimmeron Ranche," Nick Klaine wrote, "is as good as a circus." He was a party to some of the most elaborate practical jokes invented by a town known for its wry treatment of tenderfeet and green country lads who wandered into the big city. At one point, Clarke professed to have discovered a snuff mine on the Cimarron, advertised for willing miners not afraid of hard work, and placed a large quantity of his product, dug from his holding, "on market and display—at Rath & Co." Editor Klaine went along with the gag in his paper and chided Clarke for not working to get "Eastern Capitalists interested." Later, Klaine carried an item indicating that "Snuff mine stock [was] going down" and the mine was apt to be closed because Clarke had not attracted enough miners and was unjustly blaming the editor for not cooperating in pushing the project. Bill Jones was one greenhorn who fell for the line. He and a dozen others started out on foot to reach the Boss Ranch and a certain job in the only snuff mine in Kansas. They had been properly warned that Indians in the area were mean and homicidal. After walking well over one hundred miles going and coming, spraining his ankle, and hiding out nights in plum thickets, Jones arrived back in Dodge bruised and considerably wiser. Klaine next reported Red's "feather foundry" had blown up and the editor tried to promote a "green apple factory" at Clarke's and Harry Brown's place, but there are no recorded takers of this venture. "Red Clarke," Klaine explained, "with four fingers in his glass and five around it," could spin a first-rate yarn. Like Mark Twain's Captain Stormfield, Clarke claimed to have died, gone to heaven, and returned to life. When he told the celestial authorities he came from Dodge City, he explained, "they wouldn't take him below or above."[32]

Clarke's connection with Dodge had a more serious side as well. He was a member of Bat Masterson's posse that chased Mike

Rourke to the Jones and Plummer ranch in February 1878, and he had aided Bat the year before when the Dodge City sheriff arrested a man at his ranch. Nor was that all the excitement the ranch was to have that year. Clarke's unofficial press agent, Nick Klaine, explained:

> While the Cheyenne were on their way south, they camped near Red Clarke's ranche, on the Cimeron. One of them paid Red a visit and asked for liquor, which Red refused. The noble red man then drew a pistol, but Red was a little ahead of him, and with his revolver pointed at the savage's brawny form, told him to git. His Indianship never stopped running until he had crossed the Cimeron.[33]

Red Clarke's move from road ranching was a great loss to Dodge City and the Fort Supply Trail. He did, however, leave behind a spirit of lampoonery that seemed to infect Deep Hole residents. Probably Red's noblest project was his unsuccessful campaign to get the seat of Clark County assigned to his saloon at Deep Hole. By later standards, he had only scratched the surface of town-booster ridicule.[34]

After entering Indian Territory for the final thirty-eight miles to Camp Supply, the trail ran through unsettled land with no road ranches or way stations but with a number of streams to cross where good campgrounds were available. Two soldiers left excellent accounts of this part of the trail. Lieutenant Carl Julius Adolph Hunnius, on a survey expedition, kept a detailed and accurate account along with sketches of a number of campsites, and Old Cactus, the *Dodge City Times* correspondent at Camp Supply, described the terrain with affection and accuracy:

From the Cimeron we proceed over a rolling country interspersed with numerous little valleys and bluffs, with here and there a fine plateau of prairie—spontaneously like the valley—covered with rich pasture. Eight miles from Cimeron we come to Snake Creek. Here is good water and splendid grazing, but little wood, except at a distance of one or two miles from the old camping ground. Fish and game are plenty in this vicinity, and the soil of the entire face of the country is fertile and well adapted to agriculture purposes.[35]

He continued his narrative by recording the creeks with their camping prospects: five miles to Buffalo Creek; ten more miles to Gypsum Creek ("the most interesting stream on the road—

especially for mineralogist or geologists"); three miles on to Sand Creek; four miles to Devil's Gap ("the most strikingly romantic place"); and "six miles farther, down a bluff and over the luxuriant bottom of Beaver river . . . and one quarter mile south of its right or south bank, is Camp Supply." A number of the crossings did not offer good water. At both Buffalo Creek, with its wide and sandy bed, and Gypsum Creek, Lieutenant Hunnius reported the water "not fit to drink," being bitter with alkali. The road past Devil's Gap was steep and winding and made a deep impression on all who passed along it. Hunnius reported it "the finest view we had on our trip":

It is a very narrow road and on both sides you look down into deep canyons (red sandstone) and this is relieved by cedar trees, the finest we saw on the road. And all over this stretch, was a long range of hills in the distance.

Thence traveling on over still more tops of elevations, the red sandstone changed, all of a sudden, into yellow. The next big rise was 425 feet above our camping place of last night, and from this point we saw Camp Supply lying far off in the bottoms. The descent was easy; it is, in fact, a long slope for about two miles. . . .[36]

The land along the trail was to remain largely untouched until the opening of what is now Oklahoma in 1884.

During the second phase in the life of the Dodge City–Fort Supply Trail, federal influence was indirect. Troop movement and official army business still accounted for much traffic, but the major supplies for both Fort Supply and Fort Elliott were hauled by civilian freighters. Even some of the troops were transported by Reynolds' stagecoaches and other private conveyances. The federal mail contracts, which accounted for the establishment of most of the way stations and kept them in business as well as assuring the regular schedule of the passenger coaches, were important but indirect federal influences. Throughout this period the trail retained much of the character of an overland turnpike, with little local use not generated by the two forts. Settlers did not begin to file on homesteads along the route until the mid-1880s. But with the way stations in place and the trail readily and safely available, rapid migration was possible. Much of the settlement in the area was funneled down the old military route from Dodge City, where the homesteader had shipped his household goods and farm equipment and where he and his family were introduced to the Region.

The existence of the wagon road, which would bring supplies in and carry cash crops to market, reassured settlers that home-steading was possible in a country as remote and isolated as the land south of Dodge appeared to be. Before the inland towns were developed, the early settlers found the road ranches and the rela-tively quick access to the trade center at Dodge City an acceptable transitional condition. As in other instances, the federal wagon-road policy had effectively laid the basis for settlement of the land.

For the Kansas portion of the Fort Supply Trail, there was to be a third phase, which came in the late 1880s and lasted only the few years before the old ruts passed into disuse. This phase was marked by the appearance of a number of towns on the trail or near it, capitalizing on the rush of settlers to the Region and the per-sistent rumors of new railroad lines. Each of the way stations was seen as a potential townsite and an eventual station on some fu-ture rail line. Even the most unlikely spot might grow to metropoli-tan splendor.

Deep Hole was one of the sites proposed. A spiritual descendant of Red Clarke put Deep Hole, which never boasted more than one saloon and post office, into proper metropolitan perspective. George C. Walker had been plagued by requests from a number of the newspaper editors in the surrounding new towns to send news of his "town's prospects." With tongue solidly in cheek, Walker wrote the Ashland editor in 1885:

The influx of people comprises all classes, the press, the bar, the scal-pel, the pulpit, terpsichore, and the noble art of self-defence, are all repre-sented by professors who stand high in their callings. Suitable buildings and halls for the exercise of their respective talents are being erected with such dispatch as to tax the endurance of an army of skilled mechanics to its utmost tension. A company with a paid in capital of one million dollars has been formed for the purpose of manufacturing agricultural imple-ments and steamboats. The Cimarron river will be dammed two miles above this place and its magnificent water power be utilized. A mob of lobbyists will go from here to attend the next congress at Washington, and lay before the committee on river and harbor appropriations such plans and specifications for the dredging and clearing of the Cimarron river be-low here as will insure steamboat communication between Deep Hole and the Gulf of Mexico. The echoes from the unearthly screech of the loco-motive already disturb our slumbers.

This embryo metropolis is being laid out somewhat after the plan of Washington. A beautiful circular park with a fountain in the centre, which shall rival the famous one at Fountainbleau, near Paris, will be the core. Broad avenues will stretch spider-like from the shady walks of this retreat, and circular streets, like the ripples of a cast pebble on the bosom of a mirrored lake, shall band-like encompass its inhabitants. Several miles be-low the old Fort, which is so full of historic interest, there is now being laid out a driving park, as large as Lincoln Park, Chicago. That pearly stream called Redoubt will murmur through the centre and its shaded and moss bound banks be joined by stone-arched bridges.

The great humdrum of trade is now on the south side of the Cimarron, but I doubt not that in the future there will be a North Deep Hole, which will some day stretch within handshaking distance of the flourishing little town of Ashland. [37]

There was, however, one more or less serious effort to create a town at the Cimarron crossing. Deep Hole was for some time the only post office in what was to be Clark County. Consequently, there was as much reason to believe it might reach town status as any of a dozen other spots in the county. In the spring of 1887, E. G. Catrell had a townsite survey made and called the town Deep Hole. It was not the prospect of population or logic of history that prompted his action. For some time, people south of Kansas had hoped there would be a north-south railroad linkage that would pre-serve old connections within the Region. Catrell and his supporters felt that the prospects of business in many proposed towns, as well as the established trade of towns already in existence, such as Ash-land, Minneola, and Bloom, would prompt the Santa Fe to run a branch south into the western tier of Oklahoma counties. He be-lieved that one more town on the Oklahoma border would add to the prospects. It was a wasted effort, and Deep Hole continued to flourish only in the satirical pen of George C. Walker. [38]

The old road ranch and freighting park at Soldiers' Graves fared far better than its southern neighbor at Deep Hole. The quarter section on which John Glenn had established his early road ranch eventually was preempted by Charles Roby, who built a store there to supply freighters on the Fort Supply Trail. As more settlers moved into the area and as it became clear that the southern part of Ford County would be split from the original unit, the prospects of locating a county seat became more appealing. In 1883 a group of Winfield, Kansas investors began exploring the area for a likely townsite. They first selected a location west of Ashland, but on their way home over the Sun City Trail they decided the advantages of the Bear Creek crossing at Soldiers' Graves, where the east-west Sun City Trail intersected the north-south Dodge City–Fort Supply Trail with its access to the telegraph line, made it an ideal county-seat location. In October 1884 the town was platted and named Ashland. It was an immediate success, and by the spring of 1885 it had been designated the seat of Clark County.[39]

The old trail south, which passed through the center of town, continued to supply newcomers with the necessities for rapid growth, and traffic along the Fort Supply Trail returned to the volume and pace of the early years. A correspondent for the *Clark County Clipper* wrote:

Teams are now strung all along the road. Some are heavily laden with building material and move slowly on their way southward, while others loaded with passengers, land-seekers and the enterprising people who are building up a new country, whisk by on their busy errands, and soon disappear in the distance. An unusual clatter is heard at some time during the day and the four-horse stage coach, loaded to its "topmost" capacity, dashes by.[40]

P. G. Reynolds, owner of the loaded coach, was among those profiting by the new status, and he was also one of the earliest "enterprising people" to build there. The first small barn constructed for his stock he found to be too cramped, so he built another considerably larger, twenty-six by forty feet. Ashland became a dispersal point for him as he expanded his lines to Greensburg, Englewood, Cash City, and Vesta. The Ashland editor predicted P. G. would have "a good business and . . . a paying line until the railroads get here." For the few years when the old freighting trail was the major transportation link for the booming town, P. G. did indeed prosper, frequently having to add coaches and to make additional runs. One newcomer remembered the trip down from Dodge as an ordeal because of the crowded coach. "The stage," Myron G. Stevenson wrote, "was so crowded that I had to ride outside most of the time and I thought sure I would freeze to death. . . . During the 10-hour trip, it rained, hailed and snowed." Even with the arrival of the trains, passengers and mail had to be delivered to the towns that were bypassed, and Reynolds' business and the old Fort Supply Trail continued to serve the influx of new settlers for another three years. The end for both Reynolds and the trail, however, was clearly in sight, even as he built his first barn. The old ways soon were to be left behind. In March 1885 the *Clark County Clipper* boasted that the new order of things would see Ashland a temperance town. Charley Richmond, who kept the road ranch at the head of Bear Creek, closed out his stock of liquor, and Sheriff Mike Sughrue closed twelve saloons. The town was in deadly earnest; before the next year was out, Sheriff Sughrue had killed a man caught selling illegal booze when he tried to run.[41]

The town that caused the biggest shift in the trail was destined to have a short and unhappy career. In 1885, as signs of the disintegration of the Region were beginning to be clearly evident, a new town, Appleton, was chartered just south of the Ford County line in Clark County. P. G. Reynolds and the majority of the freighters moved from the old trail to an alternate route that carried them due south from Dodge City along section lines before turning east after leaving Appleton to make connections with the original Fort Supply Trail. The northern end of the abandoned road continued to be used by the farmers around Bloom, and one old-timer remembered riding a bicycle over it sometime after the turn of the century.

Appleton was to benefit from this changed route for only a brief time. After the town was platted, Reynolds again was one of the first to purchase lots. On the east side of town he built a barn large enough to stable thirty-six horses and used Appleton as his first stop south of Dodge. The town grew more slowly than Ashland, but by 1887 it had some two hundred residents who were confident that the Rock Island Railroad would soon make their town an important trade center. Unfortunately, a disagreement between landowners and railroad officials led to the railroad's bypassing the town. The residents were left with no choice but to move the mile and a half south to the new site and the new name of Minneola. Like the rest, Reynolds moved his barn and operation. By the end of 1887, there was no longer an Appleton on the map. The first

P. G. Reynolds's stagecoaches at his Appleton, Kansas, station, May, 1886. This line ran from Dodge City to Englewood with stops at Ashland and Appleton. Courtesy Rex Reynolds, Niles, Michigan.

Rock Island mail train through Minneola, on January 8, 1888, also ended regular stage runs from Dodge City through that new settlement, although Reynolds did continue operating south of there for a brief time, maintaining lines to Englewood and other inland communities. The Fort Supply Trail, however, remained open for local farm and freighting trade for a number of years.[42]

For a very brief time the town of Bloom, a mile above the Clark County line in Ford County, capitalized on the old Fort Supply Trail. In 1885, four Vanderslice brothers homesteaded a section of land, dug a well, and set up a road ranch, offering a modest stock of supplies to freighters and travelers. The mail stage from Dodge dropped mail there but did not use the ranch as a major stop. The brothers called the way station Bloomsburg in honor of their hometown in Pennsylvania. When the Chicago, Kansas and Nebraska Railroad became interested in the Vanderslice land, the South Arkansas Town Company hired a surveyor, platted a town just north of the road ranch, and dropped *burg* from the name. Growth was relatively slow as compared with the neighboring towns of Ashland, Appleton, and Minneola. At least part of the explanation for the sluggishness was reorientation of the Fort Supply Trail to Appleton and its successor, Minneola. The mail that formerly had been dropped by the Dodge stage on the old route through Bloom was now brought over from Appleton by Dad Brooks in a one-horse cart. Even with the coming of the Rock Island in 1888, Bloom did not boom, and the old trail lost all significance. In the early 1890s, Bloom failed completely, and between 1893 and 1908 it was only a "dot on the map." Unlike the trail, however, it was to revive and grow into a permanent settlement.[43]

The old military route, with its many alterations and extensions, remained an important road for twenty-two years. Throughout the period, connections with Dodge City and the towns and ranches south into Indian Territory proved a mutually profitable arrangement. The partnership was broken only when the north-south branches of the railroad that promoters had promised failed to materialize and commercial contacts were forced to follow the east-west rail lines. The Dodge City–Fort Supply Trail had served the military needs of the southern section of the Region; was a favorite of the buffalo hunters exploiting the eastern Panhandle herds; supplied the ranchers of the Region in Kansas, Oklahoma, and Texas; and finally guided farmers and town settlers who were to develop the Region in all three states. It remained until 1890 the most widely recognized road in the Region. Its passing truly marked the end of the wagon-trail economy in that section of the High Plains.

3. The Fort Elliott Extension and the Mobeetie–Tascosa Trail: The Base of the Triangle

AFTER Fort Elliott was commissioned in 1875, the trail from Kansas to Fort Supply was extended into the panhandle of Texas. Although not a part of the Military Road, the extension appeared on the maps as a continuation of the old route. Altered in detail from time to time as it adjusted to new way stations, improved water crossings, or smoother ground, the new extension remained basically unchanged until the end of the era. From the beginning the road was used heavily by nonmilitary traffic. Although it had been laid out by the army and was intended to be a link between the two forts, hide men, ranchers, and settlers all found it a useful trail south. Even after the Jones and Plummer Trail became the preferred route of the freighters, the old Military Road was more widely known outside the Region and continued to be used extensively by people living in the area.

The extension ran south out of Fort Supply, angling slightly west over rich prairie lands. About ten miles down the trail, still within the Cherokee Outlet, the marks of the Western Cattle Trail spread across the prairie for a quarter-mile or more. In 1874, under army escort, John T. Lytle drove three thousand longhorns to Dodge City over this route. By 1878 the Western Cattle Trail was well established along the ninety-ninth meridian and was used by the ma-

Fort Elliott, Texas, inspection-day lineup in April, 1880. Courtesy Boot Hill Museum, Dodge City, Kansas.

jority of the Texas cattlemen who drove herds north to Kansas. Once the cattle trail was in full use, there were times when freighters and the stagecoach drivers on the Fort Elliott extension had to wait for hours while a herd of Texas cattle passed. A few miles beyond the Western Trail, a traveler would begin noticing the heavy growth of timber to the south. The cedar trees growing there served as a lucrative second cargo for otherwise empty wagons returning from delivering supplies to either of the two forts. A Dodge City paper noted: "The wood used by our bakers is hauled from Texas by freighters who realize ten or twelve dollars to the wagon are just that much ahead as they would be coming to Dodge empty." The presence of timber also made possible a new type of construction for houses and other buildings. Wherever trees of sufficient size were found, picket walls replaced the sod used on the prairie. Posts eight or nine feet long and seven or eight inches in diameter were set vertically in a trench, which was dug according to a floor plan. Although picket houses were no more permanent than sod houses, they were considerably cleaner and just as easy to build.[1]

The first of several good camping spots and the first serviceable way station lay eighteen miles south of Fort Supply in the valley where Buzzard Creek, fed by an ever-flowing spring, converged with Wolf Creek. The way station, on the south bank of Wolf Creek, took its name, Buzzard Roost, from the stand of timber along the smaller stream. The trees on the creek had been the summer roosting place for thousands of buzzards and had been known as Buzzard Roost since the first white man came to the territory. The station changed hands frequently over the years but remained in operation until the end of the freighting era.[2]

Crossing Wolf Creek was normally a simple matter, but, as was true of any prairie stream after a rain, it could turn into a torrent as wild as its name. The force of the water and its depth were often misleading to people new to the country, as Mani Leopard learned the hard way:

The Wolf was up and still rising when the northbound stage rolled in driven by Mani Leopard. There was one passenger, an Englishman full of booze and wind. It was about midnight. They ate their lunch, put on two teams—the trail was heavy—and pulled out. At the Wolf crossing two

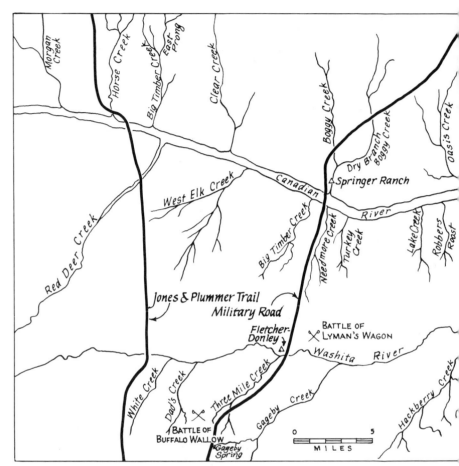

Map 3. Hemphill County Texas, showing the rivers and creeks crossed by the Jones and Plummer Trail and Military Road

miles north, Leopard got out and looked at the creek; then he came back and said, "Creek's up; got to turn back." The passenger said, "In England they pay no attention to high water, but drive right in. You Americans are such damned cowards. And I want to get to Supply." (At least that's the way Leopard told it afterwards). Leopard asked him, "Well, what do you say?" The Englishman said, "Drive in." So in they went. The stage turned over. Mani swam out. They found the passenger in a drift close by, the stage-coach and team half a mile below, and some of the mail.[3]

Buzzard Roost was a busy place. Sam Manning, who came to the Panhandle in 1874 and eventually settled in Higgins, Texas, remembered it as "one of civilization's first outposts in these parts":

Intersecting the Fort Supply–Fort Elliott Military telegraph line and overland stage and freight trail at Buzzard Roost another overland freight trail came in from the northwest and followed a southeastern course on to old Cantonment and Darlington in the Cheyenne-Arapaho country.

Hoover and Johnson, early-day merchants of Kiowa, Kansas, operated "bull-team" freight wagons over a well-beaten trail from Kiowa down through the Cherokee Strip, right by Buzzard Roost and on up Wolf Creek to their trading post in the Texas Panhandle. Buzzard Roost in the early days could have been likened to a rail road terminal of modern times.[4]

The Buzzard Roost station consisted of a two-room picket house with dirt floor and roof, a picket corral for the stage teams, "a dug out or two providing shelter for a few extra people who might sojourn for a day or two overnight," a blacksmith shop, and a "mess house" constructed of logs. The stage, going and coming from Fort Elliott, changed teams there, but the freighters and buffalo hunters also used the station as a convenient campsite. After 1883, in the bottoms just across Wolf Creek, was situated the K H Ranch headquarters of the New York Cattle Company. Although separated by the stream, the ranch and way station took on something of the character of a town. The blacksmith was kept busy shoeing the oxen, mules, and horses of the freighters, along with the ranch stock. In 1890 the mail route was changed and the way station was abandoned, but the ranch headquarters continued for a number of years to serve travelers and local ranchers in an emergency.

Ten miles farther south was Willow Springs and another well-watered camp where there was, for a while at least, a half-picket, half-dugout that served as a road ranch. Another eight miles brought the traveler to Rock Springs, where there was a way station that sometimes served the stage line. A more substantial road ranch was located near Commission Creek, still in the Cherokee Outlet, about two miles southeast of the present town of Higgins, Texas. Commission Creek was described in 1885 as "a string of clear pools twenty to one hundred feet long and fifty feet across, hung

together by a stream about a foot wide." It was easily forded, actually twice in three miles, and about three miles past the last of
these crossings was the one-hundredth meridian, marking the
boundary between Indian Territory and Texas.[5]

The Commission Creek crossing was to have a long and useful
history. When he operated the first stage line to Fort Elliott, P. G.
Reynolds had designated it as a dinner stop, and less-adventurous
folk could spend the night there. The station was known in the
early days as The Polly Hotel, named after Ephraim E. Polly and
his wife, who operated the station from 1874 until 1884. Polly had
been a pharmacist in the army at Fort Hays and was considered a
competent physician by both whites and Indians. The food and accommodations at The Polly Hotel were considerably better than at
most of the road ranches; consequently, the facilities there were
much in demand.[6]

Of all those who were given over to Polly's care and shared the
hospitality of the road ranch, by far the most notable were two
young white sisters who were rescued in November 1874 by Lieutenant Frank D. Baldwin from Gray Beard, a shrewd and seasoned
Cheyenne chief commanding some sixty lodges. The goal of rescu-
ing the captured daughters of John and Lydia German had become
a cause célèbre for the troops in the field and explains in part the
tenacity with which the cavalry pursued the Indians in the winter
campaign of 1874. The Germans were traveling in a single wagon
to Fort Wallace, on the Smoky Hill River near the Colorado border,
when they were attacked by Medicine Water's band of Cheyennes.
The parents and three of the children were brutally murdered, and
the four surviving sisters were carried off into captivity. After
witnessing the slaying and mutilation of their family, Adelaide and
Julia, the younger of the four, were driven across the Staked Plains
until they were traded to Gray Beard. Starved, neglected, and
nearly frozen, they were nevertheless treated more gently than the
older girls. General Nelson A. Miles used the rescue mission to
spur the troops to great sacrifices during the cold, wet months of
early winter.

Lieutenant Baldwin found Adelaide and Julia purely by accident.
With a small escort party, he was bringing an empty wagon train
back to the Washita base when he came upon Gray Beard's camp.

Although he had only one troop of mounted cavalry, Baldwin charged the village, scattering the Indians out onto the Staked Plains. In one of the abandoned lodges, the troopers found Julie and Addie German. General Miles had the girls escorted back to Leavenworth, Kansas, where his wife took them into her home. During the trip to Kansas the escort unit spent the night at The Polly Hotel. Mrs. Polly described the girls' condition when they arrived:

A troop of Cavalry left two white girls . . . to await the next stage to Fort Supply; these girls had been re-captured from the Indians a few days earlier. Both girls were demented from torture by the Indians who had placed cedar splinters under the girls' fingernails, between their fingers, and around their eyes. These splinters were then set afire.

The girls were between 10 and 14 years of age [actually 7 and 5] and because of their mental condition they could not or would not communicate . . . but would cower in a corner of the cabin with a blanket over their heads. They would eat only when food was placed before them on the floor, and they would eat with their hands, not seeming to know what tableware was for. [7]

Polly accumulated a sizable herd of cattle while operating the station. In 1884 he sold the road ranch and turned to full-time cattle ranching, first on the Washita River and later on Morgan Creek. When Hemphill County was organized, he was elected the first county judge. Still later he established a real estate business and became postmaster at Canadian. [8]

In 1885, Oliver Nelson, looking for a job with the Cheyenne & Arapahoe Cattle Company, followed the stage line to a point near The Polly Hotel, where he cut across to the ranch headquarters. He was disappointed to find that the ranch had all the hands it needed. Acting on a tip from the cook, he rode over to the stage station, where the company agent, Charles H. Sawyer, was looking for a stationkeeper. Nelson took the job and found the isolated station, picturesquely set under a high cliff, to be a busy place consisting of several buildings made of eight-foot cottonwood pickets. [9]

When Nelson took over the station, he found the routine already well established and the station used for a noon stop by the stage on its way from Fort Supply and for supper on the way back from Mobeetie. The schedule also allowed a travel-weary passenger to recuperate by spending the night there. The stage from the north

on its way from Fort Elliott came in at 6 A.M. one day and stopped
on its round trip headed south at 6 P.M. the next day. Between
runs, freighters, ranchers, and Indians stopped in for meals or repairs. Nelson enjoyed the feuding between the two Jacks who drove
the stage, hunted wild turkey to augment his meager table, and
observed at close hand—frequently too close for comfort—the
neighboring Cheyennes and Arapahos. However, when Nelson's
boss found the stationkeeper drunk at the Canadian crossing just
below the Commission Creek station, he offered the job to Nelson
and Nelson took it.

Nelson's new post had replaced the old Springer Ranch way station. To reach it from Commission Creek, Nelson followed the
stage trail, which continued south-southwest and entered Texas
near the northeast corner of Hemphill County. It continued southwest toward the head of Oasis Creek and crossed the Canadian
River near the mouth of Boggy Creek. From 1874 until 1883, the
major stop on the road between Fort Supply and Fort Elliott had
been Springer Ranch. Variously owned and operated during that
period, it was the best fortified landmark in the Panhandle.

In 1883, when the Springer blockhouse ceased to function as a
way station, the mail stop was moved nearer the Canadian on its
south bank and about three miles west. It was this location that
Nelson took over in 1886, describing it as "the Canadian camp":

> The Canadian camp was in the Texas Panhandle, eighteen miles south-
> west of Commission. Sand hills stretched all the way between the two
> places, with tall bunch grass and bluestem and a few hackberry trees. The
> station was on high ground, two hundred yards south of the river, several
> miles east of the present town of Canadian, Texas. There were two old
> rooms—one log, one picket—with dirt roof and floor, and a frame
> addition built on. We used the frame for the station, and the old part,
> which was liable to fall down any time, for a storeroom. I got water from a
> well six feet deep, near the river. All around was plenty of sage brush but
> little timber.[10]

The most detailed description of any stationkeeper's daily routine is Oliver Nelson's account of the life at the Canadian camp in
The Cowman's Southwest. As he described it, the life of a road
rancher was one of excitement and considerable activity. At times
his obligations to the mail contractor seemed incidental as he ex-

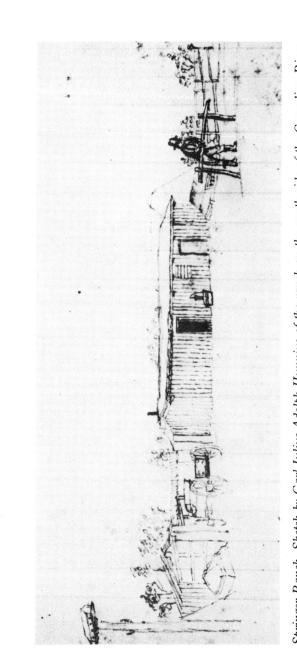

Springer Ranch. Sketch by Carl Julius Adolph Hunnius of the ranch on the north side of the Canadian River, June 23–24, 1876. Courtesy Spencer Research Library, University of Kansas.

tended aid and comfort to people traveling on the trail. Much of his time was spent in support of the army, which undoubtedly would have needed a permanent detail stationed there had the way station not existed. Nelson substituted as coach driver on occasion; ferried people, including the military, across the Canadian during high water; testified in a Fort Supply court-martial; helped capture a horse thief; tended the stock; hunted game; cooked for whoever stopped by; and engaged in the usual frontier horseplay and practical jokes.

The station may have changed since Jim Springer's day, but the Canadian River, which was the center of most of the troublesome activity, had not. The new crossing was just as dangerous and the river just as fickle as it had been and continued to be for those on the Jones and Plummer Trail farther upstream. Nelson found it to be "a treacherous stream" with ten-foot banks of caving sand:

> The bed is about four hundred yards wide, filled with very fine sand, no rocks. It has been sounded down sixty feet, and still no solid foundation. It has a heavy downslope from the west, so that in spring freshets it comes down with a roar. These rises wash channels in the bed, then fill them up with sand as soft as mush. Once a flood brought down a tree with a trunk three feet in diameter, the top pointed downstream, resting on the soft sand and sticking up twenty feet above the water. It was in sight four days, working its way down at the rate of 150 yards an hour. The January before I came a thirteen-foot stone abutment had been placed in the middle of the bed to support a telegraph pole. They had set it six feet below the sand and seven feet above, but when I got there it had sunk till only about four inches projected. By spring it was buried under three feet of sand, and had moved downstream until it broke the wire. [11]

In winter the river was even more of a problem. When the first storm, "a real hummer from the north," moved in, the river froze solid. Nelson laid poles on the ice as a makeshift bridge for the stage and other travelers. When the ice started to soften, the poles were useless. The alternative then was to chop a lane through the ice so that the wheels of the stage or wagon would be on the solid footing of the riverbed.

On one occasion the army, typically, refused to follow Nelson's advice on how to ford the river and tried to bring a loaded wagon across on the melting ice. The officer in charge forced his men, black soldiers from Fort Elliott, to stand in three feet of freezing water trying to lift the wagon onto solid ice after it had broken through, just as Nelson had warned them it would. As the officers tromped around searching for solid footing, Nelson confessed that he "walked behind the major trying to break a place so he would fall in—failed with him, but managed to get the lieutenant in." After the troopers had worked for about an hour, the major ordered them to cut a lane, as Nelson had first suggested, and they easily pulled the wagon out.[12]

For Nelson, life on the Canadian may have been full and strenuous, but it was not very profitable. After exchanging harsh words and erratic but deadly serious shots with his boss, Nelson quit his job with the stage line still owing him money. The station was turned over to a succession of short-term attendants, then closed when the Santa Fe Railroad built into the Panhandle and the town of Canadian grew up around its tracks. Nelson remained in the Region as farmer and rancher, accumulating several parcels of land. In 1890 he was forced to sell his holdings at deflated prices: a section of land in Ochiltree County went for ten dollars, and the best price he received was five hundred dollars for a quarter section. He made two runs for free land in Oklahoma, and the latter, into the Cherokee Strip, was successful. He settled on a claim near Hennessey, Oklahoma, where he lived out his life.

After crossing the Canadian River, the Fort Elliott Trail ran diagonally to Needmore Creek for about twelve miles, past Cottonwood Springs on the Washita River. A well-stocked road ranch known as the Fletcher-Donley Stage Station was maintained there on the south bank; it was established in 1875 by three old buffalo hunters, Tobe Robinson, Ed Fletcher, and Jim Donley. Robinson eventually left the partnership and moved to Tascosa, where he later became sheriff of Hartley County. The station consisted of a number of picket buildings and was remembered by the early settlers for the flowers on the sod roof and the bush arbor shading one of the cabin doors. It remained in continuous operation until the mail and stage line ended in 1889.[13]

From the Washita the trail turned south-southwest parallel to Threemile Creek. There, a particularly welcome sight for travelers was the stand of cottonwood and plum thickets clustered around a clear spring. Another nine miles brought the trail to Gageby Creek, where the settlement of the same name was later established within nine miles of Mobeetie. The last leg into Fort Elliott was over land devoid of trees but lush with grasses and other small plants. Prairie hay, tall and nourishing, grew in the draws and creek bottoms and occasionally on high spots.[14]

One of the major assignments for the troops stationed at Fort Elliott was to keep the ninety-one miles of roads and the telegraph line in good repair. As early as March 1875 they were reported busy building a corduroy base across the breadth of the Canadian River bottom. When a survey party crossed the bottom in 1876, Lieutenant Hunnius, who was in charge, reported that the corduroy road had been extended about two miles and "was awful rough and shook and jostled us fearfully." The route was always more vigorously patrolled than any of the other trails. Until 1885, escort, courier, and patrolling duty occupied much of the Fort Elliott command's time. In fact, escorting the wagon trains, carrying official dispatches, and repairing roads were about the only assignments the fort had during its last few years.[15]

Fort Elliott was destined to be the center of the first Texas Panhandle settlement following the pattern of development suggested by Lieutenant Simpson in his report of 1848. As settlers sought protection or found government jobs, concentric circles of population were established around the fort. Of the total population of 1,607 in the Texas Panhandle in 1880, 512 persons, including military personnel, resided in Wheeler County in the immediate vicinity of the fort. As a garrison town, Mobeetie grew up within the shadow of Elliott's picket walls, actually on the fort's reservation land. Beginning as a buffalo hunters' rendezvous, the settlement first was known as Hide Town and was dominated by Charles Rath of Dodge City, who picked up hides and dropped off supplies there. The name changed to Sweetwater when more settlers were attracted by Rath's business, but the place remained primarily a buffalo hunters' town, with the largest general store owned by the Dodge City merchant. Rath's firm not only supplied much of the goods needed in Mobeetie, but also served the camp on Double Mountain Fork of the Brazos River. From the Double Mountain camp, Rath, Reynolds & Co. monopolized the buffalo-hide business in the area, handling a million dollars' worth of merchandise annually for the three years the camp remained in operation. Both centers, Mobeetie and the Double Mountain camp, were tied to Dodge City by the Fort Supply Trail, so that during those early years Mobeetie was scarcely more than an extension of Dodge City's Front Street, although the Double Mountain camp also had strong trading ties with Fort Griffin, Texas.[16]

With the fort firmly established and the buffalo-hunting business exhausted, old Sweetwater quickly converted to a soldiers' town but was still dependent on Dodge City for supplies. The town's business, as described in 1879 by the Fort Griffin paper, catered primarily to the garrison:

The town as yet was but a small affair. It consists of one street about two hundred and fifty yards long. It has ten or twelve buildings on the street and several small ones off the street. All the houses except one are built of pickets and have dirt roofs. . . . Most of the houses are intended for saloon purposes, and though it appears at first sight as though the saloon traffic was overdone, yet no one complains of hard times although the garrison had not paid off for four months.[17]

The accommodating merchants furnished the usual distractions for soldiers—liquor, gambling, and women—as well as more stable fare for the settlers. "The soldiers were paid every three months," reported Dick Bussell, one of the more energetic merchants, "and we would get their money as fast as they would get it."[18]

The town became the county seat when Wheeler County was organized, changed its name to Mobeetie, and lost some of its military atmosphere. The records show that most of the voting citizens at the time of organization were scarcely of the highest order of gentility, being, in fact, dance-hall habitués and gamblers with such colorful names as Butcher Knife Bill, Feather Stone Jones, and Fly Speck. The black troops at Fort Elliott did not feel as welcome as they once had been, however, and drifted away to other sources of amusement. But the town still catered to the general needs of the garrison and was dependent on the fort for much of its trade. New hotels, banks, retail businesses, and other services required a constant stream of supplies from Dodge City. Charles Rath continued his operation there through a number of partnerships: Rath and Conrad, Rath and Hamburg, and the largest of all:

Rath, Wright, Lee, and Reynolds. All military and civilian supplies for both the fort and the town came by wagon from Dodge City. The officials at Elliott reported to headquarters that the "country in this vicinity is very thinly inhabited, and there are no resources that can be depended upon for the procurement of supplies (except Lime, Hay, and Wood), for use of the troops stationed here, consequently all stores required are hauled by wagon train from Dodge City, Kansas, a post on the A.T. & S.F. R.R., 284 miles north east from this post." Until the mid-1880s, there were never enough freighters to meet the demands of the Mobeetie merchants, and goods frequently piled up in Kansas waiting to be shipped south.[19]

Gradually the bulk of the freighting shifted to the Jones and Plummer Trail, although some traffic remained between the two forts until Fort Elliott was decommissioned, long after it had outlived its usefulness, and turned over to the Department of Interior for disposal. The last troops left on October 21, 1890. Mobeetie lost the main reason for its existence when the soldiers vacated the fort, and the town slowly faded from the scene.[20]

Since the original reason for establishing Fort Supply was tied to the federal Indian policy of encircling the Region with a chain of forts, a major responsibility for the command was supplying and maintaining communication with army contingents at Fort Bascom. The land between the forts was largely unsettled and uncharted, with no clearly marked trail until Fort Elliott was commissioned, nor was there ever to be west of Fort Elliott a trail that was fully identified and recognized. There were fixed points, way stations, and safe creek crossings, but many stretches of the prairie remained unmarked and the driver or, in the case of the mail delivery, the rider could improvise his route based on his own dead reckoning. Eventually, two more or less clear paths were developed, and the mail contractors followed one or the other, depending on the available way stations, contract requirements, and the condition of the trail.

Fort Bascom, located on the Canadian River in present-day San Miguel County, New Mexico, was provisioned and maintained largely from Fort Supply and remained active only until December 1870, when it was superseded by Fort Union on the Mora River in New Mexico Territory. After that date the army's interest in protecting a trail across the plains to Tascosa on the old route to Bascom declined. Traffic between Mobeetie and Tascosa, which was never heavy, became very erratic. Buffalo hunters rarely relied on a fixed trail, and freighters in the area tended to use the three north-south routes in reaching the Panhandle towns. The mail contractors and local settlers were the only consistent users of the trails, and even they were inclined to make their own. Garrett H. "Kid" Dobbs, who carried mail for the first contractor, Austin Barnes, on the earliest runs, observed: "Those trails [between Mobeetie and Tascosa] went in every direction."[21]

In 1880, when P. G. Reynolds put a hack carrying both passengers and mail on the line, he directed his drivers to follow a set route. However, Marion Armstrong, who took over the job of delivering mail, found the trail unmarked and was obliged to devise his own path, based on his knowledge of the country. This worked well for him but was to cost life and limb, literally, for those who succeeded him.

Of specific mail drops, creek crossings, and hack stations, the first stop west of Mobeetie was on the North Fork of the Red River some thirty miles out. Dixon Creek Station was next, about thirty-five miles on west. Another thirty-five miles across open prairie found the Bonita Creek–Canadian River crossing, leaving fifteen miles to Lahey Creek, plus the final fifteen to Tascosa. At various times, stage stops were changed and the route altered. When the first post office was established in Potter County, a new stop was made at Wheeler, headquarters of the L X Ranch, situated between Bonita and Lahey creeks. The trail was changed again while Reynolds maintained a way station on White Deer Creek.[22]

Marion Armstrong had created the first mail station when he built a dugout for his family on Red Deer Creek in 1879. This was to become a one-man station on the order of those manned by Oliver Nelson on the Fort Elliott extension and was a major stop for P. G. Reynolds' drivers as long as the more northerly route was taken. It was an ideal spot because the creek was fed by springs as well as runoff water, which ensured a convenient supply for the stage teams. The crossing near Red Deer Spring, whose clear, cool water marked the head of the creek, was a favored resting spot and had been since the earliest explorers and buffalo hunters crossed

there, finding a floodplain of considerable size, some trees that
could furnish fuel, and considerable brush. Armstrong manned the
Red River station for a brief time when it served the more southerly trail. Both routes were used primarily although not exclusively
by the mail line; they also served as individual ties between Tascosa and Mobeetie and as communication channels for some state
and local governmental agencies, which also relied on them. [23]

Extension of the Dodge City–Fort Supply Trail to Fort Elliott
was part of the army's strategy for encircling and restraining the
Indians of the High Plains. With that task accomplished, the extension, which had from the beginning seen considerable civilian
traffic, became primarily oriented to the commercial interest of
Mobeetie and Tascosa. Consequently, the two sections of the trail
from Fort Supply to Tascosa were given unequal treatment by the
army. The road between the two forts was carefully maintained;
the route beyond Fort Elliott was ignored. Since there was a more
direct road to Tascosa and the Jones and Plummer Trail was preferred by freighters headed for Fort Elliott and Mobeetie, the trail
east and west between the Panhandle towns would have faded long
before the railroad arrived had it not been for mail-contract requirements. The amount of mail delivered was light, and there
were few requests for passenger service. A stagecoach was never
used, and the route remained a hack line until the mail contracts
ended. [24]

The settlement of Clarendon in 1875 might have increased the
use of the east-west trail, but its citizens found other, more convenient routes to follow into Mobeetie and Tascosa. Furthermore,
Clarendon remained only marginally connected with the rest of the
Region. The Rev. Lewis Henry Carhart, who founded the town,
had major interests in Sherman, Texas and continued his contacts
there, although the lumber used in the early settlement and most
of the supplies during the first months of its life came from Dodge
City. After Morris Rosenfield became the major merchant in Clarendon in 1882, all of his merchandise was freighted in from Wichita
Falls. Rosenfield came to the town as the representative of a Dallas
firm, and when he established his own general store, he continued to look south for his business connections. The Fort Elliott–

Tascosa trails did little to bring the settlement into closer relationships with any of the towns in the Region.[25]

Local use of the lower base roads did, however, indirectly help keep that section of the Panhandle oriented to Dodge City and undoubtedly contributed to the development of the country. As was true of the other trails, the roads on the southern base of the Dodge City–Panhandle Region passed from existence with the arrival of the railroads. Without the necessity of freighting contacts with Dodge City, local users developed new roads leading to new centers of trade.

4. The Jones and Plummer Trail: The Freighting Road to the Panhandle

THE more centrally located of the major trails south, the Jones and Plummer, did not follow the pattern Lieutenant J. H. Simpson had outlined in his report of 1848. Neither the army nor the federal government had a role in its creation, nor was there any thought of advancing civilization through it. The founders were motivated by no more an uplifting purpose than the hope of making a profit supplying the needs of the buffalo hunters who had followed General Philip Sheridan's advice to go where the buffalo were. Since it was not a part of the federal defense strategy for the southwestern frontier, the trail was never surveyed by the army or systematically patrolled. The only military connection it had was in its service as a freighting road for wagons bringing supplies from Dodge City to Fort Supply and Fort Elliott and as an occasional alternate route for troops passing between Dodge City and the eastern Texas Panhandle.

The Jones and Plummer Trail was from the beginning a civilian road, created for commercial purposes. The two former buffalo hunters turned merchants and freighters who marked the trail saw it simply as a route for transporting supplies from Dodge City to their store on the Canadian River and returning buffalo products to the Dodge City railroad sidings. Their comings and goings carved ruts deep enough into the sod for others to follow. The chance meeting of Ed Jones and Joe Plummer that led to their brief partnership and establishment of the trail reflects the nonmilitary side of the development of wagon-road economy. For two decades of the 1870s and 1880s, the trail served as a major freighting highway while the Dodge City–Panhandle Region changed from a culture based on buffalo hunting to one solidly founded on ranching and farming.

The two founders of the trail were true but quite different representatives of the Western Plains pioneers of the post–Civil War period. Charles Edward ("Ed") Jones's life was to encompass nearly the whole of the plains experience. He was at one time or another buffalo hunter, Indian trader, Indian fighter, hide buyer, freighter, bone picker, merchant, rancher, and farmer. He came to the Region when it was an untracked prairie and lived to see it become a settled and productive land. Ed's partner, Joe Plummer, on the other hand, drifted into the Region from an obscure background, made his brief mark on the land, and moved on to new lands and ventures that are totally lost to history.

Charles Edward Jones was born August 10, 1852 at Neenah, Wisconsin. His father, James J. Jones, was an Englishman who came in 1846 with his immigrant parents to Wisconsin, where they settled in Winnebago county. James married Esther T. Clarke from New York State, and there were twelve children, Ed being the next to the oldest.[1]

As a young man just turned twenty, Ed hired out to a Wisconsin firm to hunt buffalo and ship the hides back. His salary was fifty dollars a month, substantial for a young man of his years. With contract in hand, he came to Kansas early in 1872 and for the next few years was a familiar figure in the buffalo camps in and around Dodge City. Ed claimed to have killed one hundred and six buffalo "before breakfast" as his biggest single killing. For a time, either while he was still hunting or immediately thereafter, he traded with the Indians for hides. When buffalo became scarce in Kansas, he turned to freighting supplies from Dodge City into the Panhandle.[2]

Jones gained a reputation for being a hard customer not to be trifled with, fearless, and self-reliant on the plains, whether hunting or freighting. His appearance and name added to the image. He acquired the sobriquet *Dirty Face* when an Indian fired a gun so close to him that Jones was marked by severe powder burns. His

C. E. ("Dirty Face") Jones, 1852–1935, cofounder of the Jones and Plummer Trail, circa 1885. Courtesy Bill Jones, Anaheim, California.

was a good reputation to have, particularly if backed by a certain amount of bravado; legends are made of such stuff. At one point he was driving a twelve-mule team down the Palo Duro on a dark night when someone yelled, "You halt." In J. Wright Mooar's words, "Old Jones says, 'You go to hell, you son-of-a-bitch,' and kept a-going. That fellow never said another word." Jones also knew how to deal with horse thieves. It was his custom on the trail to turn his mules loose at night, making certain his saddle horse was secured to a wagon wheel, for he knew the mules would not stray far from camp. In Dodge he announced, so that all could hear, that he wouldn't hunt his mules if they were stolen, instead, he would take his buffalo gun and hunt down four men, known horse thieves he named. He apparently made believers of the horse thieves operating in Indian Territory. On one of his trips south his mules were stolen, but the next night the leader of the gang sent one of the men back, not only with the mules, but with an apology and a buckskin money bag as well. "I brought you a hundred dollars," he explained. "The boys give it to me to pay the damages."[3]

Ed Jones knew Joe Plummer as a fellow buffalo hunter. Among other things, they were both fiddlers of a sort and exchanged instruments on occasion. However, it was not until the Battle of Adobe Walls that they became more than acquaintances. In the spring of 1874, Joe Plummer joined David Dudley as a partner in hunting buffalo in the Texas Panhandle. Dudley was an experienced hand, having hunted as a partner with Henry H. Raymond and the Masterson brothers, Ed and Bat. Plummer and Dudley, along with Tommy Wallace, set up camp near Adobe Walls to await the spring migration of the buffalo herds. They were attracted to the area by the earlier success of John Wesley and J. Wright Mooar, Jim and Bob Cator, and Lane and Wheeler. A large number of hunters in single camps or passing the time at Adobe Walls also had moved into the Panhandle early in the season in order not to miss the first good shooting.[4]

Business was booming at Adobe Walls, where a stockade, store, saloon, and blacksmith shop had been built near the site of Charles Bent's old Fort Adobe. A. C. Myers hired Ed Jones to haul in a large stock of goods, which made it possible for Jones, who was hauling hides from Texas to Dodge City, to fill his returning wagons with a profitable cargo. He rounded up a caravan of thirty wagons and some fifty freighters who could profit by the same arrangement. With the goods delivered, Jones stayed on to haul cottonwood logs from the Canadian River to build the stockade. Between Myers and Charles Rath, who also set up a store, more than seventy thousand dollars' worth of goods was freighted to an area that appeared unsettled and isolated. James Hanrahan was equally busy in his saloon helping the restless hunters pass the time until the herds arrived.[5]

The spectacular slaughter of buffalo the year before was not lost on the Indians. During the winter, Isatai, a Kwahadi prophet, had exhorted the Comanches to end the wanton killing of buffalo by driving the hunters from the plains. The prophet claimed to have great magic. "He could vomit wagonloads of ammunition from his belly" and stop bullets in midair. Quanah Parker, Comanche leader and son of white captive Cynthia Parker, also preached death and destruction, prodding the warriors into taking up arms. He proposed destruction of the hunters' base at Adobe Walls as a clear signal to the whites that the slaughter of buffalo no longer would be tolerated by the Indians. Eventually the Kwahadis were joined by braves from the Cheyenne and Arapaho reservations. The growing size of the Indian force, more than Isatai's magic, persuaded Lone Wolf and Satanta to bring their Kiowas into the effort as well. With a war party variously estimated at two hundred to seven hundred braves, Quanah rode toward Adobe Walls with confidence, supported by, but not dependent on, the protection of Isatai's medicine. Since their special hatred was directed at all buffalo hunters and not just those at Adobe Walls, the Indians set about killing white hunters wherever they were found.[6]

Besides the men gathered at Adobe Walls playing cards and drinking Hanrahan's stock of whiskey, some fifty or more outfits of varying size and strength were scattered along the area's streams, already killing buffalo. It is not known how many white men were in the Panhandle at the time, but after the attack on Adobe Walls "between two and three hundred hunters" gathered at the stores for protection. Among the hunters at work was Joe Plummer and crew.[7]

By the beginning of June, Plummer, Dudley, and Wallace had set up camp at the mouth of Red Deer Creek. Plummer knew Dudley from his own association with the Mastersons and from his frequent social contact with Dudley in Dodge City. During that first week of June, Plummer left the other two at the Red Deer Creek camp to go into Adobe Walls and buy supplies. J. Wright Mooar vividly describes the scene when Plummer returned to camp:

He came on into camp, and there was his wagon burned up, and there was his hides destroyed, and there was his two men dead in camp, and was just about half an hour until sundown. They just butchered them, that was all. Dave Dudley was propped up in a sitting position, had one of his seeds, had it cut out and fastened in his hand and it was tied around out there, and a stake drove in the ground, and his hand put on that stake so he would have to look at it.

They had him tied up and they cut a hole in the pit of his stomach and drove a wooden stake right down through here and into the ground with an ax. He had long hair down to his shoulders, and they scalped him, and took every hair of his head and ears.

They just killed the other man. They scalped him but didn't butcher him up so.

He [Plummer] was driving a four-mule team. He jumped down off his wagon, pulled his pocket knife out of his boot or belt, and cut the belly band of that near lead horse, dropped his knife, and jumped onto that horse bareback, a blind bridle, the collar on, and his buffalo gun in his hand.

Instead of turning around and going back, he went straight ahead, right into the brush. He got across the creek, into the breaks as quick as he could. He was headed up the Red Deer, and swung around that night.

[The Indians had] waited the way he was coming [into camp], and they let him get through and let him see these fellows [Dudley and Wallace]. They didn't shoot until they seed what he was going to do. He got across the creek, but they had put their horses so danged far off that by the time they got their horses and got around it was sundown, and they couldn't trail him. He said there was a hundred shots fired at him. He came right through them.

He knew how to travel and came back. He didn't get to Adobe Walls that night. It was 40 miles up there. I met him . . . the next day about half way between the Adobe Walls store and the river, . . . his horse was played out and he was walking leading his horse.[8]

Mooar and his crew accompanied Plummer to Adobe Walls, where his story caused "lots of commotion," according to Mooar. Warnings were sent to other hunters known to be in the vicinity. A survey crew from the firm of Gunter and Munson, along with its military escort, happened to be there when Plummer came in.

They followed him back to his camp to help bury Dudley and Wallace. Billy Dixon reported that Plummer found his horses still in harness. The surveyors and troop went on to Camp Supply while Joe returned to Adobe Walls. Mooar rounded up some extra men and hired an ox team to bring in his hides. Hanrahan tried to persuade Mooar and the other hunters to remain. Some were persuaded. Mooar was not.[9]

Hanrahan's arguments seemed to lose force as reports of other Indian attacks began reaching Adobe Walls. Anderson More rode in as thoroughly frightened as Plummer to report that his crew, camped at the breaks of the Washita, had suffered a fate similar to Plummer's. Since all signs pointed to a serious threat by a large force of hostile Indians, Mooar decided to return to the safety of Dodge City as soon as possible.[10]

When Mooar pulled out, Joe Plummer undoubtedly went along; he had no reason to stay, for the Indians had wiped him clean leaving only his Big 50 and his team of mules. Mooar had an uneventful return trip to Dodge City, passing along word of the murders to men he met on the trail. Two of them, one a close friend of Tommy Wallace, saddled up that night and "made a dead run for Dodge, and neither one of them was back there again." About eight miles out, Mooar's wagons met Ed ("Dirty Face") Jones shuffling along in his carpet slippers. Jones had gone back to Dodge City alone and was returning with more freight for Myers. He had heard of the Indian depredations after leaving Dodge City, but he did not know who had been killed. When he and Mooar were planning their previous trip together, they had been warned of possible Indian trouble, but at that time Jones's reaction reflected typical frontier fatalism. "If you were born to be killed by Indians," he said, "you would be killed by Indians if you went to New York. That wouldn't make any difference." Now, the actual killing and the nature of the mutilation caused him to reconsider. He stopped just long enough to inquire about who died and to tell Mooar that he had driven ninety miles without sleeping or unharnessing his eight-mule team. In spite of the danger of traveling alone, he felt obligated to continue on to Adobe Walls to deliver his cargo, which included, among other things, ammunition. There he caught a few hours sleep and, his wagon only partly loaded, hurried back to overtake Mooar at the

Palo Duro, where he felt considerably more secure among the other well-armed freighters. "You fellows can drive as slow as you have a mind to," he said. "I don't care how slow you drive." When Mooar's caravan reached Dodge City, its members learned of yet another scalping, this one within sight of the city.[11]

Neither Plummer nor Jones was quit of Adobe Walls yet. Dudley's death and mutilation were taken very hard by all who knew him. Henry Raymond said he "could not feel worse to hear of a brother's death" and hoped the government would offer "some inducement" to avenge it. He, personally, would "be glad to help slay the red devils." He and others were to have the opportunity, for more alarming news was yet to come, affecting an even larger public.[12]

On June 26, Quanah Parker and his war party attacked Adobe Walls and were soundly repulsed. Although the threat had an immediate chilling effect on the economy of the whole Region, G. Derek West saw little strategic change: "Neither side gained much advantage from the Battle of Adobe Walls. Because of their spirited resistance the whites survived, but buffalo hunting in the area was restricted for the season of 1874. . . . Some of the defenders . . . never hunted again, and the merchants suffered severe financial loss." Eventually, most of the hunters in the Panhandle returned to one of the forts.[13]

To the hunters, it seemed that the federal authorities were excessively slow in organizing an expedition against the Indians; a few ventured back into the country deemed, correctly, too dangerous for effective hunting. One of these was Emanuel Dubbs, who was persuaded by Tom Nixon to help organize a party large enough to protect itself on the open prairie; twenty-eight men and fourteen wagons were recruited. Ed Jones, who was waiting impatiently for the Region to become safe for freighting, joined the group. Once on the range, they found the party too large for successful hunting, so they split into two groups. Dubbs was elected captain of one group, with Ed Jones his second in command. As Dubbs's group approached the breaks leading into Wolf Creek, they "discovered a herd of moving objects," which they first thought were antelope but which Dubbs believed to be Indian horses. Dubbs proved to be correct, and soon the hunting party was spotted by the Indians who were driving the herd. In Dubbs's words:

We knew we were in for it. We rode back to the teams, turned them back on a run for we were on a narrow ridge, which gave the Indians all the advantage, as they would screen themselves, while we were exposed, and we wanted to make the level flat before the attack commenced. Jones and I rode along each side of the teams and with our whips urged them on. . . . Quicker than I can write, bullets were singing around and past us. The Indians came up the hollows on each side, and in a minute one of our brave scout leaders went down and his team all tangled up, and him yelling for help. We had to turn the rest of the teams back and make a corral with the wagons and hides, some returning the fire of the Indians while the rest worked. By the time this was done five horses were killed and one man shot through the hand. All the men were fairly well protected, but every once in a while a bullet would pass through and hit a horse or mule. Quite a brisk firing was kept up on both sides, without a great deal of execution on either, until about three o'clock [when] a party of fifteen Indians tried to cross the little divide from one hollow to the other. I think they thought they were out of reach of our guns. . . . We waited until they were about half way across. We raised our sights to five hundred yards . . . there were only three horses out of fifteen ever got across and only five Indians. Those who were wounded crept up behind the dead horses, some two or three fired at us, but not very long for a dead horse was very slight protection against our long shell "big fifties," and "forty-fives." This put a check to the attack for awhile. About sundown the firing ceased on both sides, and we counted up our losses and consulted what to do. We had lost nearly half our stock. But we concluded by using our riding horses we could make out to move all our wagons, by only hitching two to the wagon. There were none of our men hurt except the man who was shot in the hand in the beginning. We decided that as soon as the moon went down, which would be about 9 o'clock, we would quietly hitch up and drive back to the main camp that night. We did not think we were strong enough to make an attack on the Indians whose numbers we estimated to be between forty and fifty, with a large herd of horses.[14]

Back in camp the hunters decided to reverse roles and attack the Indians. This they did with amazing success, forcing the Indians to abandon much of their gear and extra horses. The hunters then gathered the Indian stock, consisting of seventy-nine head of horses, mules, and ponies. When they reached Dodge City, the animals were divided evenly among the men, who sold those they did not keep to replace their own losses. The general feeling was that they came out about even.

Not the least of the consequences of the Adobe Walls fight was the intervention of the army. The attack had represented more than Quanah Parker had imagined. It was an open challenge to the continued development of the Panhandle, as well as to the accepted Indian policies of the United States government. Officials in Washington could not let it go unchallenged, and the army command on the frontier was chafing to end the Indian problem with force. When Jones returned from the Dubbs-Nixon venture, he found the army ready to move.

On July 27, 1874, Colonel (Bvt. Maj. Gen.) Nelson A. Miles received orders to organize a military force designated the Indian Territorial Expedition. With eight companies of the Sixth Cavalry and four companies of the Fifth Infantry, Colonel Miles moved from Fort Dodge toward the Washita River, the Antelope Hills, and the headwaters of the Red River. Lieutenant Frank D. Baldwin was directed by Miles to organize a detachment of scouts and to advance ahead of the main force. This scout company consisted of twenty friendly Delaware Indians and seventeen frontiersmen. Among those passing the mandatory target practice and signing up for duty were men having an immediate interest in the Adobe Walls fight or in the buffalo hunting business in general. Some, such as Bat Masterson and Billy Dixon, were at Adobe Walls during the fight; others, such as C. E. Jones, Dave Campbell, and Joe Plummer, were not only buffalo hunters but had known David Dudley personally.[15]

On August 11, 1874 the scouting party left Fort Dodge. At about the same time, other units were leaving Forts Sill, Union, Concho, and Richardson. All converged on the Texas Panhandle. Baldwin pushed his men hard. On the night of August 17 a violent windstorm struck. "Had a hard time," the lieutenant wrote, "to prevent horses from stampeding. All men out except J. H. Plummer and C. E. Jones who had to be ordered a second time. These 2 men will be discharged at first opportunity." The following day the detachment marched fifty miles and camped on West Adobe Walls Creek. Early the next morning they reached the stockade at Adobe Walls, arriving just in time to drive off a new attack. They chased the startled Indians across the Canadian River and turned back only when Baldwin felt he would soon be engaging a superior force. There were no casualties.[16]

Miles (Niles) City crossing on the Jones and Plummer Trail at the Cimarron River crossing. A section of adobe was still standing on the south bank in the 1980s. Photograph by the author.

Back at Adobe Walls the hunters held council and after considerable discussion decided to abandon the stores and return to Camp Supply with Baldwin. The lieutenant advised against this but was grateful for the additional strengthening of his unit, which grew to seventy-two men. After leaving Adobe Walls, Baldwin moved down the Canadian to rendezvous with Miles. Next day the scouts again surprised a small party of Indians, killing one and wounding another. They passed the spot where Dudley and Wallace were killed, and Baldwin named the stream Chicken Creek, since he had seen a number of prairie chickens in the area. They rejoined Colonel Miles on the twenty-fourth, and, true to his word, Baldwin discharged Jones and Plummer. Along with two other men who shared their fate, Jones and Plummer were left to shift for themselves some dozen miles west of the Antelope Hills.[17]

Although they had known each other in the past, it was with Baldwin's scouts that the names of Jones and Plummer were first linked. Thrown together during the early campaign, they apparently discovered a certain affinity—including sleeping habits and disdain for army brass. From this association they formed a partnership that led first to establishing a hide-trading venture and supply depot and eventually to the trail that was to bear their names.

By the time Joe and Ed made it back to Dodge City from the Panhandle, they had worked out the details of the partnership. They knew the hostile Indians would either be herded back to the reservation by the army or annihilated. The hunters would once again be swarming over the plains, shooting buffalo and looking for a convenient place to sell hides. The need for a hide station south of Adobe Walls, yet still in the Panhandle, was clear. Freighting would remain the backbone of the enterprise, only now they would be hauling for their own profit. In Dodge City they accumulated a good stock of supplies and returned in the fall of 1874 to the hunting range, expecting to capitalize on the revitalized trade; they were not disappointed. Mose Hayes has given a first-hand account of the post they established:

Ed Jones and, I think Joe Plummer came down from the north, from Dodge, following the buffalo hunters, and built a store on the head of Wolf Creek out of cottonwood pickets. They had a dugout to keep their stores in, and they had a bar. They sold lots of whiskey, kept guns and ammunition for sale, and bought dried buffalo meat, tongues and hides.[18]

During the next few months they added a large picket house ("20x 60 of cottonwood logs and covered . . . with poles and dirt") that had a number of rooms and were soon doing a brisk business. "I delivered more hides to Dodge than any other man," Ed wrote. "In 1876, I delivered 3600 hides and in 1877 I delivered 2500."[19]

In fact, business was so good they took on a number of drivers to haul freight and supplies from Dodge City. Among them was H. E. Siders, a green kid from an eastern Kansas farm who arrived in Dodge on July 7, 1877. He picked up a job here and there but always seemed to get fired for some indiscretion, such as falling asleep on night guard. Things were not to change much after he met Joe and Ed. In Siders' words:

I again returned to Dodge and the wagon yard where I loafed a few weeks when I hired out to Jones and Plummer to pull the jerk-line over an eight horse and mule freight team to transport booze, grain and groceries for their store on Wolf Creek, being about two hundred miles south of Dodge. Had many exciting and dangerous experiences in that business driving in winter and alone . . . I was driving out of Dodge, camping on Crooked creek, some thirty miles south of Dodge; came one of those Kansas Blizzards, rain and snow. My cargo consisted of booze, horse feed and a beautiful set of furniture, for Joe Morgan who ranched on the Canadian River, (Joe had just brought a brand new wife to his ranch) some thirty miles south of the Jones & P store. I dared not turn my stock loose in the blizzard, so tied them to the wagon wheels and wagon bed, climbed in my bed in the front wagon, and to keep from freezing tapped the whiskey barrel with a straw and then nearly froze. My mules having no hay to eat, and being nearly frozen too, turned their attention to Mr. Morgan's nice furniture and literally ate it up, along with the top side boards, but it took them twenty-four hours to complete their dirty work, the storm lasting that long. I never knew how much I lowered the booze in that barrel; any way I figured it kept me from freezing. Well, when the storm let-up I moved on to the store, and was promptly fired for letting the mules eat the furniture and I've forgotten how Joe Morgan took the furniture episode. . . .

In spite of the destruction of Morgan's freight, the Jones and Plummer store was gaining a reputation as a place of refuge for a man in need of whiskey, ammunition, or a rest from whatever cares beset him. [20]

Bat Masterson found this to be true in the winter of 1878. In February of that year he was close on the heels of a gang that had attempted to hold up the Santa Fe train near Kinsley. Supported by Charlie Bassett, Josh Webb, Miles Mix, and John ("Red") Clarke, he had pushed into No Man's Land. They came close to trapping Mike Rourke, the reputed leader of the robbers, and an unknown companion near Beaver, but the pair eluded the posse. Masterson learned that Rourke and his men were headed for the Jones and Plummer place and set out in hot pursuit. Since Masterson knew both Ed and Joe, he felt they would be helpful. When the posse arrived at the Wolf Creek station, Masterson found that the gang had abandoned its equipment there and had struck out on horseback, traveling as light as possible, toward the Canadian River and Texas. As impartial merchants, the partners had been useful to both sides of the law. Masterson's possemen knew it was hopeless to follow across the Staked Plains, so they turned their weary mounts down the Jones and Plummer Trail for a slower and sadder return to Dodge City. [21]

Masterson and crew were among the last of the Jones and Plummer customers. Trade with the buffalo hunters had remained brisk throughout the 1876 season, but by the end of the 1877 hunt it was clear from the stories the hunters brought in with their reduced number of hides that the business was petering out. The partners, like others who had road ranches or trading posts, began looking for other opportunities. What was immediately available was their knowledge and control of certain grassland. *Control* is used here not in the sense of ownership but as a man's recognized range rights. For Jones and Plummer, this meant a right to the water they had appropriated and to the surrounding range. Where water was scarce, as it was in that section of the Great Plains, control included all the land around it, "for water was the sine qua non of the cattle country." Jones and Plummer had water, so they became cattle ranchers. Their old store was converted to a ranch headquarters, although many people still remembered it as a road ranch where supplies could be obtained. [22]

Ranching apparently did not set well with Plummer, and in June 1878, after Masterson's visit, Jones notified the public of the mutual dissolution of the partnership. Jones took over the assets and liabilities, and Joe Plummer was a free spirit once again. For some time Jones had been trading with his Cheyenne and Arapaho neighbors, a business he increased as he used his knowledge of the land to "locate cattle men," an interesting but not very profitable sideline. He still depended heavily on freighting to such cattlemen as Bates and Beal, Charles Goodnight, and Joe Morgan. Mixing ranching with freighting, not the best of business combinations, Jones held out for two more seasons, then sold his holdings to a pair of Burnett County brothers, Doc and Al Barton. The Bartons in turn sold control and facilities to Henry Whiteside ("Hank") Creswell, who used the old Jones and Plummer place as his headquarters. By then there could have been little of value left. As Ed Brainard put it, "I don't suppose there was much buying in that." This, plus other deals Creswell negotiated, gave him control of practically all of Ochiltree and Roberts counties and part of Hemphill. By the time he had put together the Creswell Land and Cattle Company in conjunction with a Scottish and English syndicate in 1885, one of the most influential ranches in Texas was operating out of the old whiskey and buffalo post Jones and Plummer had established.[23]

The Jones and Plummer Trail was not heavily used, nor was the population along it static. There was always change as the trail shifted to meet the needs or whims of merchants, freighters, and stage owners. Jones was probably the architect, choosing the river and creek crossings and marking the specific route. It started, or rather ended, at the partners' front door, connecting the Panhandle with Dodge City's Front Street. During its lifetime, four towns were organized close enough to it to cause it to be altered to accommodate the new main streets. After 1885 at its northern end the trail began to turn square corners, conforming to the granger's section lines. Even nature changed the details as it eroded crossings and in one dramatic instance dropped a fifty-foot section into a salt sinkhole near the Kansas line. Road ranches appeared and withered with the fortunes or interests of their owners. Although it was primarily a freighting trail, thousands of head of Texas cattle

"He Missed His Tip." Quarter-page illustration from the National Police Gazette, *October 3, 1885. It accompanies an account of Grant Wells's killing
of Robert E. Robins in an attempted holdup of the stage on the Jones and
Plummer Trail in September, 1885. Library of Congress.*

followed its ruts to the Dodge City stockyards. People then and now confused it with the Adobe Walls Trail, threatened to absorb it into other cattle trails, thought to extend it down into Texas, and accused it of wandering off to Wyoming. It remained alive and vibrant, changing and changeable, an unbearably dry and hot ribbon in summer and a life-threatening trap in the blizzards of winter.

At midpoint in the trail's history, say about 1879, a traveler journeying to the Jones and Plummer front door from Dodge City would cover some one hundred sixty eight miles, would cross six flowing streams and rivers, would observe at least four different textures of dust settling on his boots, and would wonder for hours whether he were the only traveler on the plains. If he had loaded his wagon with general merchandise at Wright, Beverley & Co. on Front Street he would start the trip by making a sharp turn down Bridge Street, heading south out of town. He would have experienced his first annoyance at having to pay the tollkeeper two dollars to take his six- or even four-team hookup across the wooden bridge; still, it was worth the price to make an easy crossing. The road out of town was flanked by cowboy camps, and the wheels of the wagon at first would have turned up fine sand as the sand hills rolled gently for a few miles and then gave over to the short grass and dark soil of the High Plains. [24]

The first possible stop was just ten miles out at the Mulberry crossing, where A. H. Dugan ran a flea-bitten store and charged twenty-five cents a bucket for watering the team. The freighters might grumble but they paid the price, for it was another ten miles before water was again assured at a spring-fed stream that trickled into Crooked Creek. In later years road ranches would be available at various points along the way, but in 1879 the traveler's eye could sweep the horizon without detecting any sign of habitation. The last tree he would have seen for many miles was the lone cottonwood on the south bank of the Arkansas River—a landmark dating back to early Santa Fe Trail days. In 1879, Carrie Schmoker traveled down the Jones and Plummer Trail to a new claim in Meade county. "In all that distance," she wrote, "from Dodge to about three miles from the site of Meade we saw not a single house, fence, field, or tree, nothing but the brown trail and on every side as far as the eye could reach, just grassy prairie land that was not green for there had been no rain for many months. On the high flats we saw a few prairie dog towns and we met a few freighting outfits going into town."[25]

As the trail approached the Meade county line it skirted the east bank of Crooked Creek and kept to the edge of the sand hills until it turned west near the future site of Fowler, crossing rich, flat prairie lands. By the mid-1880s the traveler might have rested or eaten a meal at one of the road ranches. Certainly after 1885 he could have found an excellent dinner at the Wilburn House or by the next year at Fowler could have bought from Linn Frazier's store "goods, dirt cheap, on a dirt floor" or contested the flies at the Waco House for a skimpy supper.

After turning west, the trail user went twelve miles to George W. ("Hoodoo") Brown's road ranch. Here there was not only food and drink for the passengers and fodder for the horses but sleeping arrangements if desired. Hoodoo had located near a spring overlooking an artesian valley that lay to the north of the meandering Crooked Creek. His place was a welcome refuge for all who passed along the trail.

From Brown's ranch the trail turned almost straight south over what was to be called Irish Flats because a number of Irish families settled there. Approaching the crossing of Crooked Creek, the traveler would have been impressed with the high bluffs carved by a stream that seemed gentle, even placid, and frequently went dry in late July. As was true of any creek crossing, high water could create danger even here. A young freighter, the son of W. H. Currens of Dodge City, was killed when he fell into the creek and was run over by a wagon. At the confluence (a large word for such a small transaction) of Skunk Arroyo and Crooked Creek, C. ("Little") Pratt built a store, but his name was never associated with the crossing. O. D. Lemert, a rancher who lived nearby, later (1881) secured a post office under the name of Odee. That name stuck. The store, which came to be associated with Odee, passed into the hands of John Marts, who converted it into a road ranch. At first glance it might have appeared dull and mundane and certainly an unlikely setting for romance, but Dave Mackey, a cowboy working for the Crooked L, found that it had a special charm. The

Marts had taken in Arabelle Sewell when her parents died, and she was working the day Dave passed through. Mrs. Tom A. Judy summarized the prairie romance as neat and natural as the real thing. "Belle liked his swash-buckling manner and he liked Belle. After a courtship they were married in 1884."[26]

The land changed out of Odee. The dust picked up by the wagon wheels would be sandy red from the drifted sand hills, which were covered with buck sage and yucca. In places the mounds continued shifting, barren of vegetation. It was fifteen miles of wild hills, dry as a buffalo bone, before the next water was reached at the Cimarron. At least two town builders and possibly a third tried to capitalize on the Cimarron crossing of the Jones and Plummer Trail. J. M. Byers built a store and a blacksmith shop five miles north of the state line. Rose Bud, the local correspondent to the *Fowler City Graphic*, claimed a community of three hundred, which brought the following retort from a neighboring-community reporter who visited the town and found two stores and three sod houses: "Gewhillikens! what awful families they do raise in that neck 'o woods; twenty-five to each family, and all formed in four months. Golly! what soil, and on sod too; and yet some tenderfoot will tell the innocents that nothing can be raised in southwestern Kansas." Byers did secure a post office that served the area off and on for twenty years, moving three times during its existence.[27]

When the town of Nirwana was platted, Byers moved store and stamps to the new site. Nirwana came closer than the earlier efforts to being a river-crossing town on the order of Beaver, Oklahoma. Stimulated by the land boom of 1885–86, it prospered briefly, but the general exodus of settlers from Meade County in 1888 reduced it to open prairie once again. Its site was officially located well over a mile from the river, but the Meade editor described it somewhat closer. "Nerawana," he wrote, "is situated at the intersection of the Cimarron river and the Jones and Plummer Trail on a gentle southerly slope which terminates at the river bank." There was a post office, livery stable, two general stores, a schoolhouse (which blew down in a western Kansas gale), and a park.[28]

Neither of these towns had much influence on the development of the area although they both served the trail and the settlers for a few months. The mysterious town of Ferguson probably lived only in the pages of the *Fowler City Graphic*, where it had a correspondent and its own column of news. The name first appeared in the July 16, 1885 issue announcing: "We are going to have a town on the banks of the classic Cimarron just where the Jones & Plummer Trail crosses the river. The soil is rich and water is easily gotten, but we don't want the county seat." The last statement makes it unique among western Kansas towns and undoubtedly accounts for its ghostly character. It did continue to send announcements to the Fowler paper but never gained any other recognition.

If none of these towns flourished, at least the Cimarron crossing could boast of a spectacular prairie dog town on the flats north of the river and two road ranches: Miles City on the south bank and Charles Heinz's (or Hines's) place on the north bank. Captain and Mrs. Henry A. Busing had a store and post office (borrowed from Byers City for a brief time) and some sheds and corrals, all made of sod or adobe, and the station was named Miles City. Part of the adobe walls of the store still stand. The old-timers used any of the three names—Miles, Heinz, and Busing—spelled whichever way they liked, to identify the crossing. All knew it as the Cimarron, the toughest passage the traveler had to make on his journey thus far. The river lay between hills, especially impressive to the north, marking the extent of a flat, even valley, lush with grass up to the very edge of the water. Under normal conditions it was a sandy, slightly briny stream; at other times it was a red, turbid flood. After such a flood it invariably became boggy in places, which tended to shift with each heavy rain, making a crossing somewhat of a gamble. Said Billy Dixon: "The Cimarron is commonly regarded as one of the most dangerous streams in the southwest. Its width often is three or four hundred yards. . . . It is filled to the brim with sand [that] . . . grips like a vise, and the river sucks down and buries all that it touches."[29]

From Miles City to Beaver was forty miles and another crossing. For the freighter, it was a tough pull. An old hand at freighting, José Romero, reported:

The hardest section of the road was a six-mile stretch of deep sand in the valley south of Beaver Creek. The big Studebaker wagons when heavily loaded sank into the sand almost to the hubs. When we hit this stretch of road we dropped the two trail wagons and hauled the one big wagon

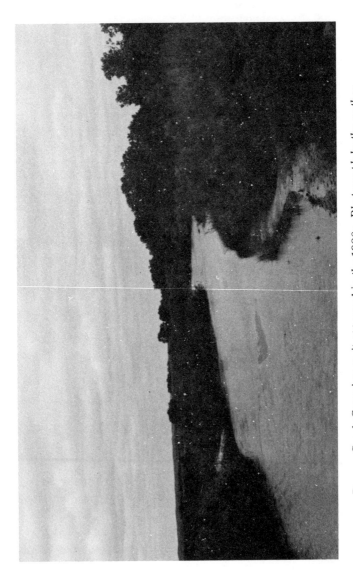

Beaver Creek Crossing as it appeared in the 1980s. Photograph by the author.

through the sand. Then we rode one mule and drove the teams six miles back to get the other two wagons. They were usually no heavier than the one big wagon and could be taken through at the same time. [30]

Sand clung to the wheels even after they crossed the river. Oliver Nelson recalled that "the trail here was loose sand so that freight teams had to double to pull down [Beaver's] Main street." [31]

The Beaver River could be as unpleasant to cross as any prairie stream, but at its peaceful best it also could be as serene as it was beautiful. The Fowler editor on a fishing trip reported it in its more benevolent state: "Nature could not have lavished her charms to better advantage. The Beaver, a beautiful stream wending its way down along grassy banks with here and there an emerald isle raising its head out of the clear sparkling water." [32]

Before they found a suitable bottom, Jones and Plummer had gone east down the North Branch of the Canadian (now known as Beaver River) for about a mile. Apparently, this crossing changed on occasion, not becoming fixed until 1880. That year Jim Lane brought a load of merchandise and his family down the Jones and Plummer Trail. He built a large, comfortable sod house: "The rafters were made of poles cut from the woods growing along the stream. Brush served in place of the ordinary sheeting and layers of sod took the place of shingles. The walls within were plastered with a mixture of sand and gypsum, dug from the hills along the stream." He opened a store in one room, which made it a bona fide road ranch. This establishment, together with a sod-walled corral, ugly as a mud fence, constituted the origins of Beaver, Oklahoma. [33]

As was true of most road ranchers, Lane made a modest living, but he lost much of his future prospects when the Beaver Town Company platted its main street on top of the Jones and Plummer Trail. The town-company agent persuaded Lane that he was a squatter with no legal rights to the land. Apparently, Lane "cheerfully relinquished" his dubious claims to the whole town for the slightly more acceptable grant of a sizable number of platted lots. If a sad day for Lane, it was a bright one for the freighters on the trail, who had a hungry customer in the town of Beaver, the earliest settlement to be established and to survive on the route. As a town, Beaver perhaps did not have all the amenities of Dodge, and prices were higher; still, it had about it the air of civilization. It could boast of tough marshals, vigilance committees, a jail, and the establishments necessary to support these essential signs of progress. But in 1879 it was just one more river to cross. [34]

Since the traveler was headed for the old Jones and Plummer hide station, he would need to pass through Oklahoma into the big-ranch country of Texas. From the Beaver River bank, the trail led up a draw (a block west of present-day Douglas Avenue) on semi-firm soil, then headed southwest over buffalo grass through the southwest section of town. Here the ruts cut across the High Plains of buffalo and grama grass, which protected the land from wind erosion and guaranteed rich grazing for buffalo or cattle. If the traveler were new to the country, the most striking topographical feature he would notice were the sinks, or depressions, of varying sizes, from a few feet to several acres in which grass stood waist high—a natural hay when cut and cured. The trail, according to Mose Hayes, who traversed it many times, went due south for approximately thirty miles to the place where the town of Booker now stands. Passing Brubaker Lake, it headed southwest toward Gillalow Lake, then went on to the Jones and Plummer Ranch on Wolf Creek just east of present-day U.S. 83. It was approximately fifty-seven miles from Jim Lane's place to Ed Jones's door. [35]

For the original Jones and Plummer Trail, this ended the trip. But the trail experienced a kind of second life when someone drove on down to Mobeetie without claiming title. Jones and Plummer Trail was awarded the honor by default, that is, common acceptance. People began drawing lines across various maps, and Jones and Plummer got its share of labels; but, more important, people simply identified the extension to Mobeetie as part of the Jones and Plummer Trail. [36]

Therefore, the traveler who wanted to cover the length of the trail had another leg in the journey to make, doubling the distance already covered to Beaver. The rapid growth of Mobeetie greatly altered freighting patterns and made the Jones and Plummer Trail far more attractive to freighters who used it in preference to other trails. Mose Hayes said of the transition:

At first the freighting to Fort Elliott was from Dodge to Camp Supply, and across the Canadian at the Springer ranch, and on thirty miles to Fort

Elliott. After the town of Mobeetie got started, more of the freighting came down the Jones and Plummer Trail to about Clear Creek and turned off to the east before it got to the end of the Jones and Plummer Trail on Wolf and continued south across Wolf Creek, up one of its tributaries, across the divide, down Horse Creek, and crossed the Canadian at the mouth of Horse Creek, about a mile above the site of Canadian, and then up Red Deer, out on the plains, and on to Mobeetie.[37]

The terrain down to Mobeetie would appear much as it had around Wolf Creek. For a few years late in its history a traveler had the advantage of breaking his journey at a road ranch. About two miles north of the Canadian on the East Fork of Horse Creek, John Gerlach had a dugout on the slope of a hill. John left Illinois in 1883, heading west intending to collect a debt owed him. When he became stranded in the Panhandle, he went to work at the Springer ranch. By November 1884 he had accumulated enough capital to put in a store with a small stock of goods. He wrote his brother and in February, George, age twenty, came down the Jones and Plummer Trail in a mule-drawn wagon loaded with farm implements and a dozen chickens. Eliminating as many middlemen as possible by hauling their own goods and raising feed and garden crops, the two brothers soon had a thriving business.[38]

Their store consisted of a main room, twenty by twenty-four feet, built of logs and covered with clay plaster. Corrals of logs were added to encourage freighters to make Gerlach's Store a major stop, since "the young proprietors handled supplies of almost every description, from lumber and coffins, to cooked meals." By 1887 it was clear to them that the railroad would drastically alter the traffic down the trail, so in the spring they moved their one-room store to Hogtown and then on to Canadian when that town was platted later the same year.[39]

If the trip to the Canadian River was routine, the crossing of the Canadian was a different matter. When Temple Houston, the brilliant and erratic son of Sam ("The Raven") Houston, the renowned first president of independent Texas, encountered the Canadian, he shook his fist at the river and declaimed, "Talk about the Mississippi being the Father of Waters when it is but an even ramrod compared to the Canadian!" Charles N. Gould summarizes the prospect the traveler faced:

Canadian River is perhaps more treacherous than any other stream of the plains. The stream is either dry or a raging torrent. The river may have been dry for weeks at a time, when suddenly, without warning, a wall of water several feet high rushes down the channel, sweeping everything before it, and for a number of days the river continues high, then gradually subsides. Following this period of abnormal flow the sand in the stream becomes "quicksand," or loose sand which appears firm but gives way suddenly under foot, rendering the stream extremely dangerous to cross. Many a herd of cattle has been mired in Canadian River, and every year loaded wagons and even teams are abandoned.[40]

Once in Mobeetie, alias Sweetwater, alias Hidetown, the traveler had reached the Mother City of the Panhandle. It had all the advantages of Dodge City: gambling and dance halls, saloons, hotels, and by 1882 two banks. Even some of the names on the store fronts and some of the prominent people were the same: Charles Rath, Robert M. Wright, Lee and Reynolds, and, for a while, Bat Masterson. Mobeetie residents built a bigger jail, but the town didn't have as spectacular a Boot Hill. And it didn't have, never was to have, a railroad. Although its trade territory extended a hundred miles in every direction, its early demise was inevitable without rail facilities. It flourished for a decade, but it was already on the skids in 1889 when half the inhabitants, along with the rest of the boomers, left for the free land in Oklahoma. What was left of the Jones and Plummer Trail became strictly a local road.

Ed Jones had marked the trail well. The watering places were spaced closer than those on many of the other trails; the terrain was smoother, or at least flatter; and as much of the sand as possible was avoided. The old Military Road was safer and the Tuttle Trail was more direct, but neither was as convenient for the freighter. By the time the way stations were in place, filling the gaps between river crossings, the Jones and Plummer Trail was a very serviceable route. Every freighter had his horror stories of chopping lanes through the ice to pull heavy wagons through a river or bogging down at a crossing or facing an unexpected blizzard, but, considering the options they had, the freighters tended to stick to the old trail.

At the peak of its freighting days, say 1880 to 1886, amazing amounts of freight passed over the Jones and Plummer Trail. But even in the beginning, almost from the first day Joe and Ed marked the route, there was heavy use. Richard Bussell described the spectacular transportation of supplies to build Fort Elliott, all moved en masse:

In the summer of 1875 one might have seen a long caravan of wagons loaded with lumber and supplies drawn by oxen and mule teams wending its way from Dodge City down the Jones and Plummer Trail. . . . For two days these wagons kept pulling up to a rise of ground about two miles from Hidetown where their freight was unloaded.[41]

Although this was undoubtedly the most impressive single venture, the Dodge City papers frequently noted the arrival of large "freighting trains." On August 6, 1878, for instance, four trains totaling fifty wagons came in from the south. It was not unusual for the large concerns, such as Lee and Reynolds and Charles Rath, to send trains of ten or twenty wagons. Lee & Ferguson purchased twenty specially designed replacement wagons at one time. Dodge City's Wright, Beverley & Company had a retail business of $250,000, much of it going into some freighter's wagon headed south. The *Dodge City Times* boasted that Charles Rath alone was shipping 150,000 pounds of freight a week to Mobeetie, all of it down the Jones and Plummer Trail. Not to be outdone, the *Tascosa Pioneer* pointed to the 119,000 pounds of goods received during the previous week. When the merchants brought in only 50,000 pounds one week, the editor called it a dull season. Each of the large stores there carried stock valued at more than $50,000, and it was estimated that each averaged between 25,000 and 50,000 pounds of merchandise hauled overland each month.[42]

Besides the merchants, there were the big ranchers, who brought in their own supplies in their own wagons or contracted with individuals to bring goods to the ranches. Supplying the ranches added a great deal to the traffic on the trail. The buffalo hunters, who created the first business boom in Dodge City, used the trail as a main artery into the killing fields. There were at least two thousand buffalo hunters in western Kansas between 1872 and 1874, when more than eight hundred fifty thousand hides were shipped out of Dodge City. A single hunter, such as Orlando A. ("Brick") Bond,

George Reynolds and O.A. ("Brick") Bond. P. G. Reynolds's oldest son and Brick Bond, buffalo hunter, bone picker, saloon and dance hall operator, and drug store owner, after a successful hunt. Courtesy Boot Hill Museum, Dodge City, Kansas.

required five wagons to haul supplies and hides, and other hunters had much larger outfits. When the herds thinned out in Kansas, many of the hunters moved south and found the Jones and Plummer a convenient route in bringing hides to Dodge City. Bone pickers, the buffalo hunters' scavengers, also fanned out from the trail, clearing the dried-bone evidence of the slaughter. Bond, a hunter turned picker, had wagons on one return trip loaded with twenty-five tons of bones, which would have required the skeletons of one thousand four hundred buffalo. In 1883 alone the bone pickers would have accounted for at least three thousand two hundred wagons loaded to the top board, many of them coming up the Jones and Plummer Trail. When the homesteaders began moving into Kansas south of Dodge City, traffic picked up considerably. Besides their own needs, farmers short on cash joined in the commercial side of freighting for brief stints. Since there was always a demand for freighting, the settlers found it a profitable if somewhat dangerous second profession. [43]

As a freighting road, in spite of its windswept exposure and treacherous crossings, the Jones and Plummer Trail served the Region well. It was to make one more substantial contribution when the southwestern portion of Kansas became, almost overnight, a favored site for new homesteaders. With homesteads filling in the land, three trading centers developed on or near the trail. Each new town added to the traffic on the trail and to the profits of the middlemen-merchants of Dodge City. Since all supplies for the new towns came from Dodge, the recent loss of the cattle trade there was offset by new merchandise orders from the Jones and Plummer Trail towns.

In February 1885, L. P. Horton and Charles P. Brown platted a town just north of the Ford-Meade county line in Kansas. Situated on a "gentle swell of the Crooked Creek," the town was named for Brown's infant son, Wilburn. Horton and Brown, the former from Michigan and the latter from Iowa, built the first store there that spring and were rewarded with instant success. Booming in the mid-1880s land rush, Wilburn had a population of two hundred within a year. [44] Frank Mathews, the optimistic editor, spread the word of newfound prosperity:

A few months ago, Wilburn was not and where it now stands the wolf, the antelope and the cayote held unchallenged dominian, save by the buffalo and the wild horse, and the rattle snake gave its fatel warning unheard by the ear of man. Today the scene is changed. One turn of the kaleidoscope of time and we see a different picture. We now have one hardware; one clothing store; two groceries; a lumber yard; a shoe shop; a large feed and livery stable; post-office; a large well conducted hotel; a blacksmith shop; two rustling real-estates firms who are always willing to give you any information desired; we also have one of the best school houses in southwest Kansas; and last but not least, a newspaper and publishing office; and yet we have just began to grow. Strange faces are daily seen upon our streets. . . . to the young man of limited means in the overdone cities of the east, who would gain a foothold where wealth and happiness be his portion; to all who would better their condition, we would respectfully, but earnestly say, come to Wilburn. We extend the invitation believing that here is a country that ere long will blossom as the rose and a town that will keep right along with the country.[45]

Much of the town's immediate success lay in its connection with the Jones and Plummer Trail. Cal Ferguson's stage, the freighting trade, the Wilburn Hotel, the Johnson and Draper blacksmith shop, and two livery barns ensured services and reasonable transportation rates to Dodge City. The future, however, lay entirely with the prospect of being on the proposed Chicago, Nebraska, Kansas and Southwestern railroad line.

In the summer of 1887 the town reached its peak. The Fourth of July celebration that summer was to be Wilburn's high-water mark. Besides the usual picnic and oratory, there were fireworks and, just like the big cities, a hot-air balloon ascension. The ascension was a nice touch, symbolizing a town on the rise. It was, however, fated to hold other symbols, not the least of which lay in the old saw "All that goes up must come down." On that bright July 4, few in Wilburn believed that the scheme for a north-south railroad was pure vapor.[46]

The hope for metropolitan status or even one-horse-town survival ended in January 1888 when the Rock Island Railroad moved through Meade County some nine miles south of Wilburn. For a time the stage continued to bring travelers through the town and drummers occasionally stopped over at the hotel. The optimistic editor of the *Argus* was one of the first to concede defeat, admitting that he was "tired of publishing a paper just for the fun of the thing." The town's death was slow, and not until 1911 did the post office move to Fowler.[47]

Wilburn's closest rival and eventual nemesis lay eight miles southwest on the same Jones and Plummer Trail. George Fowler had taken a homestead there in 1883 and had considered the site ideal for a town. He visited with Perry J. Wilden, a Dodge City merchant, and offered him a half-interest if he would plat, advertise, and bring a store and lumberyard to the town. Wilden agreed. In his words:

I hitched up my fiery black team, thru a lot of sharpened stakes in the back end of the buggy and then drove to Fowler's homestead, and after dinner we proceeded to lay out the eighty acre townsite of Fowler. We decided to have a public square with the Jones and Plummer trail running through it and to have a good well where the boys could have a chance to water their stock while they stopped and traded.[48]

On one of Wilden's return trips to Dodge City he met George and Fanny Eckert on the trail; the Newport, Kentucky couple had received a newspaper Wilden published to advertise the free lots. Wilden welcomed them as his first converts, gave them a lot, and the next day they began construction of the town's first hotel, to be known as the Waco House. On Christmas Day 1884, Linn Frazier opened the door to his half-dugout general store, and Fowler was a business community.

By the summer of 1885 the town was responding to the land boom and anticipating even more growth when the railroad came. Although in January 1886 the town lost its bid for county-seat status to Meade Center by a vote of 486 to 231, the arrival of the Rock Island made up for the loss. Fowler continued its rapid expansion until it was hit by the general exodus of the 1890s, which all but destroyed the town. For more than a decade it was without a city government and had few residents. Revival was slow, and not until 1907, when the population had grown back to 345, was the government reorganized and reestablished under an act of the state legislature. The railroad eventually brought some of the prosperity George Fowler had envisioned, but the town never reached the heights expected by those who settled it when it was served by the old wagon road.[49]

Meade Center, west of Fowler and a mile on beyond Hoodoo Brown's road ranch, had a meteoric rise. The *Topeka Daily Capital* noted that the "wonderful growth of Meade Center . . . astonishes the natives, as well as outsiders who visited the county. No town in southwestern Kansas has ever experienced such a boom." After the Meade Center Townsite Company purchased five hundred twenty acres, surveyed, and platted a portion of the land, the town was granted a charter on July 10, 1885. The first building had been raised in May, and during the two months before Meade Center received official grant of status, eighty-eight houses marked the new townsite. In one three-week period, thirty-five houses were built, and by October 1885 the town claimed two hundred houses and a population exceeding seven hundred. Early advertisements stressed its rapid growth, boasted of an opera house, thirteen wells, four daily stage runs, and, most significant of all, sixteen real estate offices. Carthage, four miles beyond Meade Center, put up a desperate name-calling fight for the county-seat vote, but Meade Center won the election handily, with Carthage coming in a distant third behind Fowler. As a result of the vote, Meade Center was designated the county seat six months before it was officially recognized as a town. The name was simplified to Meade by an act of the Kansas Legislature in 1889. As was true in Wilburn and Fowler, the early businesses catered to the Jones and Plummer Trail and the new *Meade County Press-Democrat* counted it a major victory when a stage line was persuaded to alter its route and stop in the center of town.[50]

In 1888 a report to the *Topeka Capital* described the town as a growing if somewhat primitive center of trade:

On the divide, or most commanding eminence in the country, with sloping declivities on every side, Meade Center does not look unlike the very earliest settlements on the plains—the military posts, and it is built like they were. The town is built about a central square—the parade ground of the frontier post. A flagstaff holds the central point . . . and from the mast head floated the stars and stripes. . . . The stores, the busy scene of barter on one side of the square brought to mind the quartermaster, . . . the hotels stand where the soldier's barracks might be and the cozy cottages here and there might well be taken for officers quarters, . . . the church for chapel and the mammoth two-story brick school house could be . . . the hospital. . . .

The arrival of the Rock Island tracks guaranteed the town's future. Although it suffered a population decline in the 1890s, it did not feel the loss to the extent other Meade County communities did.[51]

The rapid increase in population, bringing more than four thousand new residents to Meade County between 1882 and 1888, increased traffic on the Jones and Plummer Trail, but it was to be a short-lived boom. A major attraction for new settlers was the anticipated arrival of the railroad, which was expected to make the trail obsolete. When the Rock Island kept its promise and put both Fowler and Meade on the new line, the usefulness of the Jones and Plummer Trail as a freighting highway ended. Although local traffic continued for some time, the days of the wagon-road economy as a major economic factor in that section of the Region and for the three new towns ceased to exist.

Although Joe and Ed first marked the trail for their own freighting purposes and even though its major users were bullwhackers, teamsters, and muleskinners, the trail did serve two other important functions. From the beginning cattlemen sent their steers up the trail, and after the mid-1880s it was used as a mail route. "The Jones & Plummer Trail was more freight than a cattle trail," wrote M. W. Anshutz of Nye, Kansas, "altho many herds from Texas panhandle ranches were driven over it to Dodge in the old days." Never used for trailing cattle to the extent that the Tuttle Trail, the Adobe Walls Trail, and the Western Cattle Trail were used, nevertheless there were times and circumstances that made the Jones and Plummer Trail useful or convenient.[52]

Even Mose Hayes on the old Springer ranch, where the Tuttle Trail originated, used it, indicating that "the Bar C's, our outfit, the Seven K . . . , and Bartons used to all drive our beef herds up this Trail to Dodge." Colonel Jack Potter pointed out that some Panhandle beef herds, wanting to stay west of the Western Cattle Trail because of the fear of contracting Texas fever, used the Jones and Plummer as an alternate route. In an attempt to solve the problems associated with driving cattle, speakers at an 1885 meeting of cattlemen in Dallas recommended that trail driving be restricted to two specified routes. Many ranchers refused to abide by the guidelines that were established and preferred to use other trails, including the Jones and Plummer. Charlie Hitch recalled that in his first trail drive in 1886, from the Cimarron ranch of his brother, he headed for the Jones and Plummer and followed it into Dodge. Orrin Burright remembered the impressive sight of large herds of longhorns being driven up the trail. Apparently, both big drives from the south and small ones from the Panhandle used it. Potter remembered that in 1880 John Chisum sold "Hunter & Evean Six thousand big steers and they were trailed to Dodge City Via Tascosa and the Paladuro route to Jones and Plummer Trail."[53]

Dodge City had its last big year as a cattle town in 1885, with the Western Cattle Trail being the main supplier. By 1890 the trailing of cattle over long distances had all but ended; however, drives of a hundred miles continued and frequently followed the Jones and Plummer route. Until grangers' fences and better modes of transportation were in place, the trail was used. Even after the turn of the century herds were seen passing down the main street of Fowler, doing their best to follow what was left of the Old Jones and Plummer Trail.[54]

In keeping with a recorded history that is frequently fanciful and scrambled, the trail gained folk immortality, not as a freighting road, but as a cattle trail. In a popular cowboy ballad, author unknown, titled *The Old Cowboy*, an aged cowhand reminisces about his life on the range and trail and laments that he has "seen the good times go":

> *But many a man I worked with then*
> *Is sleeping on Boot Hill;*
> *And the last cow drive was made to Dodge*
> *Over the Jones and Plummer Trail.*[55]

The other proffered regional service was that of providing a road for stagecoaches hauling passengers and mail to outlying post offices and towns. Few stages anywhere existed for passenger service only. Mail contracts kept the business alive; passenger fare was an added margin of profit. This was especially true for settlements along the Jones and Plummer Trail. Occasionally someone would set up hack schedules between the small towns, but none continued for any length of time and all were fairly irregular.

The major mail service to the Panhandle was by way of Fort Supply. P. G. Reynolds of Dodge City had developed that line and maintained it until near the end of the era. The Jones and Plummer route was first used for mail in the spring of 1879, when weekly deliveries by hack were authorized to Tascosa via the Crooked Creek post office and the Ohio settlement at Pearlette. Various sections of the northern trail were used by mail contractors until P. G. Reynolds took over the line in 1886 and made it a major stagecoach route down to Mobeetie.[56]

For all its flexibility, the trail Ed Jones and Joe Plummer had marked remained through those early pioneering days a known guide and thoroughfare linking the panhandles of two states to the commercial depot of another. From 1874 until the last decade of the century, it was a major factor in welding the three-state region into a community of common business, economic, and social interests.

Apparently, neither Ed Jones nor Joe Plummer ever realized how important their contributions had been. Plummer remained in the area for only a brief time, with his presence in and around Dodge City for a few months after he and Jones parted company noted in the papers. He raced horses, loafed, and then was gone, west perhaps. No one knew where. An old-timer thought he had gone to Wyoming and was killed there in some fracas. There is no record.[57]

Jones left a clear trail. After selling the ranch, he continued his old line of freighting for a while. Then, according to stories written at the time of his death, he "traveled for the next seven years," whatever that means. In 1899 he purchased a ranch four miles east of old Fort Supply, where he farmed and raised horses and mules. When the strictures of age bore heavily upon him, he moved to Woodward to live with a sister. He never married. "Any girl that would have had me, the devil wouldn't have had," he said. Still, he and his fiddle, songs, and his glory tales of the old days were welcomed throughout the area. "A ready story teller, musician, singer, dance caller, no social function was complete success without him," it was said.[58]

It had been a lifelong avocation. When the first caravan of buffalo hunters and tradesmen moved down to establish Adobe Walls, they held a play-party under the prairie stars the first night out. They pegged down a buffalo hide for a dance floor and unpacked their fiddles and harmonicas. Dirty Face fiddled up a storm, buffalo hunters whooped it up, "and for comedy's sake, danced with each other." Some joys never change. Nor could he escape the familiar, the tendency to chummy nicknames. He was no longer Dirty Face. Among the Cheyenne and Arapahoe Indians in his trading days in the Panhandle, he was called Chief Coffee. That was now dignified to Farmer Jones.[59]

Jones's final days were spent in convivial leisure, "seen downtown almost every day, winter and summer." There was still something of the old courage and stamina he had when he shuffled down the trail with an eye peeled for hostile Indians:

Crippled with rheumatism and his eyesight nearly gone, "Farmer" Jones contented himself with reliving his early days experiences by recounting them to youngsters with whom he often chatted on his daily pilgrimages down town. He made two trips to town daily, one in the morning and one around midnight. With the aid of two canes he hobbled the five blocks from his sister's home to the cafe for a cup of coffee. It took him an hour to negotiate the trip but he insisted on walking the full distance, saying it killed that much time out of a long day. At night when he couldn't sleep because of rheumatic pains, he would pick up his canes, light a lantern and head for town to get another cup of coffee.[60]

Both the founder and the trail shared a common fate. In the early days they had, with resilient flexibility, probed and pointed the way for development of the Region. There followed a midlife period of solid contribution through hard, tough service, ending in a gradual decline. The Jones and Plummer Trail led new settlers to the land for new beginnings and new enterprise and sustained them once they were there. It was the compass, Mrs. Novinger remembered, in marking the direction their lives would take and in molding the memories they would hold. Certainly there were terrible memories of the trail: of the unwarranted deaths in the January blizzard of 1881; of Jim Herron lowering his dying companion from his saddle to the dust of the trail, a moment that marked the beginning of a lifelong exile for him; of the fear that must have hung over old Hoodoo Brown as he went down the trail alone to recover the scalped body on Crooked Creek, not knowing whether Dull Knife's warriors were still close at hand. The happier times were associated with a way station where a cowboy met the Kentucky girl who was to be his bride, or where the hopes and expectations of young families soared as they brought their meager possessions to a new homestead. There were those less serious recollections of district court officials getting a dunking in crossing the Canadian as the only book of statutes in the Oklahoma Panhandle floated down the stream; of P. G. Reynolds losing a prize boar hog out of his stagecoach at Bill Tilghman's ranch; of A. Bennett wheedling a drink of whiskey in place of water from fiery old Captain A. J. French on a footweary trek to Dodge City.[61]

The trail was identified with that era on the Great Plains that spanned major transitions: from buffalo hunting to ranching to farming. As long as transportation was dependent upon beasts of burden, the Jones and Plummer Trail stimulated growth and progress. In the end, progress relegated the wagon trail to near oblivion. Its death knell was the sound of the train bell as a Santa Fe locomotive pulled into Panhandle City on New Year's Day 1888. Having served it purpose, the trail gradually slipped into the dust of history, and its mark upon the land was covered by the sod like a forgotten grave.

5. The Dodge City–Tascosa Trail: The Link Between Sister Cow Towns

FOR more than a decade, Tascosa on the sandy flats above the Canadian River in Texas and Dodge City on the hills above the Arkansas River in Kansas were the liveliest cow towns in the West. The same gamblers, bartenders, and dance-hall girls at various times served the same trail-herd cowboys, determined to have a "high ol' time." The economic link that made them sister cities, although by no means a mirror image, was the cattle trade; the physical link was the Dodge City–Tascosa Trail.

Tascosa was almost totally supplied by freighters moving down from Dodge City, although some traffic continued throughout the period from 1870 to 1890 between Tascosa and Springer, New Mexico, and the Fort Bascom Trail was fairly heavily traveled for the brief period of that fort's existence. But the isolation of Tascosa made the Dodge City–Tascosa Trail one of paramount importance as long as the town flourished. Although the physical difficulties were not as formidable as those on the other two Panhandle freighting trails, the long distances between way stations and the absence of settlements made it seem longer and less inviting. The demand for goods, however, brought heavy traffic to the trail. At its peak, the population of Tascosa never exceeded 600 permanent residents, but cowboys' attraction to the soiled doves and the seven saloons on the wild side of town, known as Hogtown, and the big ranchers' merchandise requirements boosted sales far beyond the town's own needs. In 1886 the *Tascosa Pioneer* noted one hundred nineteen thousand pounds of goods received during the previous week and complained, "It wasn't a good week for receiving merchandise, either." The firms of Cone & Duran and Wright & Farnsworth each had freighting teams pulling two wagons in tandem in constant use, averaging as much as fifty thousand pounds of merchandise hauled overland each month from Dodge City.[1]

The general configuration of the Dodge City–Tascosa Trail was determined by the location of the Cator brothers' ranch, known as the Zulu Stockade. Comancheros, Indians, buffalo hunters, and soldiers had moved southward across the plains for years, sometimes following old paths and sometimes relying on their own intuition and past experiences. All kept within watering distance of the streams and generally on the high ground. There were, however, no permanent routes to that section of the Texas Panhandle until Jim and Bob Cator began making trips to Dodge City from their Palo Duro station. Because they used the same tracks and the same crossings repeatedly, their habits became a fixed trail and their home base the best–known landmark in the area. When Tascosa was founded, the trial that had ended at the Zulu Stockade was continued to the Canadian River, following a path of least difficulty over the Texas terrain.

The Dodge City–Tascosa Trail was divided into two distinct sections: the northern half followed the established Jones and Plummer Trail and also was used by freighters headed for Fort Elliott and Mobeetie; the southern half, from Beaver, Oklahoma on south, was used almost exclusively by those headed for Tascosa. W. S. Mabry's log of the northern section, given to Charles Goodnight by the Oldham Land District surveyor, reads:

Jim Lanes to Hines Crossing on Cimarron	40 miles
Cimarron to Hoodu Brown's on Crooked Creek	20 miles
Hoodu Brown's on Crooked Creek to Dodge City	42 miles

There were no surprises or independent routing on this section of the trail. It simply followed the established and clearly marked route Ed Jones and Joe Plummer had started.

Mabry's log for the southern stint was as specific as that for the Jones and Plummer section:

Tascosa to Little Blue stage stand	35 miles
Little Blue stage stand to Zulu (Jim Cator's)	30 miles
Zulu (Cator's) to Hardesty Ranch	40 miles
Hardesty's Ranch to Jim Lane's on the Beaver	35 miles

The two stations on either side of the Cators' place were selected because of their relationship to the Zulu Stockade. The Hardesty ranch, the first station south out of Beaver, was a well-protected establishment approximately halfway between the Cators' ranch and the connection with the Jones and Plummer Trail. Little Blue Station, offering the advantage of a flowing spring, was about midway between Zulu Stockade and Tascosa. The trail between these fixed points followed the logic of terrain, avoiding the sharp breaks and steep draws.[2]

After leaving Jim Lane's soddy and the narrow Beaver Valley, the trail skirted the north bank of the Beaver River, staying on high ground as it crossed the rolling hills. Horses kicked up the same red dust they had on the trail in the Oklahoma Panhandle until they recrossed the Beaver River near the place where the Palo Duro Creek empties into it. The ruts then followed the Palo Duro's west bank until they crossed Hackberry Creek, staying on the high flats above the creekbed. The country was very sparsely settled, and an 1885 traveler recalled seeing only one house between Hardesty's ranch and the Cimarron River. The flats the trail crossed were covered with short buffalo grass, and an occasional yucca bloom could be spotted; otherwise it was a barren, lonely stretch for the weary traveler. To someone looking down from the high prairie on the wooded stream, Chiquita Creek, where R. J. ("Jack") and John F. Hardesty's ranch lay, the sight must have appeared inviting indeed, offering cool, shaded comfort in summer and snug protection in winter.

The Hardesty brothers' Half Circle S Ranch was established in 1879, and for a time Jack and his brother lived at the Chiquita headquarters. However, when the ranch was finally organized to his satisfaction, Jack moved to Dodge City, leaving the management to a series of able foremen, including John Durfee and Tom Hungate. Jack, called the colonel (an honorary title), held court at the ranch on occasion when hunting and fishing parties lasting for a week or more were held. Frozen oysters and other delectables came out from Dodge, and the bumper catch of fish was salted down and returned with the guests when they left.[3]

Jack Hardesty was born in Kentucky in 1843. He and three of his brothers were caught by the Colorado gold fever and, in 1859, joined the gold rush to the mountains. Their initial mining efforts at Clear Creek were unsuccessful, so they moved on to Montana, where their luck changed dramatically; by the time they left the gold fields, all were wealthy men. At one point in his mining venture, Jack remembered casually carrying to Denver ten thousand dollars worth of gold nuggets in his money belt. With ample capital to support him, and in partnership with his brother and a number of other individuals, Hardesty plunged into the cattle business in Texas, New Mexico, Oklahoma, and Kansas. John Hardesty, Jack's older brother, established a large ranch along the Arkansas River with headquarters near where Holly, Colorado is today. The ranch on the Dodge City—Tascosa Trail was only one of many holdings but remained Jack's major base of operations for years. By 1883 it extended for thirty miles along the Beaver, where some two thousand five hundred head of cattle were branded each year. Hardesty carefully selected his breeding stock and maintained a ranch in Chase County, Kansas exclusively for breeding pure Hereford bulls. The fortunes of his cattle business suffered the usual vicissitudes of the industry, some years showing great profits and other seasons equally great losses. In 1874 he was offered five hundred thousand dollars for his cattle interests, but the severe winters in the mid-1880s brought the value down to fifty thousand dollars. The next few years saw a resurgence of his cattle business, hence the Hardesty and Holstein ranch in New Mexico, the Oklahoma Half Circle S, and his other holdings prospered.[4]

As one of the largest ranch owners in the Panhandle, Hardesty was a major supporter and organizer of the Dodge City Cattle Growers Association, which came to be called the Western Kansas Cattle Growers Association. At the peak of its power, the association had great economic and political influence. In 1884 its thirty-four members owned nearly half a million head of cattle, with most owners running their herds in the Public Land Strip, the Cherokee Strip, and western Kansas. Among other things, the association worked to prevent tick-infested stock from entering Kansas and

Dodge City, circa 1886, as seen from the south side of the Arkansas River. Courtesy Kansas State Historical Society, Topeka (Beeson Collection).

eventually succeeded in getting South Texas cattle barred from the state. The Kansans were, however, just as interested in preventing infestation in the Oklahoma Panhandle. Guards were stationed on the Western Trail, and prescribed routes were enforced. When some of the Texas cattlemen refused to comply, Hardesty and his neighbor, Ludwig Kramer, marshaled armed ranchers and cowboys to halt passage through the Oklahoma range. Although there was a direct confrontation between the contending cowboys, cool heads prevailed and the Texas herds, under the close observation of the Oklahoma men, followed a designated route south of Beaver, which prevented contamination of the Oklahoma cattle.[5]

While Hardesty maintained his business headquarters in Dodge City, he was active in the social and political life of that community. A man of strong convictions who never used profanity or forgot the social amenities, he could be stern and sharp in his business dealings. His ranch headquarters reflected his personality even when he was not present and served the travelers on the Tascosa Trail until the commercial traffic shifted from Dodge City to other railheads.[6]

Colonel Jack's penchant for parties at the ranch led to one of the Panhandle's deepest tragedies. Joe Cruse was a popular saloon owner in the settlement that was named for the colonel. In December 1887 he and his wife agreed to spread the word of a Christmas Eve dance sponsored by Hardesty. A brawling blizzard caught the pair on the prairie just west of Beaver City; when their team broke free, the couple tried to make it to shelter on foot. Eventually, the team found its way to a nearby cattle camp, and a search was organized. The Cruses were found in the open, Joe lying on his back with his wife cradled in his arms and her head pillowed on his chest. The bodies were placed in a single, pine-board coffin and buried on the flats overlooking the Hardesty ranch near the Dodge City–Tascosa Trail. Some time later, people in the area began receiving letters from a Mrs. Joe Cruse, telling of her destitute plight and seeking assistance in locating her wayward husband. The shock of this revelation only added to the tragedy because the Cruses had been a particularly popular couple in the community. The burial site above the Palo Duro within clear view of the trail, was a sad reminder to trail users that danger was always present on the open prairie.[7]

There is considerable discrepancy among contemporary accounts of where the trail ran after leaving Hardesty's ranch, but it is clear that it stayed on the west side of the creek. Freighters frequently bypassed the Hardesty place, sometimes staying on the flats a mile or more to the north. Eventually a small settlement, complete with hotel and saloons, grew on the banks of Coldwater Creek where that stream emptied into Beaver River. A freighter could—and many did—shift to a new route that placed the trail even farther north and nearer the settlement. However, the old trail remained the primary route and was used exclusively by the mail contractors.[8]

The forty miles from Hardesty's ranch to the Zulu Stockade had only Farwell Creek as a troublesome water crossing, although many draws along the way were sand filled, requiring much hard pulling by the teams. The trail came into the Cators' place from the northeast, down a sheltered valley from a fairly high, sloping hill. It was an ideal site, with ample water, timber at a nearby creek, and good grass. There in the late winter of 1871 or early spring of 1872 the Cator brothers had scooped a dugout into the side of a draw and built a corral for their stock near the headwaters of Palo Duro Creek. They became the first permanent settlers in the Texas Panhandle, and theirs was to be one of the most successful and sustained ventures in the Region.[9]

James ("Jim") and Arthur ("Bob") Cator were the obedient and very British sons of Captain Bertie Cator of Her Majesty's Royal Navy. The captain had gloried in a life of adventure, which led to decorations for various feats of valor in exotic places, including Hong Kong during the Opium War and the polar ice fields during an attempt to rescue Sir John Franklin's ill-fated expedition. Although there were generations of seamen in the lineage, Captain Cator, safely ashore as inspector of the harbor at Hull, Yorkshire, England, was determined that his sons would follow a different life. He was not seeking to pamper them with a safe, easy existance, free of the stimulation of adventure; as long as hardships and exploits were not on the high seas, he did not care how far from home or how strange the setting. In fact, his later letters to his sons reflect a vicarious pleasure in their adventures in the Wild West.[10]

After careful investigation and planning under the guidance of a highly unreliable land agent, the captain packed his sons (ages eighteen and twenty) off to Kansas—about as far from the sea as the globe would permit. The sons, neither as careful or as worldly wise as their father, lost their money to a pickpocket shortly after landing in New York City. They were obliged to work their way to Kansas, where they discovered how badly their father had been misled by his American contact. They soon learned that farming in the West, even with a substantial stake, was no sure way to wealth. So, dropping their early plans, they pooled their resources, bought five yoke of oxen and four horses, and moved on west to become freighters. By late summer 1871 they were in Fort Dodge. Having spent a year in idleness devoted primarily to hunting in the fields near home while the captain planned their destiny, the brothers shifted plans once again and joined in the slaughter of Kansas buffalo. By the time they arrived, however, the Arkansas river range was decidedly overcrowded with hunters competing for the dwindling herds. The brothers then decided to move into the northwestern section of the Texas Panhandle and build a permanent camp. For the next three years they ranged over the Panhandle, killing buffalo and transporting hides to Dodge City. The camp became a significant landmark for travelers, since it was the only permanent shelter for miles around. It also became a trading post for other buffalo hunters, who bought whatever surplus supplies the Cators had on hand. Had it not been for these customers, it would have been truly a lonely outpost. When Adobe Walls opened for business in 1874, it was their nearest neighbor, still some forty miles away. The new post gave them a sense of security, however, in knowing that there was friendly support within a hard day's ride. Quanah Parker's attack on Adobe Walls was as disconcerting to the Cators as it was to the hunters and merchants who fought off the Indians. Neither of the Cators was in the Adobe Walls fight; they were on the plains killing buffalo and heard of the battle four days later when they drove into the settlement with a wagonload of hides. Like most of the other hunters, they headed for the security of Dodge City as soon as possible. Within a month, they were back hunting in the Panhandle.[11]

In the fall of 1875 the Cators built a large picket house of cottonwood logs hauled in from Moores Creek. Designed to serve as bachelor quarters as well as to hold supplies to be traded or sold to other buffalo hunters, the house took on the dimensions of a minor fort. The corral was only a few steps away from the house, so they could keep an eye on their stock. It remained a convenient shelter for buffalo hunters until the hunting died out in 1876, then continued as a mildly active trade center for some time. Apparently it was only modestly stocked in the beginning and frequently ran low on supplies. Harry Ingerton, who traded there in 1877, reported: "They had a little store there; a box or two of sardines and some cheese, but they didn't have many supplies to amount to anything." However, billings from such Dodge City firms as Wright, Beverley & Co. and A. C. Myers Co. show a large variety of goods purchased throughout most of the period. The trail the Cators followed to Jim Lane's store in Beaver on their trips to Dodge City for supplies became an established route used by others. First buffalo hunters, then the ranchers, freighters, and mail contractors, adopted the trail and used the Cator place as a road ranch and trading post.[12]

In preparation for the arrival of a British bride, a stone house was added in the mid-1880s. From time to time other members of the family from England joined the brothers and contributed to the growing diversity of the operation. They made the shift from buffalo culture to ranching by restocking the store with goods that met the requirements of cattlemen and by moving into the cattle business on their own. Never as extensively involved as their neighbors, they found "running a supply post in a rapidly settling country placed serious limitations on the cattle business." Still, their herds were large enough to suffer severe losses in the brutal winter of 1883.[13]

Additional responsibilities and income came in 1880 when the post was made one of the stops on the Tascosa mail route. The mail stage also carried passengers, and since it was thirty-five miles one way and forty the other to the nearest station, the stockade became an important rest stop for passengers. After 1880 stables were added for the stage horses, and the Cators had one more job to tend. At the same time, Bob Cator was named postmaster. Handling mail was the least of the brothers' duties and one they had been doing informally as a favor to the buffalo hunters for some time. They continued to do so, even after the post office was established, whenever the mail was disrupted or discontinued, as it was frequently. The mail came by horseback for a brief time, then by mule-drawn hack until L. K. McIntyre, then Cal Ferguson, and finally P. G. Reynolds converted the route to a stage line.[14]

The necessity of giving the post office an official name led to its strange designation as Zulu. The Zulu War was very much on British subjects' minds and in the British press in the late 1870s as African war lords resisted, with remarkable courage and carnage, the European encroachment. It became a British war, and a bloody one, when Great Britain annexed Transvaal in 1877. Bob Cator's sister, one of the family to join the American venture, said it was because the war was a topic of considerable conversation in the family that Bob submitted the name to postal authorities. However, parental letters from England referring to the Indians as "black rascals" and "Dusty vagabonds" and the parent's strange conception of the Panhandle may have led the sons to satirize their own situation in "Darkest Texas" with a British colonial title. It was Captain Cator who first used the term *stockade* when he wrote asking his sons to define *ranch*. "I take it," he wrote, "to be a sort of Stockade."[15]

After the disastrous winter of 1883, Bob left Texas for new opportunities in Oregon. Jim remained to become an important force in the community as a rancher, farmer, judge, and banker. The post office was discontinued in February 1885 and reestablished in May of the same year with a new postmistress handling the business. Zulu Stockade, however, remained a stage station until the end of the stage era.[16]

The Cators' life in Kansas never quite equaled the adventure and exploits of the father nor was it as dangerous as the parents in England imagined. But the Cator sons contributed solidly to the development of the Panhandle, and Jim, who remained, garnered from the community the appropriate rewards of office in recognition of his service. The success of his son, who met the challenges

Dodge City and Pan Handle

P. G. REYNOLDS, Proprietor.

U. S. Mail and Express Line

Dodge City, Kan., Oct 10 1881

Robt Cator & Bro

Yours of Oct 3 Received I have not any thing to do with that 47th Bill or the Bill of Wesly Evenian But the Bill from Aug or Since August 5 I will Pay in at W B & C and Send or Bring you a Recpt As I think I will get out over the Route next week the Department has sent us a new Schedule Will you Please Sign and Return to me at Dodge and I will forward to Mr Parker and Put in the Department over P. G. Reynolds

A letter from P. G. Reynolds to Robert Cator and Brother, December 10, 1881. Courtesy Panhandle-Plains Historical Museum (Cator Family Papers).

of a new land, would have pleased the old sea captain in Hull and would have justified his early decision to send him to America.

From Zulu Stockade to the next way station, known as Little Blue Station, or occasionally as Big Timbers, was thirty miles over flat prairie generally barren of vegetation except for the ubiquitous buffalo grass. At the head of Little Blue Creek a way station was maintained by the man who broke the first sod in Moore County, his crop consisting of "copper maize." The sod house stood in a small grove of cottonwood and walnut trees that could be seen for some distance by people traveling south, although the house was situated on the side of a draw leading into Little Blue Creek. A water tank was fitted into the bank of the draw and was kept full by a flowing spring, which guaranteed water for freighters and mail-coach teams after their long haul over the dry plains.[17]

There were two routes through Moore County. The one high on the flats apparently was used when there was water in the surface ponds, and the other ran farther south, where the teamster had to travel into the breaks to find spring water. The tank at Little Blue Station was always available, even in the driest season; consequently, the stage stand there was a fixed stop for most freighters and all mail stages. The tank was also the cause of a major tragedy for the opertors of the stage stand when the young son of the way-station owner fell into it and drowned. The child's grave, on the hill overlooking the trail, joined that at Hardesty's ranch as a reminder of the unforgiving nature of the prairie venture.[18]

After leaving Little Blue Station, the trail kept to the high ground around the head of Big Blue Creek, angling southwest until it came to a large butte some distance to the left, about three quarters of a mile from the trail. At that point the road turned directly south to the head of Tascosa Creek and went down the east side of that stream, avoiding the various draws and creek heads, until it came to the sandy main street of Tascosa. The first and most lasting impression any traveler had of Tascosa was not the famous Boot Hill but the sand in the streets, even though their teams had struggled mightily pulling through the many sand draws on their way into town. Sand was everywhere. A tall, gangly girl who lived there claimed her legs were so long because she had stretched them pulling through the sand on every street and lot in town.[19]

The trip from Dodge City covered somewhere between 220 miles (P. G. Reynolds' bid estimate to the Post Office Department) and 242 miles (Mabry's calculation). The rapid-moving stagecoach took eighty-four hours for the trip, leaving Dodge City Monday at 6:00 A.M. and arriving at Tascosa Thursday at 6:00 P.M. Ox teams required thirty days for a round trip if all went well but could take six weeks if weather or animals were uncooperative. The southern half was a particularly lonesome journey, as there were few settlers and less traffic than on the other north-south trails. By the mid-1880s the Jones and Plummer section passed through country dotted with new homesteads; at one point on the trail a traveler could see six towns in Meade County. But there were no settlers below the Beaver crossing and the long stretches between way stations seemed even longer than they were.[20]

The isolation of the Tascosa vicinity made business transactions and travel difficult. Jim Cator sometimes was forced to use Jim Lane at Beaver as a proxy agent and banker because of the difficulty in getting payments to Zulu. One prospective buyer suggested that the quickest way for Cator to send goods was "by some responsible person" to Tascosa, where they could be put on a stage to Fort Elliott and then transferred to another stage, which would carry them to Clarendon, where the buyer could send a wagon to pick them up. The distance covered, as the crow flies, would have been approximately one hundred miles.[21]

Although the country between Beaver and Tascosa had little need for mail or passenger service, the stage connection between Dodge and Tascosa was essential. The first mail route between the two cities was established in the spring of 1879, when weekly deliveries by hack were authorized to Tascosa via the Crooked Creek post office and the Ohio settlement at Pearlette. The contractor, E. J. Edwards, probably left the Jones and Plummer Trail at the Mulberry crossing and followed the Adobe Walls Trail for some distance before cutting back to the Jones and Plummer somewhere above Hoodoo Brown's soddy. In between there was a stop at Pearlette, where the mail carrier changed horses, stayed overnight, and boarded with Addison Bennett, editor of the *Pearlette Call*. The hack continued on to Crooked Creek, Hoodoo Brown's, and then over to the Tascosa road at Beaver.[22]

In 1883 the Tascosa line was upgraded by order of the Post-master General, and new post offices joined those already in service. M. W. Mills of Springer, New Mexico sublet the delivery contract to L. K. McIntyre of Crooked Creek and George S. Emerson of Dodge City. Gilbert, one of the new post offices, located about one-half mile east of the future site of Fowler, was probably the new point where the Jones and Plummer Trail was picked up. At about the same time, the road ranch of Peter T. Reep on Beaver Creek was authorized as a post office.[23] Of these new moves the *Dodge City Times* editorialized:

> The Tascosa mail route is becoming a popular line. The mail matter is steadily increasing. On Friday and also on Monday last, on each day, two large sacks, each weighing one hundred pounds, were sent out from the Dodge City postoffice. Mail matter increases when it is known that the facilities are ample and the mail is carried promptly and safely. On the Tascosa mail route, Mr. McIntyre, contractor, gives the work his special attention. The mail arrives and departs promptly, very rarely is there a delay, and then upon the most unavoidable circumstances. It is proposed to increase the service on this route to three times a week. Some weeks ago a petition, signed by the residents along the route, was sent to Washington, asking for the proposed increase. The business along the route and the interests of the stockmen and residents, demand the increase. Information has been received from Washington that the proposed increase will be made. The growing interests of this western country demand increased mail facilities.[24]

The editorial was over optimistic about the volume of mail headed south. In fact, it was difficult to keep agents and contractors interested in a line to such sparsely settled areas. Many of the early carriers lost money and quit the business. Addison Bennett recovered some of his costs in serving one Tascosa line that went broke by taking a bill of sale for the pony stabled at his place. In 1883, when Tascosa went without mail for some time, unhappy patrons discovered the carrier had quarreled with his boss and simply quit. No one took over. M. W. Mills spent several weeks in Dodge City trying to subcontract the route, but without success.[25]

In 1885 enough new post offices were authorized along the trail in Kansas to make full service profitable. Four new stations— Wilburn (March 9), Fowler City (January 13), Meade Center (July 30), and Byers (September 24)—brought mail coaches back to the

Zulu Post Office, the first permanent settlement in the Texas Panhandle. Zulu Stockade was established in 1872.
Courtesy Panhandle-Plains Historical Museum.

Jones and Plummer section of the Tascosa Trail. Cal Ferguson, who had been associated with W. M. D. Lee in freighting, took over this new route. He began by running a stage on Tuesdays and Saturdays from Dodge City to Tascosa, with daily runs to the local towns and post offices of Wilburn, Crooked Creek, Pearlette, Fowler City, Belle Meade, Spring Lake, Meade Center, and Carthage. After a brief trial, a number of these smaller stations were forced to make individual pickups at one of the other towns because of the lack of business. [26]

Ferguson's ticket office was two doors down from the Dodge House in Dodge City, and his Tascosa stage left at 7:00 A.M. After a dinner stop at Fowler's Waco House, it was on to Meade Center for supper and a change of horses. An all-night ride to Beaver ended the Jones and Plummer phase of the trip. Ferguson had purchased new equipment for this expanded route; it had "improved springs" and "cushioned seats." It was a good run and apparently profitable, although somewhat erratic. Unfortunately, he was driven out of business by a fire in a neighbor's house in Dodge City that spread to his livery barn and destroyed much of his stock, coaches, and feed. P. G. Reynolds, the Fort Supply mail contractor, bought Ferguson's remaining assets and took over the route. [27]

Reynolds made several changes in the line, such as putting on an eight-passenger coach, "well painted and finished, very attractive"; changing meal stops; and designating express agents in conjunction with other express lines, such as Wells Fargo. The Reynolds operation continued until his death in 1888 and for a while after that under his son. [28]

The citizens of Tascosa held out great hopes for the coming of the railroads. The inconveniences of wagon-road transportation, they believed, would end and new settlers with new needs would stimulate business. As a county-seat town, Tascosa seemingly had a bright future. Merchants could expect the mail to be on time, they would no longer run short on supplies, nor would they be required to keep their own expensive freighting teams on the trail. Except for the brief period when P. G. Reynolds held the contract, mail never seemed to reach Tascosa with the same regularity it arrived at other post offices. In 1886, just before Reynolds took over, the editor of the *Tascosa Pioneer* lamented: "The mails continue to come in with their irregularity and infrequency uninterrupted and unthreatened." Although business was good, all believed the railroads would make it better.[29]

In the spring of 1888 the long-anticipated railroad reached Tascosa. True, the Canadian River lay between the town and the tracks and it was not until February that the Fort Worth and Denver City built a depot across the river, but this was a small inconvenience in view of the old system. A bridge was built to connect Tascosa's main street with the depot; according to *Tascosa Pioneer* Editor Charles Rudolph, "the depot is just as close to town as it can be, and as it need be." W. M. D. Lee, the town's most important customer, had opposed the bridge because of his real estate interests elsewhere and the higher taxes bridge construction required. He even threatened to abandon the town, and he eventually did leave the Panhandle. His ranching business was not only a serious loss to the Tascosa merchants but an omen of what was to come.[30]

The railroad did not bring growth; in fact, it contributed to Tascosa's decline because businesses and townspeople began moving to more flourishing points along it. The loss of trail herds, which had stimulated Tascosa's economy, was another major blow. Within a year it was clear that the town was dying. For Dodge City's sister city, it was to be a slow, lingering death aggravated by the drought and ruinous cattle diseases of the late 1880s and ending in the devastating flood of 1893. These disasters adversely affected the population in the surrounding trade area, and the new shipping points and rival towns drained much of what remained of Tascosa's income. All hope of recovery faded when the Chicago, Rock Island and Gulf, which might have made Tascosa an important station, laid tracks to Liberal, Kansas and missed Tascosa by fifty miles.

As for the Tascosa Trail, ranchers still used it and continued to secure most of their supplies from Dodge City until 1892, but by then the rail lines and new roads had changed the course of commerce for both merchants and ranchers. A new road was built to Liberal, and Jim Cator's records after 1892 reflect the shift of his purchase orders away from Dodge City to the new and closer town. Still, the stage line from Meade to Beaver and Hardesty continued in operation until after the turn of the century, and freighters continued to haul supplies from Beaver to Tascosa.[31]

Although Tascosa lived on until World War I, it had ceased to be an important center of trade for a dozen years. New towns, new railroads, and new highways irreversibly altered the pattern of traffic, and the old north-south link between Dodge City and the Tascosa Panhandle area was broken. The demise of Tascosa ended the usefulness of the trail. When the once proud seat of government for nine counties, having a population of nearly eight hundred ("counting cowboys, the ranchers, Mexicans and all"), ceased to function, the trail died, too. As was the case with other trails, sod covered the old ruts and new farmers in their newly fenced fields plowed them under. Only an occasional highway sign and a few local history buffs were left to mark its passing.[32]

6. Freighting: A Grimy Business Fit Only for Peculiar Men

THERE is a tendency in describing the developing West to people it with stereotypes. There were cowboys, nesters, miners, ranchers, schoolmarms, prostitutes, gamblers, homesteaders, and outlaws. Each, it would seem, knew his or her place and did not stray from it. No category of western types has been more universally depicted with unfounded uniformity than the freighters. Penny dreadfuls, regional novelists, history buffs, and professional historians have painted them with a broad and unvarying brush. Rarely were the freighters made the center of any great drama; instead, they were allowed to blend into the scenery as quaint, humorous, somewhat disreputable characters of a predictable type.[1]

Expressmen, freighters, in fact all who were involved in moving wagons down the trail were lumped together as unfortunates caught in a dusty, monotonous, and unpleasant trade. Even the serious scholar found them a strange and peculiar lot:

> For all that may be said in his behalf, a teamster possessed few of the refinements of life and little of the dash and flamboyance that made other types of frontiersmen legendary figures. He belonged, by and large, to a class of illiterates. A teamster's face, hands, and clothes (including frock pants tucked into jackboots, checkered shirt, and broad and sloppy-brimmed felt hat) were invariably and indescribably dirty and grimy due to constant exposure to dust or mud and to the back spray of tobacco juice squirted into the prairie winds. Nor was he considered the soberest of

men. He drank more than his thirty-five dollar monthly pay with keep would allow. He brawled long and hard before extended trips, and enroute he not only patronized saloons where he found them, but was even known at times to have raided the liquor in freight. At such times and places he often became involved in quarrels, but seldom in gun fights.[2]

When distinctions were made among freighters, the role of the man within the wagon crew was considered most important in determining his characteristics. The wagonmaster was "almost invariably a powerful figure . . . forceful enough to impose his authority on men who were themselves tough and often restless. By the very nature of their job, they had to be strong, brave, and tireless. They had to know how to exact obedience to their commands. On the other hand, they were profane, hard drinking, fighting men who could handle a revolver or bowie knife and were 'often guilty of barbarous tyranny.'" The bullwhackers who drove the oxen, on the other hand, "were anonymous men," "taciturn and often peculiar." "The chasm," we are told, "separating the wagonmaster from the muleskinner and bullwhacker was wide, and in turn the teamsters looked with no small degree of condescension, if not scorn, upon the swampers and 'cavvy boys.'" Among the teamsters, the muleskinner held himself a notch above the bullwhacker, the notch representing about ten dollars more per month in pay. Cooks, when there was a separate assignment, bore a striking resemblance to the cattle-drive cook, having a heart of gold, the charm of an irritated porcupine, unsanitary but superior culinary abilities, and a vulnerability that made them the butt of campfire practical jokes. At the lowest level were the herders, or cavvy boys, who looked after the extra stock: green kids, earnest but error prone. Taken as a whole, teamsters were "hard-bitten men" who "stuck together" and "remained in a class to themselves."[3]

Such one-dimensional categories are not very useful in describing individuals in the wagon-road business of the Dodge City–Panhandle Region. Furthermore, such stereotyping promotes a superficial understanding of the people who settled the Region, for nearly all of the wagon-train personnel remained in the West to become farmers, stockmen, merchants, or community leaders—the eventual permanent settlers.

In truth, teamsters, confined as they were to a dusty, slow-moving routine, did not compare favorably with their more glamorous peers in stagecoach and riverboat settings. They had neither the dash nor the flair of a stage driver, nor did they possess the aura of authority and adventure of a Mississippi sidewheeler captain. In the words of R. D. Holt: "The old-time freighter was no picturesque character, as was the cowboy. . . . In frontier communities, however, he was not ranked as low in the economic and social scale as were the sheep herders."

Even though teamsters may have ranked low in the transportation hierarchy of their day, there was no single freighting type. Nor was there within the wagon-team hierarchy a fixed position. Individuals who made their first trip down the trail riding jerk line became wagonmasters on later trips. Henry Walker estimated that on the overland trails nine out of ten who started as teamsters were advanced to wagonmaster for faithful service. Probably the same ratio could be found in the Dodge City–Panhandle Region. There are many instances of men who worked on all levels. Robert M. Wright began his career trudging alongside twelve yoke of oxen as a hired bullwhacker, eventually drove his own freighting wagon, and ended life as a leading Dodge City merchant sending dozens of wagons down the trails. Fellow townsman George Reighard served his apprenticeship as a civilian driver for General Custer before he accumulated enough capital to buy his own outfit. Undoubtedly, the individual's reaction to the business of hauling freight changed with changed status; personalities, however, did not. A peculiar muleskinner was likely to be a peculiar wagonmaster. If certain skills or behavior were required to manage a large train but were not needed for a single six-mule hitch, they could be developed, but the style and manner of each man remained unique, perhaps even peculiarly unique. The business did not create a type or fixed caste.[4]

There are, however, a few generalizations that are applicable to the total business of freighting in the Region. First, it is safe to judge the job of any freighter on the trail to be monotonous and unpleasant. Second, because of the working conditions, few men thought of freighting as a career in the same way ranchers or farmers thought of their occupations as a lifetime commitment. Finally, the types that do emerge are based on economic status within the frontier society rather than their position within the freighting trade. Of these three generalizations, the first is the most obvious and the most easily demonstrated.

The working conditions of the freighter, whether wagonmaster or bullwhacker, were tough, tedious, and unpleasant. Trudging beside a bull team moving at two miles an hour or a mule train at two and a half miles an hour was a monotonous job. At the end of a hot day spent in a cloud of dust churned up by teams and wagons, all members of an outfit were "indescribably dirty and grimy." Cleanliness was not a matter of personal preference but depended upon the availability of water. Night camp near a creek might allow removal of the grime during the balmy summer months, but winter gave no such relief. Rain and blizzards added their own dimensions of unpleasantness.

All walked except those who rode the jerk line. Few wagons came with seats, and standing precariously on the wagon tongue was not particularly restful. Walking in winter had the added advantage of staving off the cold, and in the summer walking was preferred to the stifling confinement of a high-sided wagon, even if it had been equipped with a seat. Since the loaded wagon traveled no more than twelve or eighteen miles a day, the stint was not considered grueling to men accustomed to walking. Far more wearing were the natural hazards of the trail. Crossing swollen or frozen streams was not only dangerous but required great exertion under considerable stress. There a man might have to wade through freezing water leading reluctant animals, chop ice lanes to secure sound footing, or heave and haul on a mired wagon.[5]

Most teamsters slept on the ground winter and summer. In winter, two buffalo robes, fur side in, wrapped in a tarpaulin, made for a fairly comfortable night. The tarpaulin was essential during the rainy season. Rest under adverse conditions might be difficult but was not impossible.[6]

A hard life is frequently associated with hard liquor, but there seems to be little evidence supporting the image of freighters as universally heavy drinkers. Alexander Majors of Overland Trail fame was not the only boss convinced that sober, industrious men made the best drivers. Although there is no record of the kind of solemn oath Majors extracted from his employees, which required them to refrain from all profanity, gambling, and drinking, the teamsters in the Region seemed no more addicted to alcohol than any other plainsmen. William E. Lass's assessment of overland crews also was near the mark for those in the Region. "The bull-whackers' proclivity for whiskey," he wrote, "was easily exaggerated." Under certain conditions, drinking while on the trail could be positively dangerous. W. F. Reynolds' death on the Fort Supply Trail in a severe blizzard in 1881 was believed by his fellow teamsters to have been the result of whiskey. He was walking behind his horses and wagon, which were following a small freight train. Five miles north of Bluff Creek the wagonmaster noticed that Reynolds' team was following them but the freighter was missing. The crew reported that Reynolds was under the influence of liquor at the time, and they assumed he perished in the snow. Drinking and driving did not seem to mix, even in the nineteenth century.[7]

Although the Dodge City paper noted with enthusiasm the arrival of four large wagon trains and predicted the crews would make "times quite lively during their stay," freighters in Dodge City did not stage the wild binges or hurrah the town to the same extent the cowboys did. The dangers of associating with these "hard-bitten men" with resultant deadly gunfights and quarrels were not great. Freighters did brawl and there were shootings but, again, never to the extent of the trail-herd cowboys. Ike Berry, who freighted between Dodge City and Fort Supply, killed a man with cold calculation because of a personal insult. One of the Lee and Reynolds employees, Captain Wheeler (the title had carried over from Civil War days), was killed by an unknown hand. Wheeler's body was found in back of a saloon the morning after "a high old spree . . . and some quarrels." One of the most publicized killings was that of a young black wagon boss who worked for Lee and Reynolds. William Gibbs and a wagon-train cook, Joe Campo, exchanged shots in the street at Fort Supply after Gibbs fired Campo. The cook was wounded slightly, but Gibbs, seriously wounded, was hospitalized in the fort's infirmary for some time. Gibbs remained at the post recuperating and creating trouble in general, apparently "spoiling for a fight." An insult directed at George Thomas' wife led to another shootout. Thomas was more accurate and persistent than Campo, and after wounding Gibbs he chased him into a butcher shop, firing his navy six-shooter until Gibbs lay dead on the floor. In spite of these incidents, death was far more likely to come to a freighter as a result of weather or an accident at a river crossing than from any other source.[8]

Monotony and more money, rather than hazards, hardship, or hard customers, drove men to look for better ways of making a living. Working conditions plus their own restlessness forced all freighters, regardless of status, to leave the business. One of the marks of most men who came to the frontier, whether teamster or homesteader, was their willingness to try anything once. Freighters not only moved up, and sometimes down, through the freighting hierarchy, they also moved out of it at the first opportunity. Like most frontiersmen, freighters were inclined to be multifaceted and multitalented individuals (jacks-of-all-trades). For them, freighting was considered only a means to some other end. All saw, or thought they saw, greener pastures down some other trail. This was as true for big operators, such as W. M. D. Lee, who left the business and moved into the Texas world of high finance, as it was for George Reighard, who took over a second-rate hotel in Dodge City. Few stayed with freighting as long as Casimero Romero, who lasted from 1882 to 1887. Only Charles Rath remained in the freighting business throughout the entire wagon-road period in the Region. When they left the trail, the freighters scattered into most of the occupations available on the frontier. Ed Jones and Monchy Russell, like many others, turned to ranching; Romero and Reighard became hotel operators; Willie Hutchinson converted his freighting teams to livery horses; Bat Masterson gained fame as a lawman; J. J. Long and Robert Wright became prosperous merchants.

Difficult as it is to find fixed-personality patterns or uniform characteristics in the men who drove wagons, there were some similarities of attitude and action based on status. Day laborers and owners of a freighting outfit had different motivations and expectations. Among those on wages, troopers and civilian teamsters working for the army certainly understood that their jobs required responses different from those of men in charge of a single wagon carrying freight for Dodge City merchants Henry Beverley or Jacob Collar. Even more distance separated an entrepreneur like W. M. D. Lee, who had fifty or more teamsters on the payroll,

from a man like Chris Schmoker, who occasionally loaded a farm
wagon for a single trip into the Panhandle. Lee's status in the Region, as well as his approach to his enterprise, resembled that of
eastern industrialists in both action and business attitude. Other
men, for instance Willie Hutchinson, who hauled freight over the
same trails Lee used, might have adopted Lee's patterns if he had
achieved Lee's status and economic power. But he was not so
blessed, and Lee was.

Lee and his partner, A. E. ("Albert") Reynolds, were representative of a small group of men who can be considered wagon-road
entrepreneurs. As part of a multistate operation, these two men
put together the largest freighting organization in the Dodge
City–Panhandle Region as a service arm of their other enterprises. In the early fall of 1869, Lee and Reynolds formed a partnership to obtain a federal license to trade with the Cheyenne and
Arapaho tribes and to secure the post tradership at Camp Supply.[9]

Long before they began dealing in the Region, both men possessed the basic characteristics and attitudes typical of eastern entrepreneurs. Both had served apprenticeships in the same or similar
businesses before 1869. Reynolds, who was born in 1840 in New
York, worked in his father's store until 1865, when he set up his own
general store in Leavenworth, Kansas. Using connections he had
cultivated there, Reynolds secured the position of post trader at
Fort Lyon, Colorado in 1867. Lee, who was a year younger, was
born in Eaton, Pennsylvania, but his father soon moved to Portage,
Wisconsin. A former Portage resident, J. B. Fargo, gave Lee his
first job: driving a wagon for Wells, Fargo from Missouri into Kansas. When the war came, Lee served in General Philip H. Sheridan's
quartermaster corps and stayed on at the end of the war as a civilian employee.

Combining their talents, the two men focused on the new venture their drive, ambition, and experience in procurement, marketing, freighting, and manipulating government contracts. Of their
pooled resources, by far the most important was the experience
they had in securing government licenses. Lee did the early footwork, ably coached by Reynolds, in consulting those who had influence in granting licenses, including Enoch Hoag, the central superintendent of Indian affairs at Lawrence, Kansas; Brevet Colonel

A. D. Nelson at Camp Supply; Brinton Darlington, agent for the Cheyennes and Arapahos in Oklahoma Territory; Secretary of War William W. Belknap in Washington, D.C.; and Brigadier General J. M. Hedrick at his home in Iowa. Finally, with what can only be labeled as a substantial bribe (one thousand dollars in cash and the promise of a fifty-five-hundred-dollar annual retainer) to General Hedrick, a close friend of Secretary Belknap, the partners were in business; the all-important license and monopoly had been secured. Without the initial capital and the knowledge of whom to consult, the prize would have gone to other men. In fact, the post tradership had been awarded before Hedrick was contacted by Lee, and Belknap had to be persuaded to rescind the order. Lee's tenacity, his cynical understanding of how to tap the federal government's largess, and his willingness to risk time and capital to achieve his goal had secured for Lee and Reynolds the right, in part an exclusive right, to supply some five thousand Indians and military personnel with goods and services. From the initial foothold at Camp Supply, the partnership expanded to include transportation of army baggage, troops, cordwood, grain, hay, and building materials. Over the next ten years, the partnership grew and expanded into other nonarmy-related activities. Both men displayed the same boldness of action that had secured the early contracts. Each took on separate partners and with them ventured into all phases of the buffalo-hide business, merchandising through general stores, stagecoaching, contract freighting, Indian trading (including whiskey, guns, and ammunition), and ranching. When they acquired the 29,440-acre LE Ranch in Texas, ranching came to dominate all other considerations, but until he left the Panhandle Lee remained active in a dozen regional activities.

Supplying Lee's and Reynolds' vast commercial and ranching empire was a monumental undertaking. Lee's ability to organize and to risk men and money successfully was an essential element in the effort. Since their freighting operation was one requiring a continuous stream of wagons on the trail, Lee developed a system of small units, each under the control of a wagonmaster. A number of these men—among them Andy Jard, L. N. York, and Gus Miller—became familiar and respected figures in Dodge City. The trains usually consisted of six to twelve wagons of the Schuttler freighting type, pulled by six mules or seven yoke of oxen. A single unit, or outfit, required ten to fourteen men. For a time Lee experimented with an eight- or ten-mule hitch pulling three wagons that could haul a railroad boxcarload of goods. Since Lee and Reynolds supplied the needs of towns, garrisons, Indian reservations, buffalo camps, and ranchers, their cargoes were quite varied, including everything from beads and bracelets to fencing and guns. Contracts were negotiated with the army for handling "the baggage of the 23rd Infantry": two hundred cords of wood, six hundred tons of hay, a "bull train of oats" and another of flour. A single contract with Charles Goodnight to supply his ranch with six months' supplies, including sixty-seven miles of barbed wire, required a train of thirty wagons. The newspapers in the Region were inclined to record only the total tonnage of Lee and Reynolds shipments. One story reported the shipment of 200,000 pounds in April 1878, and between July 1, 1882 and February 1, 1883 some 901,923 pounds went to Fort Elliott, 1,806,155 to Fort Supply, 323,588 to Mobeetie, and 198,668 to Tascosa, plus another 788,733 pounds between Fort Supply and Fort Elliott. When Reynolds joined Rath in supplying the Double Mountain camp on the Brazos River, the already heavy volume of traffic became heavier.[10]

Unable at times to keep up with the demand, the company hired individuals to haul separate loads, but Lee usually tried to keep any source of profit within the partnership. This was as true in small matters, such as adding billiard parlors to the Camp Supply facilities, as it was in large ones, such as preserving the exclusive right to the Indian and hide trade for themselves and their partners. At one point Lee and Reynolds ordered from Chicago twenty wagons with wheels six inches higher than those of ordinary wagons; the wagons were designed especially for crossing the Arkansas River without wetting merchandise, thereby saving the toll on the Dodge City bridge.[11]

The pair knew how to ingratiate themselves with the army and with Indian agents and apparently secured "special rates on railroad lines east of Dodge City." Part of the favoritism shown by Indian Agent Brinton Darlington stemmed from his gratitude to Lee, who had been a friendly witness in a court-martial at Fort Leavenworth. Lee also had the loyalty of those who worked for him. One of them,

Marion Armstrong, wrote that Lee "took good care of his employees, feeding them well and paying them good wages." Although it was impossible to operate as large and diversified an enterprise as the Lee and Reynolds company without making enemies, Lee's contributions outweigh the damage his ambition and singleness of purpose might have caused. He came to the Region with the instincts of the nineteenth-century entrepreneur (in local parlance, he was a plunger), and his training there merely sharpened these characteristics for his later career as "a rancher, a deep-water entrepreneur, and an oil producer." He did not accept the Region on its terms alone but tried and succeeded in altering the environment for what his generation thought was a better setting. His biographer's summary confirms a positive assessment:

> In 1869, when Lee made his first effort to establish a trade in Indian Territory, the Southwest was an open wilderness of unrealized potential. But by good fortune and force of character, Lee was able to use his intelligence and adapt himself to a new environment. The ten years that he was engaged as an Indian trader served to harden the mettle of the future cattleman, entrepreneur, and oil producer. In a very real sense, Lee began his independent adult life with the August, 1878, ride out of Indian country into Texas. Left behind were events that he chose to forget, but, nonetheless, events that shaped both the man and the frontier.[12]

A. E. Reynolds matched his partner in boldness and energy. On the strength of a letter from Lee, Reynolds bought half-interest, sight unseen, in the LE Ranch. In 1881, in a move calculated to unnerve Reynolds and acquire sole ownership of the ranch for himself, Lee suddenly gave his partner the choice of buying all or selling all of the partnership. Given only ten days to decide, Reynolds rode to the nearest railroad station and caught the train to Denver, where he consulted a Scottish company that he knew might like to invest in a large ranch. Securing the approval of company officials, Reynolds had to make a round trip to New York to secure the funds. He rode back to the Panhandle ranch and presented the amazed Lee with cash in time to clinch the deal. With A. E. Reynolds as general manager and his brother, C. F., as local operator, the LE brand became one of the prominent marks in the Region. The Reynolds brothers sold their holdings in 1902 and returned to concentrate on their mining interests in Colorado.

Lee and Reynolds were not the only entrepreneurs who found the trails south to be paths to great enterprise. Although not as successful as either Lee or Reynolds, Charles Rath of Dodge City was just as aggressive in developing his diversified enterprises, and he possessed many of the same essential characteristics and attitudes that were necessary to become a wagon-road entrepreneur.[13]

Rath was born in Sweetwine, Ohio and grew up on a farm there. He received the barest rudiments of formal education but became a self-educated man while serving as a freighter on the old Santa Fe Trail. As a bright and ambitious nineteen-year-old, he signed on as a teamster, freighting as far west as Bent's Fort in Colorado. In the shade of a wagon with the tongue hoisted as a back rest, he read anything that came to hand. For a time he clerked in Bent's store, where he discovered a completely new culture. He took to wife a thrice-married Cheyenne woman who counted among her former husbands the well-known scout Kit Carson. Roadmaker (Rath's personal name for his Indian wife, Making Out Road) bore him one child, taught him much about Indian life, and helped him develop proficiency in the Cheyenne, Arapaho, and Kiowa languages, knowledge that he put to good use in his later life.

In 1858, Rath left his bride and Bent's Fort to establish a road ranch near Ellinwood, Kansas on the Arkansas River. He was joined there by several members of his Ohio family, including his brother Chris, who became the first of many partners. He continued his work as a teamster with his own wagon, hauling freight to Fort Hays for the army. By 1860 he had started accumulating land around Ellinwood, helped to organize the town of Beach Valley, and acquired another ranch near Lyons, Kansas on the Santa Fe Trail. The war years were spent trading with the Indians (as was the case with W. M. D. Lee, the goods included whiskey and firearms), hauling freight for the army, and looking after his property. Although he sustained considerable financial loss when the Ellinwood ranch was raided and burned by Indians, he managed to expand his holdings during the war. Among other ventures, Rath secured a contract to supply mules, oxen, and equipment in grading the roadbed for the Santa Fe Railroad as it moved west across Kansas, furnished meat for the track crew, and increased his land holdings. In 1870 he married Caroline Markley and the couple moved to Topeka, where he could look after his many business interests. The Census of 1870 listed his occupation as freighter and his personal wealth at fifteen thousand dollars, certainly substantial capital to use as a working base for his entrepreneurial ambitions.

As the tracks moved west, Rath followed. William C. Lobenstein, a dealer in pelts and leather at Leavenworth, had purchased buffalo robes from Rath while Rath was supplying the railroad with meat. When the Leavenworth merchant received an order for five hundred buffalo hides to be sent to England for experimental purposes, he called on Rath and A. C. Myers, another merchant who had also sold hides to him. The hides left over from that shipment started the American buffalo-hide industry, made Lobenstein the largest hide buyer in America, and put Rath in a business that would make him a fortune. [14]

Although Rath became one of the most successful hunters in the West, he continued his freighting operations through the partnership with his brothers. In 1872 he moved to Dodge City, where he established the Charles Rath Mercantile Co. in partnership with Robert Wright and A. J. Anthony. In Dodge City, his major interest shifted to the buffalo trade: buying hides, meat, and bones; tanning hides; supplying hunters on the prairie; hunting with his own crew; and freighting the harvest to Dodge and supplies to the prairie. In his first major hunt, organized exclusively to bring in hides, Rath had an outfit of twelve teams, six to eight mules to the wagon, and a crew of twelve men. He was one of many hunters to kill more than one hundred buffalo in one stand. Robert Wright wrote of him:

My old-time friend and former partner, Charles Rath, was a great hunter and freighter. No one handled as many hides and robes as he did, and few killed more buffaloes. He was honest, true and brave. He bought and sold more than a million hides, and tens of thousands of buffalo robes, and hundreds of cars of buffalo meat, both dried and fresh, besides several carloads of buffalo tongue. [15]

When the Kansas herds were decimated, Rath moved south. In a short time he had established trading posts at Adobe Walls (which cost him at least fifteen thousand dollars in the Quanah Parker raid), at Fort Griffin in partnership with Frank E. Conrad (the post sutler there), at Sweetwater with Henry Hamburg, and on the Palo Duro. The most spectacular of his ventures was made in partnership with Lee and Reynolds when they combined forces to establish a trading and hunting camp near the Double Mountain Fork of the Brazos River. Lee was incensed by the encroaching traders and was determined to control all the hide business remaining on the Southern Plains, if only as a partner. By January 1877 the camp was doing business with some one thousand hunters who dubbed it, variously, Reynolds Town, Reynolds City, or Rath City. Supplies and hides were taken either from or to Dodge City or Fort Griffin. Rath led the expedition down from Fort Supply, following the directions of a compass fixed to his saddlehorn. Trailing behind him was a caravan of wagons, including one loaded with men, shovels, picks, and axes to clear the trail and make stream banks, draws, and washes passable. The lead wagon was followed by fifty or sixty others, under the direction of John Russell, loaded with everything a hunter might need, including a disassembled saloon and brothel. Individual hunters, their wagons, and crews joined to make a caravan of more than two hundred wagons. By the end of spring, the partners had transported more than one hundred thousand hides to the railroad sidings and Lee was close to realizing his ambition of controlling the buffalo-hide business in northern Texas.[16]

A major task for Rath, as it was with W. M. D. Lee, was to keep the wagons rolling. The volume of his freighting business was immense. Robert Wright indicated that he and Rath had shipped out of Dodge City two hundred thousand buffalo hides, two hundred cars of hind quarters, and two cars of tongues. The *Dodge City Times* boasted that in 1881 Rath was shipping one hundred fifty thousand pounds of freight a week to Mobeetie, where the partnership of Rath and Conrad handled some one hundred thousand dollars worth of merchandise annually. The Hamburg partnership at the peak of its operation kept a bull train on the road continuously, hauling one hundred forty thousand pounds each trip and making a round trip every twenty-four days.[17]

Wright recalled the startled reaction of a Kansas City warehouseman at the size of one of Rath's orders:

Charles Rath & Company ordered from Long Brothers, of Kansas City, two hundred cases of baking powder at one order. They went to Colonel

W. F. Askew, to whom we were shipping immense quantities of hides, and said: "These men must be crazy, or else they mean two hundred boxes instead of cases." They said there were not two hundred cases in the city. Askew wired us if we had not made a mistake. We answered: "No; double the order." Askew was out a short time after that and saw six or eight carloads of flour stacked up in the warehouse. He said he now understood. It was to bake this flour up into bread.[18]

Rath dispatched wagon trains in all sizes, from a single load to caravans of a hundred or more wagons. Handling what Rath considered a minor assignment in the offseason in 1883 required delivery of more than eighteen thousand pounds of raw wool from a rancher south of Fort Elliott. Wrote Judd Crawford, a Dodge City pioneer:

I can see Rath's train yet, starting across the bridge, one way traffic. Sometimes they would be tied up for two hours at one end, then the other way around. Two wagons were hooked together and twelve or fourteen mules hitched to it, sometimes three wagons together and twelve and fourteen mules hitched to them. If he started out with a team, he would ride on ahead for he could not [afford to] spend twenty days with a train.[19]

As was true of Lee and Reynolds, Rath had to depend on wagonmasters, such as Billy Dixon, George Aiken, and Thomas Nixon, to see the wagons through. Eventually he divided his enterprises, placing Fred Bond in charge of his eastern Kansas operations and Joseph Minor in charge of the bull trains in the Panhandle. By then, he had acquired a number of small freighting lines and had expanded his regular line down to Santa Fe, New Mexico. With the Double Mountain partnership ended, Rath vied with his old partners, Lee and Reynolds, for government contracts, and it was not unusual to read in the Dodge City papers that Rath was in the East "looking after government freight contracts."[20]

Although the freighting process was fairly stable, Rath did experiment with new equipment and acquired wagons with higher wheelbases and shorter beds. By far his most daring innovation was the acquisition of a steam-propelled "road engine . . . intended at first as the motive power to haul freight wagons." When he tested it on the main street of Mobeetie, it caused a sensation but proved impractical. Eventually he used the engine to run a sawmill.[21]

By the mid-1880s, Rath had acquired a reputation as a plunger

This photograph of wagons loaded with buffalo hides on a Dodge City street was taken in 1872, and several copies were made. Courtesy Kansas State Historical Society, Topeka.

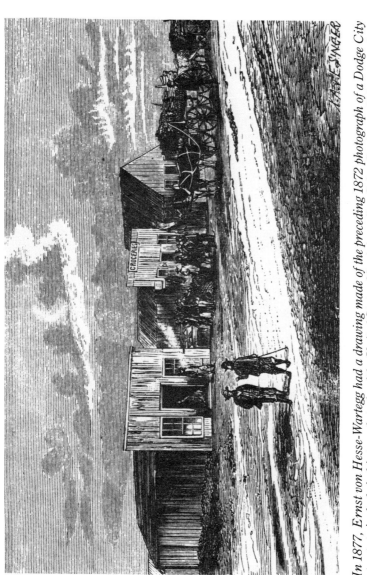

In 1877, Ernst von Hesse-Wartegg had a drawing made of the preceding 1872 photograph of a Dodge City street, to include in his travel study of the United States, Nord-Amerika: Seine Städte und Naturwundes, Sein Land und sein Leute, which was widely circulated in Europe. Courtesy Kansas State Historical Society, Topeka.

backed by enormous wealth. He was, in fact, spreading his operation in too many directions, not always on a sound basis, and as a result his wealth suffered. After the Adobe Walls disaster, William C. Lobenstein had backed him with capital, and over the years Rath returned the favor to many of his friends. He also invested heavily in cattle and land in and around Mobeetie. However, he was still willing to go outside the Region if the opportunity were presented. He received a contract for eighty thousand dollars to grade roadbed for the Atlantic and Pacific Railroad in New Mexico, and he applied for a number of patents, including several versions of earth scrapers and one for a folding egg crate. It is not clear whether he invested heavily in these.

As his interest shifted south from his Dodge City base, his luck seemed to run out. There was a costly divorce, his third unsuccessful marriage, many lawsuits, and failing investments. Rath had always been generous in making loans and backing partners; now many of them were reneging on repayment. The biggest loss was his investment in land and town lots in Mobeetie. When the railroad bypassed the town, land values fell dramatically. Eventually, Rath lost the empire he had built on freighting and the buffalo trade. In 1889 he tried to make the run on foot into the Cherokee Strip for free land. His final days brought him to eking out a living on a downtown street of Trinidad, Colorado, grinding out music on a borrowed hand organ. He died July 30, 1902 at the age of sixty-six.

As long as the buffalo trade had fueled the market, Rath had prospered. In the words of his biographer:

Surely no one risks as much in capital and effort as Charles Rath did to get the buffalo trade. Generally, although he had many partners, he took care of the traveling end of the business, having made many good connections through the many years he had been going east. Throughout it all, he seems to have kept on good terms with his partners, business associates, the hunters, and customers in general. [22]

He had attempted to adjust to the changing economic environment, as W. M. D. Lee had done so successfully, but he had failed to gauge the effects of the railroads on his other enterprises and had invested too heavily in one location. This, plus his personal losses in divorce settlements and other legal matters, had destroyed his base of operating capital. He remained in the freighting business too long, hoping it would continue to be a cushion for his other ventures as it had been in the past. Clearly in command of many of the essential attributes of a successful entrepreneur, he resembled W. M. D. Lee in many ways. Rath possessed tremendous drive and energy, a willingness to risk and experiment, an ability to organize and use other men's labor to his own advantage, understanding of the necessity of manipulating government agencies, and the self-confidence that inspired trust by others as well as personal assurance that he could control multifaceted operations with success. His ultimate failures were largely a matter of personal misfortune, misplaced trust in other people, and a run of bad luck. His contributions to the development of the Region were positive and of considerable proportion. Even more than Lee, Rath demonstrates to what heights of success a wagon-road entrepreneur in the Region could climb—and how far he could fall.

Another category of freighters were the small, independent operators, individuals who considered freighting, for a time at least, to be their major occupation. They owned their outfits, contracted to deliver cargoes, and regularly or occasionally employed other men as teamsters. They did not possess the characteristics of a Rath or a Reynolds, nor did they aspire to become entrepreneurs. Their major considerations were that each would be his own boss and would make enough profit to move into some other enterprise where he would continue to control his own life. Like Ed Jones, a few might put together a single large train for some one special project, but primarily they drove their own teams on a single or tandem hitch. Most of the wagons in the early period were driven by independent owners who maintained a limited outfit and remained active for only a brief time.

Typical of this group, but not necessarily a model frequently duplicated, was George Reighard. Born in Pennsylvania on February 1, 1847, he came to Fort Hays in 1867 as a government freighter, riding the jerk line to Camp Supply via Fort Dodge. As a muleskinner in Colonel Custer's Seventh Cavalry supply train, he made the first trek down the Military Road to the site of what was to become Camp Supply. On these trips, Reighard never ceased to marvel at the number of buffalo on the plains. The army supply train, he reported, frequently traveled for a hundred miles through a continuous mass of buffalo that were slowly grazing northward: [23]

Often we would be stopped by a group of a few hundred that was so compact it blocked the way and we would wait until it drifted past and a lane opened ahead of us.

I have read of a Russian ice breaking steamer battling its way through the ice floes . . . , how it would nose this way and that along lanes between the floating ice cakes. In much the same manner we navigated through that vast drifting herd of buffaloes. [24]

The immensity of the herds and the sounds they generated were awesome. When a herd was some miles off, the sound was "like distant thunder," but at close range it reminded Reighard of the pounding and clattering of his own freight train crossing "a high, long wooden bridge." On one trip the press of the massed buffalo overturned six of the heavily laden freight wagons.

After two years as a government teamster, Reighard joined a crew of hunters shooting buffalo just east of the trail he so often had followed down to Camp Supply. In the vicinity of present-day Ashland, he personally killed two thousand buffalo, seventy-nine in one stand, and the crew skinned another three thousand on nearby Sand Creek. As was true of other hunters, Reighard believed the herds to be indestructible:

Pity? No, I did not feel it. It was business with me. I had my money invested in that outfit; if I did not butcher the buffalo there were many other hunting outfits all around me that would, so I killed all I could. . . .

In the early '70s we did not think we were exterminating the buffalo herds. There were 3 million buffaloes then, enough, we thought with the natural increase, to supply the market for a hundred years to come. It was natural for us to think that, the herds were so large. [25]

In the winter of 1872, drifts piled high against Reighard's camp on Crooked Creek, leaving him snowbound for over a month. With supplies running critically low, he harnessed his four-mule team and cut across the prairie, hoping to make it to Dodge City. But when he reached the Military Road, he and his team were so exhausted that he turned south toward Camp Supply, eventually making it to Kaufholz's and Beauregard's soddy in the shelter of Bluff

Creek. The road ranch was an inviting sanctuary, so much so that he "just holed up" and, before the snows melted, bought the ranch and its stock of supplies. For this "old" buffalo hunter (age twenty-five) in need of "a breather," the ranch had the feel of a peaceful refuge, although it was isolated and vulnerable to attack in the heart of disputed Indian country.[26]

Up to that point, his life had been overcharged with excitement and adventure, beginning with an enlistment in the Twenty-second Pennsylvania Cavalry at age sixteen. He fought at Spotsylvania Court House and Cold Harbor, where he was wounded. When he was not hunting adventure, it had a way of finding him. He was present at two killings in or near Dodge City in which he had no stake and witnessed only by chance. He was a passenger headed for Dodge when the wounded Grant Wells shot a drunken cowboy named Robbins, who was attempting to rob the stage. And he was in the Lady Gay the night City Marshal Ed Masterson and policeman Nat Haywood attempted to calm the boisterous Oburn cowhands whooping it up under the influence of considerable whiskey and high spirits.[27]

The road ranch was not to be nearly as exciting as Reighard's casual, unintentional encounters; still, it was a lively spot visited by freighters, buffalo hunters, Indians, and soldiers stopping by for food, fodder, and shelter. In March 1873 he took as a partner George Oakes, another Camp Supply freighter and Indian fighter who had survived the Beecher Island fight. They began hauling with two wagons, picking up freight in Dodge for delivery to Camp Supply. When Oakes left for parts unknown, Reighard and John ("Red") Clarke, who had the road ranch down the trail on the Cimarron, became partners and continued the freighting trips. Then, in 1877, Reighard traded Silas Maley the Bluff Creek ranch for the Great Western Hotel, situated at the south end of the toll bridge in Dodge City.[28]

The future, Reighard believed, lay with cattle ranching, and he decided to invest in rangeland, but before he was able to complete a deal he learned that he could sell his freighting equipment and stock for a good price in Deadwood, South Dakota. To pay for the trip, he loaded his wagons with flour and coal and headed north. In Deadwood the demand for goods and freighters was so strong he remained there for a year; eventually he sold his mules and wagons, returned to Dodge, married Miss Anna Gyles, and set up a ranch just across the Arkansas River near Chalk Beeson's old COD range. He gradually accumulated a substantial herd of longhorns, but in the Blizzard of '86 he suffered irrevocable losses. From a herd of more than two thousand two hundred head, he lost all but one hundred. As was the fate of many other Great Plains ranchers, the storm ended his cattleman days. He turned to farming, purchasing land just east of Dodge and remaining there until the infirmities of old age forced his retirement. He died August 22, 1936.[29]

Reighard's experience was fairly typical. Not having the capital to invest in as large a train as Romero, he was forced eventually to seek some other advancement. After the buffalo were eliminated, ranching had an enormous appeal to anyone with even limited capital who could start small and gradually stock the range. Reighard had neither the inclination nor the mental and material assets to become an aggressive entrepreneur, but he did have enough drive and imagination to attempt other enterprises with more rewards than freighting. As an independent freighter he tried to develop the business as an auxiliary or extra source of income, but long before the wagon-road economy ended, he, like his fellow independent operators, turned his talents to a less dreary and exacting task.

Freighting was an easy business to enter. Anyone with a team, wagon, and spare time could set himself up as a freighter. Ranchers, farmers, and merchants frequently hauled their own produce and supplies for convenience or because of the uncertainty and expense of hiring someone else. This group of casual or part-time freighters, sometimes referred to as shotgun freighters because of their scattered trips, constituted the third and eventually the largest group of drivers on the trails.

Many shotgun freighters came from the ranks of men changing jobs or occupations. Freighting was a good transitional trade. Hauling contracts were negotiated for limited times and did not tie a man down. Gossip picked up in the towns and camps the freighter visited brought news of other opportunities. And freighting equipment was easily disposed of or converted to other uses.

One group using freighting as a bridge between jobs were the old buffalo hunters; by 1878 there were many of them in the Region.

Their relentless efficiency had cut their hunting careers short, so the Big 50s were put aside to gather dust while leaning against a wall in the back bedroom. Meanwhile, the hunter had to make a living, so the old survivor, still in his twenties and thirties, took whatever opportunities came to hand. Since many had acquired teams and wagons as part of their hunting equipment, the shift to freighting came easily. In Dave Bowers' words: "After all the buffalo was gone, we went to freighting, hauled to headquarters for ranchers from Dodge City, Kansas, or from Fort Worth. We hauled groceries, dry goods, corn, whiskey in barrels, and beer in quart bottles." After a brief stint as freighter, the hunter usually heard of some new opportunity and the "old" buffalo hunter became an "old" freighter.[30]

Ranchers, on the other hand, found they had to be permanent, if only part-time, freighters. Many did not feel comfortable depending on hired wagons, so they maintained their own outfits. M. H. Loy remembered meeting the ranchers from the Panhandle in "long trains coming up to Dodge for their first load of goods in the fall to do through the winter. They drove six or seven yoke of oxen or the same span of mules." Other ranchers found it cheaper to hire freighters to bring goods to the ranch. Ed Jones made a contract with the Bates and Beal ranch to deliver four hundred thousand pounds of freight. He used ten wagons and fifty head of mules and oxen to haul twenty thousand to thirty thousand pounds per trip.

Such large assignments were not unusual. José Romero, Casimiro's son, explained that freighting for ranchers always meant heavy loads because of the nature of the supplies. Barbed wire and other necessities were either heavy in themselves or were ordered in bulk. "A box of bacon," Romero explained, "would weigh four or five hundred pounds." Fencing the cattle range increased traffic into the ranch country, and a trip was just as profitable if a return load could be found. Occasionally, firewood or some other product was available; one freighter reported he made an extra one thousand five hundred dollars in one season by bringing back a load of bones each trip.[31]

The bone boom not only solved for a while the problem of finding a profitable return load but also stimulated many settlers to join the freighting business as part-time freighters and bone pickers. Advertisements circulated widely on the plains alerted folks to the easy money and great demand. One of the lesser-known bone buyers in Houston sent out a broadside calling for a thousand tons, and the Dodge City buyers expected even bigger amounts; the response was gratifying. Any homesteader could buy survival until better times came by delivering bones to the Santa Fe siding in Dodge City. When L. K. McIntyre and his partner found themselves with no food and no money, each hitched his team to a wagon and started for Dodge City, going in separate directions and picking up bones en route. It was the low mark in their venture, but the partners survived to prove up their claims. Even the established freighter found bones a profitable cargo. Tom Nixon, better known as a hunter of live buffalo, boasted of returning one of Charles Rath's freight wagons filled with bones. Romero found the margin of profit much increased as long as bleached bones could be found on the prairie. The result was that bones were piled in ghoulish heaps several hundred yards long and six to eight feet high along the tracks in Dodge City. In 1883, thirty-six carloads weighing more than eight million pounds were shipped from there.[32]

Before bones were used to fill the returning wagons, the hide business sometimes served the same purpose. Ed Jones became involved in Adobe Walls when he needed cargo for empty wagons headed south to pick up hides. Firewood was a good return cargo used by many freighters. The demand was high in Dodge City and at the forts, but as a return cargo it was less desirable because it required hard work and was more time consuming than picking up bones.

As land was taken up by homesteaders, the new farmers became another major part of the freighting traffic. Few could afford to pay freighters to haul material and supplies to their homesteads, so, like the ranchers, they became frequent travelers on the road. Others found hiring out to deliver a wagon load of supplies to the Panhandle or Dodge City a convenient and important supplement to their farm income. A farmer down on his luck and lacking ready cash could hitch his plow horses or a span of mules to a farm wagon and become a freighter for one or two trips. Carrie Schmoker Anshutz remembered that the droughty times from 1879 to 1881 along the Kansas border converted many a farmer to teamster. Some left the country, she recalled, "none could make a living farming so . . . turned to freighting, some to bone picking." Freighting over long distances was a tough business and not for the faint of heart. One farmer-freighter was caught in a blizzard that buried all the sleeping men in snow packed so tightly that they had to be rescued by soldiers from Fort Dodge. Safely back in Dodge, he wrote his friends: "So much for freighting on the frontier. My advice to farmers is to attend to their farms and let freighting alone." But when times were hard and the team idle, the homesteader tended to ignore hardship. [33]

Others saw freighting as a more or less permanent auxiliary enterprise and, since there was always a demand for it, considered it a second profession. William Henry ("Willie") Hutchinson fit into that category. He was the son of Elijah Hutchinson, who brought his grown and married children to homestead in Meade County, Kansas. Willie was truly a jack-of-all-trades and attempted many while connected with family operations in Meade County. Using the Hutchinson Road Ranche as a base, Willie operated as an independent freighter on the Jones and Plummer Trail. As long as the family functioned as a unit, he could afford to be gone for three or four weeks, making deliveries to Mobeetie, Tascosa, or some isolated ranch. He also profited by picking up a load of bones for the return trip. Eventually, however, freighting became too disruptive to his other efforts and he converted his teams to the livery business in Fowler. He built a livery barn at Wilburn in Ford County, graded the first streets in Fowler, initiated the petition to survey and improve roads north to Dodge City, and ran a hack between Fowler and Dodge City. A man of many talents and much ambition, he farmed, raised sheep and cattle, served as justice of the peace and trustee of Fowler Township, represented the Independent party in Ford County, and was a charter member of the Democratic party in Meade County. He remained active in the political and business life of Meade County for fifteen years, until 1895, when the effects of tuberculosis forced him to leave. Seeking the one known remedy of that day, a high, dry climate, he moved to Carlsbad, New Mexico, where he died in 1899 at the age of forty-three. [34]

Freighting was a means of supplying the cash requirements of the Hutchinson clan, and Willie was able to accumulate stock for his livery and road-building activities. When the brothers moved to separate operations, Willie found more convenient and profitable uses for his time and energy. His willingness to risk, to diversify, and to work hard might have propelled him into the entrepreneur class if he had not been plagued with ill health.

Regardless of status, entrepreneur or night herdsman, shotgun or full-time teamster, freighting in the Region was pretty much the same for all. Dirt and grime accumulated on wagonmasters in layers just as it did on the cavvy boys, the winter's wind chilled indiscriminately, and wagon tongues broke with complete impartiality. By the late 1870s, when wagon freighting reached the Region, most of the innovations and improvements of equipment had been tested and a fair degree of uniformity developed in the day-to-day operation. It was an old, established business.

The work began early. In the growing season, when the bull trains carried no feed or fodder for the stock and depended on grazing the oxen on prairie grass, the train started about four o'clock. Depending on the distance to a good camping or grazing spot, the wagons kept to the trail until near noon, hitched up again at four, and drove until dark. The lead position in the train was a highly favored spot, not only in terms of pride in being first, but also because it was freer of dust and the teams were easier to control. Consequently, there was usually a good-natured rush to see who could get off first. If mules were used, the order of the day was altered but little; the grazing time was shortened at noon, but otherwise it was the same sunup to sundown routine. [35]

The major difference between overland freighting and that in the Region was the size of the trains. Rarely was there put together in Dodge City a full train consisting of twenty-five or more wagons under one wagonmaster. Those who reported mile-long trains snaking down the trail were actually seeing several individual units joined loosely together for social contact and cooperation in corraling at night and crossing difficult streams. Generally a train consisted of six to ten wagons, with the average outfit (single owner) having three wagons and fourteen to twenty horses, mules, or oxen. After the mid-1880s, single or double wagons were seen most frequently.

Trains of ten or more wagons, if they used the wagons for a corral, would park parallel, with a chain or rope closing the ends. Most units, however, did not corral the stock. Some carried a night herder, who slept in one of the wagons as it rocked along during the day; others simply hobbled or let the mules loose, knowing they would not stray far from camp. Another technique was to stake out a mare wearing a bell and turn the mules loose, knowing they would remain close to the bell mare. The night herder was usually a boy in his teens, along more for the adventure than the pay. The advantages of smaller units were many, and since there was little danger from outlaws or Indians after 1875, the earlier compelling reasons for the larger, slower caravans no longer existed.[36]

In one respect the Dodge City trails appeared to serve the teamsters far better than the typical overland routes. Food in the Region was abundant and varied; at least the choice of meat was nearly unlimited. José Romero, freighting out of Tascosa, reported that quail, prairie chicken, turkey, duck, antelope, buffalo, and deer were to be found in abundance all along the trail and were part of the daily fare. Way stations were available along the line and occasionally a freighter did buy a meal, but generally a grub box replaced the grub wagon of the larger overland trains. Most wagon outfits were small enough that the teamsters prepared their own meals. Soda crackers, cheese, bacon, coffee, bread (pan bread most frequently), and canned peaches were staples, supplemented by whatever meat the countryside offered. Usually, three meals a day were provided; unless inclement weather or haste dictated otherwise, they were cooked. Since the trails were used so heavily, camping spots where water, and possibly fuel, were available were well known and the necessity of the wagonmaster's scouting ahead was eliminated. In the smaller units the cook was designated on a daily rotating basis. Orrin Burright traveled with a three-wagon crew on many occasions and described a routine that was fairly typical:

Our freighting crew was just one of the many such outfits that could be seen coming and going along the trail most any time of day or night.

We got our goods all loaded very early in the morning and were ready to leave Dodge City by sunup. We did not have a chuckwagon as the cattle drovers did, but each crew carried its own groceries and cooking utensils and we made camp as we stopped beside the trail and cooked our noon meal, fed our teams and gave them a short rest before starting on the way again. About sundown we again stopped and cooked our supper, also on a campfire, and fed our teams and staked them out for the night with two armed guards always on duty throughout the night.

Everything was astir in the camp at daylight and several men took care of the animals, greased the wagons, checked the gear and harnessed the mules while another man prepared breakfast. Then we started again towards our destination. [37]

Larger units had a cook and a cook's wagon, usually referred to as a utility or trap wagon, loaded with spare parts, feed for the animals, and food and bedding for the freighters. Even a ten-wagon train might keep a special horse-drawn trap wagon. After all the other wagons were on the trail, the cook cleaned up the campsite, hurried to pass the train, and had a meal ready when the rest of the wagons arrived. [38]

Little was added to the old debate over the relative advantages of oxen over mules or vice versa, but the champions of one animal over the other were just as certain as they always had been since the days of Josiah Gregg. Many felt strongly that bull outfits were superior and made freighting profitable. Oxen could winter themselves on the open range, required less expensive equipment, had better footage in sand and mud, were gentle, tractable beasts not easily stampeded, and cost less. On the other hand, they were slower, became footsore more easily, and were subject to more diseases. One unfortunate freighter pulled into Dodge City with one hundred head of healthy oxen, but before he could settle his business and leave, sickness decimated the animals and he did not have enough left to pull the empty wagons. [39]

In spite of these handicaps the early trains made more use of oxen than they did mules. "At Tascosa," a resident reported, "you would see ox teams with trains a mile long. They did most of the freighting in the summer because the oxen could live on the grass. There were a few freight outfits that drove mules and ran all winter between Dodge and Tascosa." Blacksmiths who specialized in shoeing oxen could be found along the trails. Sam Manning nailed hundreds of shoes on cattle at Buzzard's Roost, and a blacksmith shop near Beaver on the Jones and Plummer Trail kept busy for many years. If the train could not reach a blacksmith, the ox that was tenderfooted was thrown, tied down, and shod on the spot.[40]

Men who preferred mules found them particularly adept at plains freighting. All agreed that in town a team of mules was far more maneuverable in loading and unloading a wagon, but the true test was in the long haul on the trail. There the mule's endurance and resistance to the extreme heat of summer and cold of winter were legend. Mule trains moved more rapidly on the open, level prairie, and mules could survive on dry grass as easily as a steer. Charles Goodnight claimed that a mule could smell water farther than any domesticated animal. "If the wind was right [a mule] might detect water six or seven miles away," he said. As important as that might be on the open prairie, it gave little advantage on set trails; however, freighters claimed that the mule needed fewer waterings a day, and this was important. Although a mule was believed to be able to stand more abuse from a driver than any other animal, the clinching argument in the mule's favor was given by Captain John Mullian. Mullian, who later became a road engineer, denied the stubborn, uncooperative nature of the beast. If they were not mistreated, he claimed, but handled "as you would a woman with kindness, affection, and caresses, you will be repaid by their docility and easy management."[41]

As draft animals, horses became more popular as the trails improved, even though old-timers still preferred mules and mules were almost always used in winter hauling. From the beginning, most large and medium-sized trains brought a few horses along to help with river crossings and for messenger and scouting purposes. Horses were better swimmers and were easier to control in a running stream. Mules were totally unreliable in water, appearing at times "determined to commit suicide by keeping their noses down." According to one old freighter, mules "simply give up if their ears gets wet." Another swore that they were the "greatest cowards in water and would prefer drowning to swimming." Mrs. Frances Roe told of the near drowning of the commanding officer in the Arkansas River at Fort Dodge. The team on one of the wagons broke through the ice "and being mules, not only refused to get up, but insisted upon keeping their noses under water." The officer tried to hold the mules' heads above water but was wedged tightly between two animals and nearly drowned. "I can fancy," Mrs. Roe wrote, "that there is one mule still chuckling over . . . having gotten even with a commanding officer!" Oxen were handicapped by short legs and an inclination to become disoriented in a fast-moving stream. J. Wright Mooar, however, denied the charge as it related to his oxen. He had no trouble in crossing a swollen stream while he was hauling hides out of the Panhandle, he said:

A damned mule, he would get ugly and would lay down and die, and a horse would get scared and drown if he could. Them oxen would swim all right, and when their feet struck a bar, they'd pull, and there was enough of them that they could get the balance of them and pull the wagon when they hit a bar. All of them on the bar could pull and those that hadn't crossed could pull, and there would be some of them pulling all the time. We put across twenty-two hundred hides . . . [in one] day.

Since the stream crossing was the most dangerous part of the journey, horses eventually became the preferred animals. [42]

Techniques developed over the years made any of the three types of teams effective. The brute strength of a bull team made it particularly useful in crossing the wide, sandy bottoms of the Canadian and Cimarron rivers. Since most freighters pulled in tandem, they perfected a quick and efficient method of taking the wagons across one at a time:

There were lots of sand draws from Dodge to Tascosa. You crossed the Cimarron, the Beaver, and the Blue. The freighter would drive up and drag the trail wagon. Then he pulled his lead wagon across and came back with the lead cattle. Some of those cattle had sense like a Mexican sheep herder. With three yoke of oxen, the trail wagon was pulled nearly up to the lead wagon. Then one yoke of oxen pulled the wagon up while the driver guided the trail tongue so that the ring would go over the gooseneck. The bull whacker talked to those oxen until they eased the wagon up, because they knew if they missed it they would have to be hitched on to pull the load back. [43]

The custom of pulling wagons in tandem made the Schuttler wagons built in Jackson, Michigan popular. These wagons were less expensive than most because the company used cheap convict labor, but it also had eliminated the characteristic Conestoga overhang to permit a shorter hitch, making possible the use of wagons in tandem. Studebaker wagons were widely used, too, but wagons of all descriptions could be found on the trail. Shotgun freighters pressed into service whatever they had, in many instances flat-box farm wagons. Old Conestoga, Murphy, Chicago, Turnball, over-hauled army discards, and home-modified wagons were used. If the cargo needed protection, the wagons were covered with sheets and bows, the distinctive canvas top of the covered wagon. [44]

One special service in the Region required specific adjustment of the usual freighting wagon. Buffalo hides were loaded on all kinds of makeshift conveniences, but the big buyers, hunting outfits, and freighting concerns made specific adaptations. Panhandle hunter Robert Parrack described hide wagons as being "similar to a hay wagon." To keep from losing the load on rough trails, special care was taken in both the loading and construction of the wagon bed:

The hide frames on the wagons had sharp spikes about two inches long, turned upward. These spikes held the loads in place. In loading the hides on the wagons, the freighters stacked them as high as possible. Then the loads were pulled down by tying one end of a rope to a solid part of the wagon. The rope was drawn across the load and the free end was wrapped around one of the hubs. The team was started up, which caused the rope to be drawn tighter, and the hides were pulled down. The load was then tied securely with ropes, and more hides were placed on top of the load.

Frank H. Mayer acquired a huge wagon that required a twelve-mule hitch. It was equipped with a nine-inch tread, flat iron wheels, and a bed of one-eighth-inch steel. Most wagons, however, had a normal frame; some owners removed the sides and set posts at the four corners. [45]

The loads of large wagons on the trail sometimes weighed five thousand or six thousand pounds. A good rule of thumb was one thousand pounds for each animal in the team, but most wagons carried lighter loads. Freight rates were determined by weight and volume. If an article was heavy, the rate was determined by weight; if it was bulky, the charge was determined by volume. Household furniture was figured by volume; a four hundred-pound case of bacon was figured by weight. Packing was a problem with any wagon because of the jarring the load took as it bumped along the trail. The use of bran, grain, or hay, which could be sold or used on the return trip, made a convenient cushion. Unlucky teamster

W. B. Beaird reported that it rained on him almost constantly during his trip and as a result the corn in the bottom of his wagon had sprouted by the time he reached his destination.[46]

The trips all seemed to take about the same time on the trail, if the weather held and there were no accidents. Eighteen days to Tascosa from Dodge City was considered a good run, and sixteen days to Mobeetie was judged to be about average. Occasionally a freighter boasted of better times, and Ben J. Jackson's trip from Mobeetie to Dodge City in fourteen days was worthy of note in the *Dodge City Times*. Teamsters were usually hired by the day for one trip, a custom that added to the temporary nature of freighting. Pay was at the unskilled-labor level. On a monthly basis, the army, which established a scale others followed, paid laborers thirty dollars a month and teamsters thirty-five. Wagonmasters, with the added responsibilities of supervision, received seventy-five dollars a month and were not hired on daily basis.[47]

In spite of low pay and unpleasant working conditions, the wagon yards in Dodge tapped an almost bottomless reservoir of men who were out of a job and low on cash. Any farm boy knew enough about animals to qualify as a teamster, jerk-line rider, or cavvy boy. Specific freighting skills were simple and easily learned. The experience of H. E. Siders was typical. He had been fired for incompetence from a number of jobs, but he knew that if he "loafed around the wagon yard" long enough someone would take him on. There were always jobs available and the wagon yard in Dodge City was an unemployment agency of considerable importance. Anyone could put up with a few days of dust and toil to get a grubstake, and after a few months on the trail a young man of ambition could accumulate the funds necessary to begin homesteading or continue searching for better prospects.

There never seemed to be enough freighters. A *Fort Griffin Echo* correspondent wrote of the Mobeetie merchants' plight:

Freighters is the scarcest article in the Panhandle. It is impossible to get goods and building materials here to supply the demand. Hamburg & Company keep a full train on the road that hauls 140,000 pounds at a load to Dodge and return every twenty-four days, and this does not keep their house supplied with necessary goods. Truly Mobeetie is booming.

The post trader at Fort Elliott complained to the *Dodge City Times* that he had 100,000 pounds of freight in Dodge he couldn't get wagons to haul. "His opinion is," the editor commented, "that there are not enough teams on the road to supply the demand of corn alone in the Panhandle during the winter." In 1883, 30,576,575 pounds of freight was unloaded at the Santa Fe depot in Dodge City for civilian use, plus an additional 3,576,575 pounds for the army. Receipts for freight at Dodge remained high through the mid-1880s. In May 1884 the Atchison, Topeka and Santa Fe Railroad unloaded 5,253,080 pounds of goods. The poorest month that year, February, saw 1,865,170 pounds deposited on Dodge City docks.[48]

The end of the wagon-road economy and the end of the need for a new supply of freighters came with the spread of the railroad network throughout the Region. Sometimes the end was as abrupt as the arrival of the first train, but generally there was a slow, gradual decline, with some trails and roads serving the wagon traffic well into the new century. Just as Dodge City had been the terminus for feeder lines into the Panhandle, new towns in Kansas, Oklahoma, and Texas became depots for shorter connecting lines. Where freighting by wagon continued, it was as an auxiliary to a new transportation system. By 1890, however, freighting was no longer a major industry. By then the growth and development of the Region, which the wagons had sustained, had become dependent on new mechanized modes of transportation.

7. P. G. Reynolds: Mail Contractor and Entrepreneur of the Wagon Road

LAND, capital, and labor without direction do not produce anything; the catalyst for productive yield lies in the efficacy of the fourth factor, the entrepreneur. Although all four components are interdependent, the managerial role is the essential creative force. If the entrepreneur is effective, the enterprise prospers; if not, the other factors may for a time carry the project forward, but eventually it will fail. The entrepreneur, as F. W. Taussig has said, "stands at the helm of industry and guides its operation." He is the driving force in a capitalist society.

In the Dodge City–Panhandle Region a number of creative entrepreneurs, men such as W. M. D. Lee, Charles Rath, and Casimiro Romero, used the wagon roads to develop profitable and reasonably efficient ventures. As compared with transportation facilities in the more settled areas of the United States, the wagon-road service was slow, costly, and primitive. But considering the frontier nature of the territory, the utilization of capital and labor was sophisticated enough to support fairly large operations. Since it was a time of transition, the early developers were able to make the first substantial modification of the environment that would permit more intensive use of all four factors of production.

The entrepreneurs of the road were attracted to the frontier from widely different backgrounds, lured, as were others, to the West by the expectation of a new start and the conviction that success, honor, and power were clearly within grasp. Although their personalities reflected the diversity of their upbringing, there were certain characteristics, certain attitudes toward life, and certain convictions about themselves and the new environment that were held in common. These traits and predilections set them apart from the wage-earning freighters, cowboys, and farmhands, who were used by the entrepreneurs to further their own ambitions.

As a rule the entrepreneurs were older than the typical plainsman and had already served an apprenticeship in a related activity before coming to the Dodge City–Panhandle Region. W. M. D. Lee was only twenty-nine when he began his career at Camp Supply, but he was experienced as a driver for Wells Fargo and had served as quartermaster in Sherman's army during the war and as a civilian immediately following the war; Casimiro Romero had already built an empire based on sheep, complete with its own town, when at the age of forty-nine, he organized his first freighting outfit. The entrepreneurs considered themselves self-made men, but all brought with them to the Region either capital or, more important, some grant of privilege, license, or contract. Romero had cash; Lee had a contract as post trader, a monopoly of great value. There is no question that their greatest motivation was the expectation of making money. Like the cattle barons, whom they resembled, they came in the hope of accumulating wealth and power over the years. This contrasted markedly with the cowboys, freighters, and buffalo hunters, who sought wages to gratify immediate needs and pleasures.

Nearly all entrepreneurs in the Region during the 1880s invested in cattle. The difference, therefore, between the cattle kings and the leaders of commercial enterprise became quite blurred at times. It is difficult to separate the businessman in Colonel Jack Hardesty or Ham Bell from the rancher. In most matters, the two types thought alike and frequently joined forces to advance their common cause. The major distinction was that the entrepreneurs of the road were not committed to a way of life to the same extent as were the cattle kings; consequently, they could make major adjustments in their business with more ease and a clearer conscience. They apparently felt little compunction in totally changing their means of making a living. When he became convinced the ranchers would someday dominate the land, Romero sold his sheep empire, which had taken years to develop and which rivaled neighbor Charles Goodnight's cattle holdings in size and value. Lee shifted partners and property frequently, left his lucrative sutler's post, and plunged into large-scale ranching with no sign of regret. It is reported that when he eventually left the Region, Lee never again mentioned his life there.[1]

As businessmen they were willing to take large financial risks, but such boldness did not mean they took their enterprises lightly. "A man might as well be dead as to lose his property," Robert Wright said when weighing the options of facing death if he stayed to drive off an Indian attack or saving his scalp by running and leaving his stock. All were prodigious workers and pursued the business at hand with inordinate drive and singleness of purpose. The worst charge one could lay on any man was that he "was not much force," meaning he was lazy.[2]

Business reverses were accepted philosophically as being in the nature of things, the luck of the draw, a setback but never a catastrophe. Robert Wright concluded that "out of great conflict rises a period of prosperity . . . this endurance of adversity, equipped people with courage." Wright undoubtedly would have denied the charge, but he and his peers unmistakenly endorsed the same principles of social Darwinism that the eastern industrial moguls of that day endorsed. The strong ought always to prevail, they believed, and any successful entrepreneur knew which man deserved his status. They prided themselves on being good judges of character, and they entered into partnerships and other business relationships with little more than a handshake and dissolved them with scarcely less bother. All used the partnership to pool capital and share talents. Few men tried to build a sizable enterprise on their own. They were quite willing to experiment with new methods and, like most Americans of that age, they were fascinated by new technology and put much reliance on improved equipment and mechanical gadgets.

As was true of other Gilded Age capitalists, they were politically conservative, were leery of federal or even state government, and were champions of home rule. The government's police role, which included ridding the plains of unproductive Indians, curbing the lawless, and protecting the arteries of commerce, was their concept of the extent of useful governmental powers. Lee was never reluctant to call for military protection of his hay parties and teams or demand escorts for his mule trains when they were in hostile territory. The entrepreneurs were, above all else, strong law-and-order men. Most, however, reflected the cynicism of their eastern counterparts in accepting the financial rewards of governmental policy described as the Great Barbecue by Vernon Louis Parrington. They willingly accepted free lands, government contracts, and policies that supported their private enterprise.

In social attitudes, the entrepreneurs of the Region acknowledged their role as models of community decorum, which placed them a cut above the rest of the people. They accepted the obligation of propriety, married good women, raised industrious sons and dutiful daughters, saw to it that their families attended church, worked to advance the community, and generally eschewed politics beyond their own immediate environs. In short, they tried to be good and contributing citizens and accepted the role of leadership as a natural obligation of class.

Philander Gillette Reynolds, the Dodge City mail contractor, was one such contributing entrepreneur. As much as any single person, he used the trails to change the cultural and economic environment of the Region. By keeping the lines of communication open within and contacts with life and commerce outside the Region, the "good and productive population" could and did evolve. In his case he was not required to seek new enterprises when the organization he created became obsolete, since his death coincided with the closing of the era of the wagon-road economy.

There is a portrait of Reynolds made at the end of a life fast closing. The beard is glorious—it falls to his chest in a graceful, tapered flow—patriarchal, and venerable, worthy of the Eastern Orthodox sacristy. Although it is a portrait of an old man, the eyes are clear and calm, reflecting an inner assurance and an open gentleness. Still, there is the beard. Considering his life and other people's judgments of him, it seems incongruous, an affectation. It is a reminder that we can know little of a man's private motives from his public presence alone.

Philander Gillette Reynolds (at least the name does justice to the

Philander Gillette Reynolds, 1827–1888, Dodge City mail contractor and stage operator on the trails south into the Texas and Oklahoma panhandles. Courtesy Rex Reynolds, Niles, Michigan.

beard) left little by way of written record of private (or, for that matter, public) concerns. Other men found him affable, courteous, accommodating, good natured, honest, trustworthy, and attentive to business. In demeanor, they used such words and phrases as *dignity, grace, uncomplaining, philosophical, suave, a man of natural strong disposition.* His profession required him to be durable, exacting, and frugal. His convictions were Christian and Republican. He was probably as Victorian as Dodge City, that Babylon of the Plains he lived in, would tolerate. He supported the church, adjured liquor, and championed public probity. He hoped, he believed that Dodge would become a more settled, law-abiding place to live and conduct business. In short, as a product of his time, he was the kind of careful entrepreneur required to move the frontier of the West from a raw, undeveloped prairie to the more ordered, and settled community.

Long before a Reynolds coach rolled across the Kansas plains, the transportation business was ingrained, almost second nature to the Reynolds. The first recorded ancestor of the stage owner was Christopher Reynolds, born in 1530 in County Kent, England. He and his sons engaged in trade and commerce and with his brother, Nathaniel, formed a shipping company. Twin grandsons brought the business to America, and the family remained in some phase of freighting generation after generation. By the middle of the eighteenth century, Elmira, New York was headquarters. It was there, on November 3, 1827, that Philander Gillette was born, the youngest of three brothers. When he was ten, his parents moved to Coldwater, Michigan, still involved in the freighting trade but primarily engaged in farming; here P. G. was educated and grew to manhood. Both his older brothers attended Wesleyan Seminary at Albion and he probably did, too. Milton W. was to put his education, which was completed at the University of Michigan, to use as the editor or owner of a dozen newspapers in Oklahoma, Nebraska, and Kansas, including those at Parsons, Lawrence, Geuda Springs, and Leavenworth. Milton W., considered an authority on Indian affairs, was present at both the Fort Smith Council (September 1865) and the Medicine Lodge Council (October 1867). Under the pen name Kicking Bird, he gained national reputation as an exponent of solving the Indian question by settling Indians on private lands and opening the reservations to white settlers. In a busy public career, he was elected to the state legislatures of Nebraska, Kansas, and Oklahoma and did much to foster settlement in the West. George A. Reynolds edited a paper in Oklahoma, the *Indian Progress*, with Elias C. Boudinot, as Indian agent for Kansas, and he, too, found his way into the legislative halls at Topeka.[3]

The Joseph Hard family, also from New York, moved to Coldwater about the same time the Reynoldses got there. On December 29, 1852, P. G. married Lemira P. Hard. Lemira was a small, rather self-contained woman who took the rigors of life with evenhanded courage. It was a personality trait that would be useful to her in the kinds of settings in which she was to spend her life. Two sons were born to the Reynoldses in Michigan: Eddy Niles in 1854, who died in infancy, and George Alexander, who was to become P. G.'s partner in the late years of the stage business in Dodge City.

In 1856, Reynolds joined his brother-in-law A. H. Hard of Lawrence, Kansas in operating a stage line and maintaining a large livery and stage barn. Apparently other members of the Hard family moved to Lawrence about the same time as P. G. and Lemira. Under A. H. Hard's tutelage, P. G. learned the stage and mail-contract business. Three more Reynolds sons were born in Lawrence: Charles Laymon (October 25, 1860), Sidney ("Sid") Philander (December 4, 1867), and William Milton (April 30, 1870). Charles and William Milton died in infancy. Other members of the Reynolds family found Lawrence a friendly base of operations. Brother Milton W. had visited there and in the spring of 1865 formed a partnership that purchased the *Kansas State Journal*. In the years ahead he was to become owner of two other Lawrence papers.[4]

During the years when William C. Quantrill was masquerading as John Hart in Lawrence, he made the acquaintance of P. G., undoubtedly through stage connections. As Quantrill moved about the country on his mysterious errands, P. G. had occasion to extend him assistance and favors. They became more than mere acquaintances but were not close friends. The attitudes of the two men toward slavery were decidedly at odds, and they seem to have had little in common except their business contacts. The Hard-

Reynolds livery was a station on the Underground Railroad, helping to spirit slaves to freedom. It was an important station, and at the time of P. G.'s death the Dodge City editor reported that "hundreds of these people in eastern Kansas remember Mr. Reynolds and love him as they love their lives." These were hardly the credentials that would endear him to Quantrill.[5]

Still, when Quantrill rode into Lawrence at dawn on August 2, 1863, he had given orders not to burn P. G.'s property. Unfortunately, the ban did not extend to P. G.'s neighbors. As the guerrillas separated into small bands to loot, burn, and murder, there was no way to prevent the spread of destruction. With houses going up in smoke and flames, it was inevitable that the Reynolds home would catch fire. George Reynolds, then six, was playing on a rope swing in the yard, oblivious to all danger, while the sacking proceeded. Once his house was on fire, however, George remembered the rush to save what furnishings could be removed. Some of Quantrill's men rode up and, learning whose home was ablaze, aided in removing some possessions and extended their apologies, for what they were worth, to Mrs. Reynolds for the destruction. A few items were saved, and charred possessions were passed down from generation to generation as grim reminders of troubled times.

As for the livery and stable, all was lost. In the words of the *Kansas Cowboy* editor, "not a hoof left of his horses and nothing of the buggies but burned iron smoldering in the embers." What was not burned was looted, and the stock was driven off. The loss was estimated in more inflationary times to be $30,000. In 1887, however, when P. G. Reynolds and W. H. Hard appeared before the Board of Claims, they received $4,010 for losses sustained by the firm Hard & Reynolds during the raid. P. G. did not witness the destruction of his home, but it is doubtful that his presence would have altered events much. He was in Nebraska on business at the time, and when he returned and saw his property destroyed, he said to his wife: "Well it is alright if you and George are safe." He seemed to view all calamities calmly and philosophically. Throughout his life he accepted business reverses as part of the price of risking capital and managing a business.[6]

Whatever the amount of the loss and however calm and philosophical P. G. might be, the Lawrence affair was a serious setback. The line and franchises were intact, but it must have taken considerable time to restock and get business moving again, judging from the Kansas Stage's experience the previous year when its mules were stolen by Jayhawkers and weeks dragged by before they were back in full operation. But eventually the Hart and Reynolds equipment was replaced and the stages ran again. It was to remain P. G.'s major occupation while he was in eastern Kansas.[7]

He did, however, engage in other ventures while in Lawrence, including contracting to furnish telegraph poles in Oklahoma, which undertaking proved an additional liability. The arrangement was to collect them into rafts and float them down the river to the place of delivery. While this arrangement was being effected, the river rose and, in spite of all efforts, took them away. In this he sustained a loss of ten thousand dollars. "Well," he said, "I reckon it is alright. We ought not complain at what seems Providential." Nothing ventured, nothing gained. The risks were always present on the frontier for those who assumed the role of entrepreneur in a dynamic, changing economy. The trick was not to give up but to find new opportunities for additional risks.[8]

P. G. was now seriously in debt, so he began looking for that new and better opportunity to recoup his losses. For some time he had been interested in a railhead connection for a stage line and had visited Dodge City on several occasions. It is not known with certainty just when P. G. moved to Dodge City, although it appears that he came alone and was joined later by his family in 1875. When the decision to move west was finally made, his business connections in Lawrence were to come loyally to his aid, lending him capital, equipment, and stock. Furthermore, he had secured, through bid, a contract to deliver mail to the military outpost at Camp Supply. As he arrived in the unofficial capital of the Dodge City: Panhandle Region, P. G. clearly conformed to the profile of the typical entrepreneur of the road. At forty-eight he was older than most of the men on the streets of Dodge, he had the advantage of having some capital in the form of equipment and stock, he had served as stagecoach operator and mail contractor for most of his adult life, and, more important, he had the grant of privilege in the form of a government contract.[9]

Dodge City was a town of exceptional energy and excitement when P. G. set up his line in 1875. The three blocks of false-fronted stores on Front Street, the heart of the West's wickedest city, were firmly established. The Peacock, Long Branch, Alamo, Saratoga, and Beatty and Kelley's saloons, as well as Hoover's Wholesale Liquor Store, were trying to prevent any traveler from leaving Dodge still feeling thirsty. The commercial firm of Charles Rath, which had done so much to tie the Panhandle to Dodge City, was at its peak of activity. The names of established merchants, such as Collar, Wright, Zimmermann, Fringer, and Bell were to become legendary, even mythical, a hundred years later in the hands of Hollywood. Then, too, Dodge had its Boot Hill as a symbol of reckless and lawless life in a wide-open town. The winter and spring of 1872–73 had seen fifteen men killed with their boots on, and Boot Hill began accumulating fresh mounds at an alarming rate.

For all the familiar faces, buildings, and action, however, Dodge City was in its first phase of transition. The years 1872–74 had made it the buffalo-hide capital of the world. By 1875 the great kills, when a man could slaughter fifty to one hundred in one stand, were over. Hides still came in and buffalo bones piled high along the tracks, but the brief and bloody harvest had accomplished all that General Phil Sheridan had hoped. Mari Sandoz called Dodge City "the daughter of the hide men"; it was soon to become Stanley Vestal's "Queen of Cowtowns." During the winter of 1875, the Santa Fe Railroad built the first stockyards there, and Dodge became the major shipping point for Texas, Oklahoma, and Kansas cattle. Where hunters, soldiers, border ruffians, and freighters had walked the dusty streets, now cattlemen, cowboys, and freighters were to dominate.

The transition made substantial and immediate changes in the town's business and social life. The buffalo men had been a raw, rough, and untamed lot who required comparable entertainment and limited supplies. While the cowboy was no more sophisticated, his gratification required more spirited, more immediate, and more boisterous entertainment. Whiskey off the tailgate of a wagon was enough for early buffalo hunters, and a bar under a roof, no matter what its surrounding, was more than adequate for the later ones. A cowboy wanted something a bit more fancy for his few days' fling. The southern sympathies of the cowboy also required certain adjustments; new names appeared on the entertainment palaces: Nueces, Lone Star, Alhambra. More important, the cattleman's ranching needs required far more variety and far more expensive supplies.

Still, Dodge lost none of its notoriety, none of its saloons, and none of "its motley crowd of sinners" in the transition. But it was clearly a town and not a stinking, brawling depot for hides and dead flesh. Officially incorporated in 1875, it had a functioning city government; it showed signs of being a permanent address. If Dodge merchants catered to the likes and dislikes of the boys going up the trail, it was plain to see that it would grow and one day would be peopled with honest and stable folk. Women other than soiled doves were filling residences north of Front Street. And Dodge was booming. Above all else, it was clear that a man could make a dollar in Dodge City.

It was a good time, 1875, to bring a new business to town, and it was a good business that P. G. brought. Transportation, whether by rail or hoof, was to be the lifeblood of Dodge City. The need for quicker and more certain connections between Dodge, the transportation center, and the range, the production center, favored an efficient and regular stage route. P. G.'s coaches were to furnish an important link in the transportation network for a town maturing as a cattleman's center.

The Reynolds family fit smoothly into the life of the town. It was not as if they were brash newcomers in an old, entrenched society; all Dodge Citians were newcomers. If P. G. had needed an old, established sponsor for reference, there was A. J. Anthony, who had been post trader at Fort Dodge as early as 1867; few had been around longer than he. He signed the Dodge City Town Company charter in 1872, homesteaded a mile west of town, and served as county treasurer and county commissioner, and he had championed every progressive move the town had made. Anthony certainly could have vouched for P. G.'s character, since both he and Reynolds were in the stage business in Lawrence at the time of Quantrill's raid. Mrs. Reynolds found that none of "the leading social lights" had been in Dodge more than two or three years. Alice Wright, Calvina Anthony, Carrie Rath, Amanda Webster, Sally McCarty,

Matilda Zimmermann, Sara Evans, and Jennie Collar all came in 1872. A new family there to stay was an addition welcomed by the movers and shakers of the town. A new family with strong moral conviction was even more to be desired. When P. G. and Brothers O. J. Wright, R. W. Evans, R. G. Cook, and A. J. Anthony helped organize the first denominational church, the Evangelical Christian Church, the good citizens of Dodge were indeed gratified.[10]

Although the Reynoldses were busy with the stage line, they continued to play a modest role in Dodge City's social and political life. P. G. served on the school board, represented community speculators in the Dodge City Mining Company, was appointed to review petitions for new roads, and as a charter member, helped establish yet another denominational church when the organizational meeting of the new Methodist Church met in the Reynolds home. In social attitudes, P. G. and his family adhered to established principles of the entrepreneurial class and accepted the role of community leadership without undue pretentions.[11]

Reynolds devoted considerable time to local politics. He was named to the executive committee of the Ford County People's Mass Convention in the fall of 1879. The convention succeeded in defeating the Dodge City Gang's candidate, Bat Masterson, and putting George Hinkle into the sheriff's office. As a member of the conservative property-owning faction, P. G. had his first—but not last—encounter with Bat. His only bid for office was for that of county treasurer, where he ran well in the outlying areas but did not carry Dodge City. His toughest political job came in 1884 when he was chairman of the district senatorial convention which split into two factions holding separate conventions in Garden City and Larned. His conciliatory efforts were not enough to calm hostilities and two candidates were nominated. He served on a number of local and state Republican party committees, was a delegate to the state Republican Senatorial Convention in 1884, and served as a delegate to and president pro tem of the state congressional convention in 1886. But P. G. was basically interested in Dodge City and regional affairs. Inevitably, his pride in his adopted community and his concern for his expanding business brought him into that strange turn of personal, philosophical, and political events known as the Dodge City War.[12]

The central figure, if not the major instigator of the Dodge City War (or the Saloon War, as it is sometimes called), was a cocky, bantam-rooster gambler named Luke Short. He stood five feet six inches in his polished boots and weighed a full one hundred forty pounds without his six-guns. In 1883 he bought Chalk Beeson's half-interest in the Long Branch Saloon. His female entertainers, particularly his piano player, and his easy familiarity with the cowboys and cattlemen made for stiff competition. Furthermore, the shift in ownership came as Dodge City prepared to hold its city elections, always hotly contested affairs. The explosive blend of personal, economic, and social animosities was to reach a critical state after that election.

There is a temptation to treat "The War" as comic operation of little significance except to the private fortunes of the individuals involved. If it had been only a business war, sparked by Luke Short's hiring an attractive young woman to play the piano and let her melodic notes waft through the plank walls of his establishment to entice thirsty cowboys to desert all other dens of delight, the episode would deserve a light touch. And certainly the flurry of misinterpreted telegrams between the chief executive of Kansas and Dodge City law officers, the posturing of "known gunmen" on the streets (surely at high noon), the declaration of neutrality by the sovereign state of Atchison, Topeka and Santa Fe, and the purple passages of newspaper vilification, portrays Dodge City as the "Beautiful Bibulous Babylon of the Frontier" it was reputed to be.[13]

However, for many of the solid citizens of Dodge City who had established homes and businesses there, much more was at stake. The conflict, as they saw it, had to do with reform. As the bitterness between the two rival saloon and political factions grew, both attempted to convince those not directly involved that they and their supporters were *the* champions of law and order. The press, both in Dodge City and throughout the nation, was quick to choose sides. A Kansas City paper, first hearing of the conflict from Luke Short, reported that "W. H. Harris, of Harris & Short, proprietors of the Long Branch Saloon . . . represented the quieter and more reputable element" while his opponent "was representative of the tougher element of the sporting fraternity." The *Dodge City Times*, on the other hand, found the anti-Short faction to be "good and law abiding citizens" intent on driving "the lawless element" from the city. [14]

In March a mass meeting had selected a slate for the upcoming election, headed by Luke Short's partner as candidate for mayor and supported by the remnants of the old Dodge City Gang and the *Ford County Globe*. Their administration would have been business as usual, catering to the cattle trade and the sporting ways of cowboys and gamblers. An opposition slate was put together by another group of citizens, with Larry Deger as the mayoral candidate and several prominent businessmen (Robert Wright, Ham Bell, H. M. Beverley, George S. Emerson, and Henry Sturm) running for council positions. This ticket was vociferously and intemperately supported by Nick Klaine and the *Dodge City Times*. It was a reform ticket, so much so that the early contender for the mayor's spot, Alonzo B. ("Ab") Webster, withdrew, since he was associated with the saloon business and it was felt that this was an inappropriate credential. Deger and crew won the election by a comfortable margin. [15]

Reform ordinances to curb vagrancy and prostitution were quickly passed by the new council. No one, not even the most vociferous reformer, expected them to purify immediately "the wickedest city in the West." Nick Klaine pointed out in the *Times* that not even John P. St. Johns, the ardent Prohibitionist governor, had been able to close Dodge City's saloons, which were still flourishing three years after Kansas had voted itself dry. "These things would continue in some manner, no matter who were the Mayor or Councilmen," Klaine editorialized. "We are satisfied and contented if these things are conducted properly, orderly and decently." [16]

This attitude was supported by the non-saloon and non-cowboy business community. This is not to say that the community was anti-cowboy or anti-cattleman in sentiment. But Klaine, for instance, had written many articles encouraging farmers to settle and praising the great agricultural prospects of the area. There was room, he wrote, for more than stock raising. The future of Dodge City lay in "the settlement of the country." The business community, including P. G. Reynolds, endorsed this concept. Dodge City needed to look to its image if it was to attract settlers and new business. So the reform measures were easy to push through a council dominated by merchants and store keepers. Enforcement was another matter. [17]

Naturally, and unfortunately, Luke Short felt the reform sting first when his singers were arrested as prostitutes. At first he simply shrugged off the arrests as a petty annoyance; the fines would be only one of those trifling costs of doing business. But when he learned that the rival saloon entertainers had not been jailed, he strapped on his six-guns and headed for trouble. As he stood outside the jail, Special Officer L. C. Hartman saw the fired-up Short striding toward him. In his haste to get off the first shot, the officer missed. Luke returned the fire just as Hartman tripped and fell, with timing only a Hollywood stunt man could have duplicated; the bullets harmlessly kicked up dust in the street back of him. Thinking he had killed his man, Short rushed for cover and barricaded himself in a nearby saloon, ready to defend life and honor with a sawed-off shotgun. Negotiations eventually dislodged Luke, who was immediately arrested, bonded, and ceremoniously rushed out of town by the officers of the law and a sizable posse of citizens.

Luke's first appeal for justice was to Governor George Washington Glick, suggesting the state militia might be needed to reestablish his rights in his own saloon. He next turned to real firepower, his old friend Bat Masterson. With typical generosity, Bat rushed to his friend's defense. A citizen had been deprived of his rights and property, Bat felt, and the governor of the state of Kansas should do something about it. Governor Glick seemed to understand and to sympathize. He fired off a number of telegrams to the Dodge City sheriff, George Hinkle, apparently urging him to protect the rights of all the citizens of Dodge City. The sheriff seemed unable to get the message straight. He thought the governor was ordering him to arm the town to prevent the likes of Masterson and Short from taking over. Luke and Bat could see that they were getting nowhere through legal channels. [18]

The press next reported that Bat was recruiting his own army, including Wyatt Earp, Charley Bassett, and Doc Holliday. Eventually, Dodge City saw a contingent of gunmen drifting into town, including Shotgun Collins, Frank McLane, Texas Jack Vermillion, Don Tipton, Johnny Millsap, Johnny Green, and Wyatt Earp. The governor, aware of most of the rumors and some of the facts, dispatched Adjutant General Thomas Moonlight to sort things out and prevent bloody confrontation. Once again the militia was promised, if needed. Somewhere along the line, the Atchison, Topeka and Santa Fe Railroad central office, acting like a benign sovereign power in an international dispute, wired its local agent: "Considering your relation to the Company and our large interest in Dodge City, I think you should hold yourself aloof from both parties to the existing troubles. Do everything you can to allay excitement, and to prevent any hostilities to the company." Naturally, all this was reported with fine coloring by the press in Chicago and New York. Such was the Dodge City War.[19]

P. G. Reynolds was one businessman who saw The War as a law-and-order issue and not a matter of saloon-owner preference. It is not known whether he was a member of the posse that saw Luke Short on the train out of town and later met the train Sheriff Hinkle thought was carrying Short and Masterson back into town. However, he was vitally concerned in seeing that Governor Glick heard the citizens' side of the fracas. Furthermore, he had for some time held Masterson in low esteem. Back in 1880, he and twenty-three other businessmen, professionals, and city officials had signed a petition denouncing Bat for arresting "the Hon. D. M. Frost," an arrest, the petition claimed, which was "made solely to gratify [Masterson's] revengeful feelings." He now signed a telegram, along with other Dodge Citians, telling the governor that he had been misinformed and asking him to authorize an impartial investigation.[20]

When tension continued to mount and rumors of coming bloodshed continued to circulate, P. G. joined eleven other citizens (immediately dubbed the Twelve Disciples by the barroom crowd) in traveling to Topeka to present their side of the story to the governor face to face. Their mission was primarily one of defusing the explosive situation without sacrificing the reforms that had been initiated. The meeting was productive. Glick wrote Sheriff Hinkle congratulating him on his efforts to keep peace and assuring him that he was not required to protect Luke Short at all costs. The directive must have confused and delighted the sheriff, who finally had gubernatorial instructions he could carry out with enthusiasm.

Eventually, a compromise was worked out and Short was allowed to return and manage his property. The reform ordinances were kept on the books but not enforced. For the moment, Luke Short, Bat Masterson, and the status quo had won.[21]

But The Dodge City War forecast changes that were inevitable. Bat and the gunmen soon left town, and Short, after a brief stay in the hostile climate of Dodge, sold out and left for New Mexico. The reform-minded buisnessmen remained. The various citizen groups P. G. had joined made it clear in dealing with the governor that they were men of substance and stability. The 1880 petition was signed by sixteen professionals or businessmen; if they did not list their official titles, they indicated their business connections. Henry Strum, who was in the liquor business, concealed the fact by referring to himself simply as "a capitalist." The point they wanted to make was that theirs was not only the party of respectability, it was the wave of the future. Nor was gambling per se the target. If conducted with proper decorum, gambling was a lucrative business bringing welcome dollars to the town's economy. But the "wild and wooly cowboys" and "aging gunmen" had given Dodge an unhealthy reputation. If the town was to attract new business and stable settlers, its unsavory past had to be buried. On August 18, P. G. and four other businessmen (George Hoover, Morris Collar, Charles Dickerson, and R. Gaede), representing both saloon factions and the business interests, presented the mayor a petition requesting a review of "the gambling interests," which were in need of "considerable bolstering." They urged a return to a peaceful status quo and an end to Glick's Guards, a pro-Short unit of the state militia organized by authority of the governor. Order, not blue laws, was what the business community desired.[22]

This cooperative gesture toward business harmony was a short-lived interlude. Toward the end of the month, P. G. was with yet another delegation when they were told by a representative of the railroad that if the Dodge City officials did not "make an effort to suppress vice" the new one hundred thousand dollar rail facility would be located either west or east of them. The threat of one railroad official carried more weight than all of the reform-minded businessmen, the militia, or Luke Short's gun-toting friends.[23]

If Dodge was to continue to grow, it had to create a law-and-order atmosphere that would encourage commerce, for its preeminence in the Panhandle Region was being challenged. The town's new role would have to look beyond the cattle trails, which had blessed Dodge so abundantly in the past. Men, like P. G., whose business depended on the roads to the Panhandle could see that a new era was at hand. Nick Klaine, who long had advocated change, was now joined by voices once heard only in support of the status quo. Within a month of the railroad's threat to move facilities, all businesses were required to close on Sunday. Klaine boasted in the *Times* that "the last relic of the frontier has given up the ghost." Within three years, the *Dodge City Kansas Cowboy*, created exclusively as a journalistic spokesman for the cattle industry, editorialized:

The day of the cowboy in his pristine glory at Dodge are almost numbered now, and varied interests are rapidly springing up, the quiet pursuits of agriculture and manufacturing will soon take the place of the once great cattle interests, and with them will come the better element already there, and the lawless will disappear before the higher civilization as has the Indian and buffalo, and Dodge City from a rough frontier town, will soon emerge into an embryo city, virtuous and good, and discarding the vicious and lawless elements of society, and we believe she is even now undergoing that change.

It took several more years to tame the town and make it see the value of being a more localized center of trade, but the bloodless Dodge City War was a major step in bringing in settled business interests to replace the Luke Shorts and Bat Mastersons of the early and more exciting cattle town. The Dodge City dominated by cattle interests was to become a lively memory but, nonetheless, only a memory.[24]

Despite his involvement in The War, P. G.'s ventures into politics remained marginal. He dutifully participated in local affairs when some major issue needed support, but the excitement of political strife was never a lure. Politics, even local politics, was a time-consuming hobby he could rarely afford because his coaches and mail contracts were demanding—at times more than one man could manage. His convictions regarding the role of government, his distrust of meddling by Topeka politicians and functionaries, his staunch advocacy of law and order reveals him as a nearly archetypal representative of the Western Plains entrepreneur.

Both of P. G.'s sons took an active interest in the stage line, and George, who was ten years older than Sid, became a full partner. Somewhere along the line, George had acquired a good working command of the Cheyenne language. This may have come from mingling with the Indians who loafed around the various stage stations, or there may have been longer, closer contacts with them at the agencies. Since both uncles, George and Milton W., were closely tied to Indian affairs, serving at various times as Indian agents, and with George publishing a paper that carried columns printed in Cherokee, Choctaw, Chickasaw, and Creek and Milton W. being a nationally recognized authority on Indians, young George could have learned the language from family contacts. A brief and rather cryptic note appearing in the Dodge City paper indicated, if nothing else, the intimate contact the Reynoldses had with the Indians:

Mr. Whitebird, a Cheyenne Indian, who lives at Ft. Supply, was in the city last week and was chaperoned by his cousin, Mr. George Reynolds. Mr. Whitebird is brother-in-law of Amos Chapman, the well known Indian scout. Whitebird is a civilized Indian and was in the city purchasing supplies. [25]

At any rate, young George early acquired fluency, and by his twentieth year part of his assignment was visiting the Cheyenne agency at Camp Supply "looking after the interests of his company." He also served as interpreter for the seven Cheyennes who were indicted for murders committed in Kansas during Dull Knife's Raid in 1878. A widely published series of pictures shows him seated with the Indians on the steps of Ford County Courthouse. Wild Hog, labeled "Dull Knife's Right hand man," is leaning very close to George because he was fearful of the flashes made by the photographer's equipment. These warriors were mauled severely in the field before they surrendered, and their trip from Leavenworth to Dodge was a nerve-shattering ordeal. Heavily manacled and harassed by mobs in Topeka and Lawrence, two were still suffering from battle wounds, one from attempted suicide, and all were uncertain of their fate. They must have been unnerved to know that they were now at the mercy of Sheriff Bat Masterson, who had fought at Adobe Walls and in the Red River War. George befriended them throughout their stay in Dodge, and for years he was remembered by the Cheyennes as "the white man they could trust." George's close contact with the Indians before and after Dull Knife's Raid undoubtedly accounts for the Reynolds line's being free of Indian harassment. [26]

George drove the Dodge City–Fort Supply and Fort Elliott route longer and more frequently than any other driver. In P. G.'s later years, George contracted for mail lines directly and undoubtedly was in some sort of partnership with his father before that. As early as the Census of 1880 he listed himself as a mail contractor. The Reynoldses were a very close-knit family, and the stage operation was on such an intimate family basis that it is difficult to discern business relationships. When George married Lida Norwell of Belpre, they lived with his parents at the Second Avenue home. Naturally, George took over all the lines when P. G. died. [27]

Sid, the younger son, began riding and driving the stage at an early age, but his main assignment was that of clerk, making out waybills for passengers and patrons. Sid attended the first public school established in Dodge and was the first student from there to attend Kansas University, where he studied music and business. He returned to his hometown and helped his father until 1888, when he began working for First National Bank. He was to serve many years as city commissioner and as finance commissioner, the position he held at the time of his death, using talents sharpened in the old stage office. [28]

As P. G. grew older, with his sons taking on some of the responsibility for his expanding stage lines and with Dodge City becoming more settled ("civilized" was the way townsmen put it), there was time and opportunity to relax and enjoy life more. P. G. and Mrs. Reynolds attended parties and frequently had guests in the home. He was active in the International Order of Odd Fellows; on his fifty-fourth birthday, there was a surprise party; later a wedding anniversary attracted all the important Dodge City figures; the couple went to the exposition at Santa Fe; and there was a long vacation and pleasure trip to St. Louis, Chicago, New York, Boston, and Michigan.[29]

One of P. G.'s personal indulgences furnished the whole town with amusement and provided an authentic frontier atmosphere for newcomers and visitors. He, or perhaps George, had acquired two tame buffalo, brought in while calves and fed from a bottle. According to Robert Wright: "They were so exceedingly tame and docile that they came into the back yards, and poked their noses into the kitchen doors, for bread and other eatables." The buffalo received national attention when a troupe of entertainers visited Dodge City in 1886. The group's large and noisy band marched down Bridge Street, then passed the Reynolds home, where the leader, dressed in "a big bear-skin cap" and shining regalia, made a near-fatal mistake. As the musicians trooped by the back yard, where the buffalo were showing signs of restlessness, "the band leader stepped out of the rank, shook his baton, and flourished it right in the buffalo's face." The *Globe Live Stock Journal* told the story:

> The buffalo that runs about town is accustomed to the music of the Cowboy band, it's western in appearance and does not interfere with the peace and happiness of the buffalo, but there are some things that the buffalo won't stand, and among them is a strange lot of men blowing horns, marching through the streets, headed by a drum-major dressed in red trimmings and a wooly hat. Yesterday the buffalo observed the Simon Comedy Company's Hussar band parading the streets and took exceptions, and with head down and tail up charged the band. The music ceased with the first bellow of that wild animal, and the band done some excellent running. It was the worst broke-up parade you ever saw. The buffalo took possession of the streets, while the band roosted on fences, porches, and small shanties.[30]

It was not the last of the affair. That evening as the band played in front of the opera house, "some mischievous person" turned the buffalo loose on it one more time. In the words of Wright: "That was enough. They not only threw away their instruments, but took to their heels, shouting and hollering, almost paralyzed with fear."[31]

The buffalo antics were not always directed at strangers. Long-time Dodge City resident Bill Jones described another rampage:

One day when he [Reynolds' buffalo] was going through everything he could find he discovered a salt-barrel in a back yard, with a few cabbage leaves and a little salt in the bottom. . . . He rammed his head down in the barrel to get at the cabbage leaves, and when he raised his head up, of course, he raised the barrel too. . . . About the same time someone threw a bucket of hot water on him, and the fun started. He ran over everybody and everything that got in his way. He finally reached the street, and down town he went, through several fences, and against several houses. He ran into a wagon, over a buggy, and finally into a millinery store on Bridge Street. Of course, all the girls that were working there and all the lady customers had seen that buffalo hundreds of times; but they had never before seen him with a barrel stuck on his head. They all gave a scream or two, and out of the back door they went. For a few moments he had the store all to himself. He did quite a lot of damage to the show cases and the millinery goods, and then out at the back door he went, just as the last woman disappeared over a high board fence in the rear of the store.[32]

As P. G. prospered in Dodge he began diversifying his activities and acquired a ranch on Ash Creek. Profits from ranching in the early 1880s were so attractive that anyone in Dodge with surplus capital or access to credit invested in cattle and rangeland. However, P. G.'s ranch, with its blooded stock of "graded Shorthorn of the celebrated Tipton-Anders county," was no more than an auxiliary to the stage business and occupied little of P. G.'s time. As Dodge City's population increased, so did the inner-town traffic, and Reynolds established a city bus and transfer line with Henry Tisdale as partner. There was also some limited single-consignment freighting business. Although any one of these enterprises might have occupied him full time, P. G.'s basic interest remained with the stagecoaches and the U.S. Mail.

Typically, when P. G. listed his occupation, he said he was a mail contractor. He worked at this with dedication and singleness of purpose, but it was one facet of his life in which he did not follow the usual entrepreneurial pattern. Although he undoubtedly had the opportunity, he did not participate in Vernon Louis Parrington's Great Barbecue. Reynolds might well have been one of the privileged who received the unearned benefits of governmental largess; the opportunity was there. Because of conditions in the Region, the contracts granted by the Post Office Department were vulnerable to graft and became some of the juiciest morsels on the federal spit. Reynolds was one of the first mail contractors and held contracts throughout the Star Route Frauds. Mail lines all around him—and some routes he had held previously—were involved. The table for the Great Barbecue was set, but Reynolds did not sit down. Perhaps he was too small an operator or perhaps he was not known to the Washington crowd and therefore was not invited to the feast. He, in fact, may have been a victim. His own conservatism and code of honesty, however, more than circumstance, kept him from getting his fingers burned as a participant.

Reynolds found the transporting of mail on the western frontier an exacting business requiring good public relations, a reputation for integrity, and considerable luck. The enterprise was also highly competitive, leading to failure as often as to success. But he soon discovered that beyond the requisites of personality and character, a successful contractor had to meet two other requirements: a contract for a specific line or lines, either through direct bidding or by subcontract, and adequate equipment and stock.

Early in the history of the post office it was determined that transporting the mail belonged to the private sector. The meshing of a public system with private operation seems to encourage error and fraud; indeed, some societies assume that it cannot be done without greasing the gears. In the United States, determining where legitimate profits stop and graft begins has always been a difficult problem for the government in dealing with private enterprise. When supervision is at a distance or falls into greedy hands, corruption is inevitable.

Even under favorable conditions, keeping the postal system advancing as rapidly as the expanding frontier would have been difficult. For those who came early to the West, there was always the feeling that the federal government was not doing enough: not enough stations, not enough routes, not enough deliveries. "Had the mail service been in the same condition in ancient days that it now is in this country," a Panhandle editor wrote, "Paul's Epistle to Titus and others would never been received in time for publication in the Bible." Establishing post offices was easy; the bottleneck was in delivering the mail to them.[33]

Before federal delivery routes were established in the Region, receiving mail was a sometime thing. Passing cowboys, freighters, and soldiers made what deliveries there were. Going to and from Dodge City for supplies, Bob Cator performed the service for folks around Zulu Stockade until 1883. Down in the Texas Panhandle, Austin ("Dad") Barnes made a business of gathering outgoing letters at ranches, posting them in Dodge City, and bringing letters to the ranches when he returned. For this irregular service he charged fifty cents per letter each way. Until the star routes were established, this was the best the Region could boast.[34]

Naturally the Post Office Department and legislators were under constant pressure to improve delivery. Post offices sprang up like mushrooms. Meade County, Kansas, through which the Jones and Plummer Trail ran, had a population of only 3,596 by 1890, but between 1879, when Pearlette became its first town, and 1890, it had twenty-seven towns, most platted between 1885 and 1888. All thought they deserved regular if not daily mail. Petitions endorsed by senators, the press, and tax-paying citizens poured into Washington in support of the requests. For instance, Panhandle and Dodge City residents were joined by the Dodge City newspapers in supporting the army in trying to step up deliveries to Camp Supply, and in June 1878 more than two hundred people from the Region signed a petition for mail delivery from Dodge City on a tri-weekly basis.[35]

The Dodge City papers gave strong editorial support for improved service to both Camp Supply and Fort Elliott.

The question now is will the Postoffice department favor our humble petition. We hope the good people of Dodge City will lend their mighty influence to this requisite project and assist us in consummating their devoutedly wished object.

The Pan Handle is filling up very rapidly by come-to-stay settlers and this practically is the only mail facilities to all that scope of country, as the writer was informed that so far one mail arrived at Elliott from Fort Bascom and it bro't one letter and that was taken about 30 miles below Elliott. The mail all go by the Camp Supply route. . . .[36]

When P. G. was denied a service increase two years later, the *Dodge City Globe Live Stock Journal* ran an editorial blaming the "rather cheeky" Texas politician who resented Dodge City's dominance of trade for the delay and calling on citizens to assist the Fort

Supply community in its efforts. For postal authorities, sorting out priorities and responding to the various claims while operating an economical department was difficult if not impossible. The rapid growth of the West and the clamor for more post offices and routes contributed to the Star Route Frauds.

Then, too, the system of assigning routes and contractors was unwieldy and open to abuse. The 1845 law reforming the assignment system had provided for competitive bidding, the contract going to the lowest bidder without designating the mode of delivery except that the mail had to be carried with "celerity, certainty and security." Those routes on which the mail was carried by horseback, stage, or hack with celerity, certainty and security were indicated by an asterisk, or star, hence the term *star route*. To encourage more efficient use of the lines and to help keep the cost of postage down, carriers were encouraged to use conveyances that could serve other purposes, such as carrying passengers; thus the stagecoach developed as the main means of transporting mail in remote areas. The income from passenger and express-freight fees made lower mail bids possible and, consequently, lowered postage rates. In 1878–79, when Dad Barnes was charging fifty cents a letter to Dodge City, the rate for first-class mail in the rest of the United States was three cents, sealed packages were three cents for each half-ounce up to a limit of four pounds, second-class matter was two cents a pound for newspapers, the third-class rate was one cent for each two ounces, and registered letters were ten cents. Postage was so cheap that cowboys in Mobeetie took great delight in sending special-delivery letters to anyone whose name came to mind, just to see the postmaster jump on his horse and rush to deliver the "urgent" message. Mobeetie washerwomen were the recipients of several such special letters.[37]

Delivering mail by passenger coach became such an essential part of the system for star routes that there developed the practice of submitting with the mail bid a so-called improved bid in which the time, frequency, or mode of conveyance was improved in exchange for enhanced compensation. The second assistant postmaster general was responsible for reviewing improved bids and allotting the extra compensation. The large number of such bids for servicing remote areas, where it was easy to falsify distances and the number of patrons, opened the way for considerable corruption. For most of the western states and territories, star routes were the typical assignment, and each year the number of improved bids increased. In 1872, for example, there were 4,506 designated star routes in Kansas; by 1883 there were nearly 11,000. In Indian Territory all but 73 of the 2,364 routes were so designated. Checking the legitimacy of requests for extra consideration became increasingly difficult, even if postal authorities had desired to do so.[38]

The bidding process was open to abuse at both ends. The same men bid for many of the same routes. If the lowest bidder defaulted or rejected the offer, the contract moved up to the next-lowest. By means of back-scratching exchanges, bidders could manipulate both the amount and the recipient of a bid. Furthermore, the successful bidder did not necessarily deliver the mail on the line; he could subcontract to anyone at a negotiated figure, who in turn could sublet to another person. Because of subcontracting, it was frequently impossible to determine who was actually operating a particular stage carrier or how much he was receiving to carry the mail. This was as true of P. G. Reynolds as it was for other operators. For instance, evidence indicates that P. G. began the first private service on the Camp Supply line in 1875 and continued it until his death in 1888. However, he was not the successful bidder at times and may have been a subcontractor for some of the period.

At the time of his death, Reynolds was in partnership with Henry Tisdale and they were operating the Southwestern Stage Company. It is possible that Tisdale had been the successful bidder for a number of lines and the partnership was a variation of the subcontracting system. Henry Tisdale was an old acquaintance from P. G.'s Lawrence days. The native New Yorker entered the stage and mail-contract business in Lawrence early on and he also chartered the Panhandle Stage Company, operating lines in Texas. One of the most persistent of the bidders for government contracts, Tisdale entered forty-two bids for star-route service in Texas alone from 1879 to 1882 and was low bidder on only one. This does not mean, however, that he did not operate a number of lines in Texas.[39] The difficulty of determining who was in charge can be illustrated by this news item from a Dodge City paper:

L. B. Williamson, present proprietor of the Mobeetie and Fort Supply Stage line, was in the city Wednesday and Thursday having come up from Mobeetie over P. G. Reynolds line, on his return home. . . . H. Tisdale of Lawrence, Kansas, was awarded the route at the general letting, and will take charge after July 1st.[40]

The lines open to bidding were a few miles to several hundred miles long. One of Tisdale's 1879 bids was for the Fort Elliott–Fort Bascom route (which was to figure prominently in the Star Route Frauds), 270 miles, and another was for the Lawrence–Carbondale line, which paid six dollars per round trip of 32.6 miles. A star-route contractor sometimes found it necessary to put several routes together, either through bids or subletting, to make an operation successful.[41]

As western immigration burgeoned, the mail-contract system ripened for plucking. When a ring of corrupt government officials began manipulating improved bids, obscure and occasional bogus routes, and subcontracts, it is estimated that the government was defrauded of four million dollars. In the trials of 1882–83, fraud was proved on ninety-three routes, but no convictions were obtained. The trials were replete with legal delays, charges of jury tampering, impassioned testimony by such well-known frontier figures as Generals William T. Sherman and Nelson A. Miles, and the legal bewitchment of Robert G. Ingersol.

The Dodge City–Panhandle Region was in the thick of things. The second assistant postmaster general, the inside man, had requested an additional $43,413.52 in one month for Indian Territory routes alone. A number of routes P. G. Reynolds had or was to serve were singled out, and H. M. Vaile, who had contracts for routes out of Camp Supply, was at one point in the proceedings judged guilty of conspiracy on a vote of nine to three but escaped conviction. The biggest fish caught in the investigative net was U. S. Senator Stephen W. Dorsey of Arkansas, who was indicted in the investigation that was begun during James A. Garfield's administration; Dorsey also was the biggest loser. Robert G. Ingersol's legal fee was one-third of Dorsey's ranchland and cattle in New Mexico. Reynolds had received one of his most important subcontracts from Senator Dorsey's brother in 1878. After several weary months of litigation, only two minor and partial indemnifications were won. The trials, however, did much to arouse public demand for improved postal service, and they clouded Chester A. Arthur's future as president. [42]

There is no doubt that mail service in the Region, as in other parts of the West, suffered during the period when spoilsmen were awarding grateful and cooperative bidders fraudulent contracts. Oklahoma resident Fred Tracy recalled conditions as he remembered them:

In 1881 there was another "Star Route" established through the "Strip" from east to west, from Camp (Fort) Supply . . . to Springer, New Mexico. On this route one man made one trip through on horseback, then for a time he would go from Camp Supply up the Beaver (River) to some cattle ranches, loaf around a few days and go back. For such service it was claimed the government was paying one hundred thousand dollars a year. [43]

Cowboy David McCormick topped Tracy's story:

You remember that Star Route scandal? They bumped Uncle Sam for a few million. One time we sent up some letters by this fellow. He carried it on horseback. This old fellow ordered a jug of whiskey there. They had a hell of a time until the whiskey give out. They branded the cats and dogs and everything. . . . This was at Fort Bascom, where this fellow lived. The whiskey give out and the fellow said, "We'd better start." So he brought the letters he had taken up to mail all the way back with him. That was the kind of mail service we had. [44]

After the trials started in 1882, mail contractors were watched closely, especially those in the Panhandle, since two routes, Fort Griffin to Fort Elliott and Fort Elliott to Meschita Falls, were singled out during the trials as prime examples of abuse. Any irregularity or delay was viewed with suspicion. Understandably, M. W. Mills, who lived in New Mexico and was known as a politician of sorts, being "a representative in the Territorial Legislature," found it difficult to find someone willing to subcontract a line out of Tascosa in 1883. [45]

P. G. Reynolds' primary business throughout the dismal period of fraud and rumors of fraud was with star routes. At one point he accompanied Dodge City Postmaster Herman J. Fringer to meetings "representing the star route service" and was described at the time of his death as "one of the largest star route contractors doing business with the government." He escaped all association with scandal and in spite of the adverse publicity that mail contractors in general received, he was much praised for his service. In the words of Cape Willingham, one of the earliest Panhandle pioneers on P. G.'s line: "'Star route' was the first mail service to amount to anything."[46]

Once delivered, mail was handled carelessly at many post offices. The contents of a bag would be poured on a table or floor, and patrons would pick out their own. Stamps and money orders were handled in a similarly irregular fashion. Delivery was another matter. Once on the hack or coach, the locked bag was treated with great care and there are few recorded instances of loss. Horses were killed and drivers froze to death, but the mail got through. P. G.'s record was exemplary.

A visitor to America noted: "Everything new is quickly introduced here. There is no clinging to old ways; the moment an American hears the word 'invention' he pricks up his ears." No entrepreneurs responded more quickly to new inventions than those in transportation. The equipment P. G. used had evolved over so many years that by the 1880s it had nearly reached its limit of adaptation. Reynolds made certain adjustments in his coaches, hacks, and wagons, but basically he was interested in using the best that had been developed. At least part of the explanation for his success lies in the fact that his equipment was from the beginning better than that on most lines in the West. He and others found that in sparsely settled areas requiring few deliveries, a horse or buckboard was all that was needed. Tascosa, the last outpost in the Region, never got beyond hack service on its east-west line, and when Reynolds put on a buckboard, it was considered an upgrading of service. His other lines, however, were supplied with the best equipment he could buy or build.

The hacks or buckboards Reynolds and other contractors used in thinly populated areas should not be confused with the fragile, graceful vehicles seen on the streets of a city. Reynolds' hack or buckboard may have fit the same generic description, but the similarity ended there. A buckboard is generally described as a four-wheel vehicle having a platform set on springs that carry the seats. Reynolds' hacks were locally constructed and consisted of a wagon bed on which two spring-supported seats were mounted, usually covered with a canopy and open on all sides. Normally there was room for the mailbags, three passengers, and the driver. Strength and speed were major considerations; comfort held no priority. Three passengers filled the hack, four made it unpleasantly crowded, and Mose Hays of Springer Ranch found five passengers intolerable:

I got on that old mail hack and went to Camp Supply. I went up there to Fort Dodge to see about them. The first night out we changed horses, and there was three great big huskies got on and then there was another fellow and that made three in the back and three in the front. We got rid of these old hobos, and then there was just three of us then. Then I got down in the back and caught up some on my sleep. We paid the man twenty dollars extra to get us to the train in Fort Dodge the next morning.[47]

Another winter traveler had a much better time of it during the Blizzard of '86 by burrowing into a pile of buffalo robes in the back of the hack and not peering out until he reached Hoodoo Brown's road ranch. Buffalo robes and tarpaulins were standard required equipment for winter travel. Summer passage was considerably more pleasant and a decided improvement over a stuffy ride in the stagecoach, provided the hack was not overcrowded. The dust that engulfed a coach in stifling clouds was dissipated in a hack, where the breeze could blow straight through. Even under the best of conditions the rider could expect to arrive at his destination windblown and covered with dust, looking like he had spent the day in a mine shaft.[48]

There were a number of variations on the hack, including homemade caricatures of a coach. Reynolds apparently used one of these on the Dodge City–Fort Supply Trail after he shifted his main line to the Jones and Plummer Trail. Fred Tracy missed his ride two days running in Dodge City because he didn't recognize the vehicle standing in front of the hotel as a stagecoach. The Englewood coach he was waiting on turned out to be a spring wagon with a canopy top of canvas and looked more like a prairie schooner than the Concord coaches Tracy had seen pictured in magazines.[49]

When possible, P. G. used standard stagecoaches on his lines. They were good for business and gave the impression of security and stability. Customers along the way appreciated the effort.

When Reynolds added a coach to the Dodge City–Camp Supply route in 1878, the Camp correspondent to the *Dodge City Times* saw it as an optimistic sign of progress. "It is reported," he wrote, "that Mr. Reynolds intends putting on the route between this Post and Dodge City, heavy four horse Concord coaches. This looks like business, and implying from the number of passengers traveling over the road, that there is a special demand for locomotive power."[50]

All accounts of Reynolds' stagecoaches refer to them as Concord coaches or "after the Concord style." Pictures of his equipment, however, show them to be considerably different from the standard Concord coach found in the East. The original Concords were light, elegant works of art: brightly colored, usually red, with fixed, glazed windows and an original scene or fancy scrollwork painted on the side. The narrow tires on sturdy spokes and forged-iron axle bearings created wheels impervious to water and capable of long wear at high speed. The Concord was a thing of beauty and durability, suited perfectly to eastern turnpikes and established roads. The slight, forward rocking motion caused by the through-brace suspension of three-inch-thick leather straps made for an easy, comfortable ride. The prime virtues of a Concord coach were light weight, speed, attractiveness, and extraordinary durability.[51]

Travel in the West posed unusual problems, so Wells, Fargo hired J. Stephen Abbot to redesign the coach for rougher western terrain. The result was two types of far less elegant and far more practical vehicles labeled with descriptive titles: mud wagon and celerity coach. The major difference between the two was the sturdier construction of the mud wagon. Instead of the delicately curved body of the Concord coach, the front and back of the Abbot models were straight, perpendicular to the floor. The front boot extended farther out over the rear team, and the back boot of canvas was nearly as large as the front one. The throughbraces were suspended to accommodate the flat-bottomed body. This arrangement resulted in a rougher ride yet provided some cushioning to absorb bumps and jars. The roof of the western coach was covered with canvas, and canvas curtains were rolled and strapped at the top of the window and door openings. The mud wagon had no hinged doors. All models had leather seats that faced each other front and back, with the Concord and the celerity having a third seat in the middle facing front. Finally, the tires were wider on the western coaches, more suitable for mud and sand. In short, the western coach models sacrificed elegance and style for stability, sturdy construction, and economy.

Reynolds' coaches resemble the western version more than the eastern. At least two styles are shown in pictures of vehicles on his line, and there may have been other types. Reynolds undoubtedly modified designs to meet his own requirements. The coach in *The Last Hook-Up*, although it resembles a mud wagon, does appear to have unique features, particularly the boot in back. Since some of his coaches were built by Pat Sughrue, a Dodge City blacksmith better known for his exploits as a peace officer, Reynolds could easily have altered construction. P. G. was convinced that good profits required good equipment, and he continued to add new coaches to his lines almost to the end of the era. James R. Quinn reported that in the summer of 1887 the coaches on the Tascosa run were "well painted and finished, looking very attractive," and as late as January 1887 a Dodge paper noted that Reynolds had put three "new Concord coaches" on his mail routes. [52]

All coaches were designed to carry mail; passengers were always a secondary consideration. If the stage was carrying a full quota of passengers, each person had sixteen inches of seat space. No trip in summer could have been very comfortable. One fat lady or a paunchy drummer could turn a sweltering, dust-clogged stage into a nightmare. At such times the seat on top alongside the driver was a prize spot, even though its occupant was exposed to the blistering sun. News that P. G. sent a special coach to Fort Supply loaded with "sixteen colored troops" speaks volumes on the subject of troop treatment and army economy and presents a bleak picture of an uncomfortable twenty-hour ride. [53]

Maintaining good stock—horses and mules, the other half of a well-equipped coach—was a constant worry for P. G. As the number of animals he needed grew to meet his expanding lines, so did the problems of keeping serviceable stock well fed and cared for. In 1884 the *Dodge City Kansas Cowboy* indicated that Reynolds "kept 50 teams on the road," a number that had grown by the time he joined Tisdale to one hundred fifty head of horses in the partnership alone. Earlier in his operation he had used mules to a greater extent, even the small, unpredictable Spanish type. As business improved he turned to horses almost exclusively, although mules were kept for use in foul weather.[54] P. G. probably and his son George most certainly enjoyed good horses, and at least one coach reportedly was drawn by "four spirited, well matched and well-groomed horses." It was a luxury, however that the stage lines could not often afford. Matched pairs and Morgan breeding were for town buggies and show. P. G. needed strong but inexpensive horses with reasonable speed and endurance. The Morgan breed was preferred by all coachmen. Ralph Moody explained: "Although short-legged and weighing less than a thousand pounds, he could outpull any other horse on the frontier and outwalk, outtrot, and outrun any horse ever matched against him." The horses pictured in the various Reynolds hitches may have been descendants of Justin Morgan's marvels, but they reflect more than a hint of less reputable plow-horse breeding in their recent ancestry. Those in *The Last Hook-Up*, seem very ordinary. They appear to be somewhat spavined and muleheaded, and at least one sports a parrot lip. These were work animals, not show horses. Maintaining stables of the size Reynolds needed meant that availability, not class, ruled purchases.[55]

As did all big stockmen, Reynolds registered his brand, a large R on the horse's left hip, and to ensure wide recognition the brand was shown in Dodge City newspapers for an extended period. Lost stock, whether strayed or stolen, was not uncommon. In September 1879, Reynolds followed a herd of horses stolen from him to Ryansville and on to Kiowa, where they were recovered. The best protection was good stables and sound fencing. The Dodge City stables were situated for a time at the corner of Vine Street and Third Avenue and on Second Avenue across from the Reynolds home. Both sites were close enough for P. G.'s personal supervision, but he also had to rent stable space from time to time, even in Dodge City. When he extended his line past Camp Supply and added new teams in 1878, he leased Henry Sturm's facilities; in Mobeetie he used the Miller Stable. He also built stables and barns at various stations along the line: Appleton, Ashland, Wilburn, and

Fort Elliott. Although P. G. concentrated on graded Shorthorn cattle at his ranch on Ash Creek, it also served as pasture for his stage horses. He used barbed wire for fences there; in fact, he constructed some forty miles of barbed-wire fence in the Panhandle in 1882 and added nine miles to it in the summer of 1884.[56]

Feeding such a large number of horses scattered from Las Vegas, New Mexico to Granada, Colorado was a monumental task. At times P. G. used his own crew to put up hay—one hundred tons in the summer of 1887 at Bluff Creek alone. More frequently, however, he contracted for it from various people. Ben Haywood, a former stage driver who was farming near Wilburn, received a hay contract from his old boss. Haywood's contract was large enough for him to subcontract with neighboring farmers to put up their hay on shares; from the vicinity of Wilburn he worked north to Dodge City looking for suitable crops. Where Reynolds maintained his own stations, as at Buzzard's Roost, the stationkeeper was responsible for summer feed, but winter hay and grain were provided by P. G.[57]

Any attempt to reconstruct P. G. Reynolds' mail-contract business in detail is bound to fail because his financial records were destroyed years ago. It is clear, however, that after the first few years his operation was far from simple and was conducted by a number of separate companies with a variety of names. At the time of his death, one of the Dodge City papers noted that he was operating "six different stage lines leading in all directions from this city."[58]

Generally, P. G. operated alone, although, like other entrepreneurs, he did not hesitate to use organizational devices to secure contracts and capital. The partnership was the most popular form of business organization in early Dodge City, and men like Charles Rath and W. M. D. Lee had many partners during their business careers, frequently maintaining partnerships with a number of different men at the same time. Lee's propensity for such arrangements has led to considerable confusion about his relationship with P. G. Since the Lee and Reynolds firm was a prominent freighting concern and since P. G. was equally prominent in the transportation of mail, it is easy—and was at the time—to assume that P. G.

was the Reynolds in the Lee and Reynolds partnership. He was not. Albert E. Reynolds, Lee's partner, may have been a distant relative ("about a second cousin," according to one of P. G.'s sons), but P. G. was never associated with him or with W. M. D. Lee in any business venture.[59]

Apparently, P. G. was sole proprietor of the first stage line from Fort Dodge to Camp Supply; it remained his bread-and-butter line until 1886, although there may have been brief periods when someone else carried the mail. At times in the early days, four hundred pounds of mail per week was sent to the post, and during 1877 Reynolds was paid $2,600 for a biweekly run. In 1878 he was awarded a new contract at the greatly reduced sum of $761. "It is presumed," the *Dodge City Times* editorialized, "that an increased passenger travel will partially make up the expense in carrying this mail as the contract is extremely low." Even after he shifted his route to Mobeetie away from the Dodge City–Fort Supply Trail he kept a stage, under the aegis of the Southwestern Stage Company, going south by way of Ashland.[60]

P. G.'s first extension beyond Camp Supply came with a subcontract in March 1878 to deliver mail to Fort Elliott, alternating with a government team. On a new route as the first civilian carrier to Fort Elliott, Reynolds held a contract only until July 1 and was paid six hundred dollars for once-a-week delivery. When the contract was extended, the operation was known as the Dodge City & Panhandle Stage and U.S. Express Mail Line.[61] An advertisement for it in the Dodge City papers took the form of a box and a brief paragraph describing the service:

P. G. Reynolds, proprietor of the stage line from Dodge City, Kansas, to Elliott, announces 185 miles made in 40 hours and $35 for the round trip. The mail runs daily on Mondays, Wednesdays and Fridays. The line is well handled, and even ladies, alone and unattended, are entirely secure. If continuous passage of two days and nights should be too much for frail nerves, passengers can wait over at Camp Supply, midway, and rest. Meals are fifty cents each can be had at most of the way stations. The Wednesday morning train from Dodge connects at Fort Elliott for Clarendon.[62]

The contract apparently was one of the improved bids because P. G. received double pay. The stage ran day and night, leaving

Dodge City at 7:00 P.M. and arriving at Fort Supply twenty hours later, with the same distance and time for the trip to Fort Elliott, requiring, the *Ford County Globe* noted with considerable understatement, the "rapid movement of the ponies on some of the stations." The number of deliveries to Fort Elliott varied from time to time, and P. G. worked hard, strongly supported by the military and the Dodge City press, to get more deliveries to the post and neighboring Mobeetie. As the fort's importance declined, more emphasis was put on deliveries to Mobeetie. By 1886, when P. G. bought out Cal Ferguson, the Jones and Plummer Trail was being used and the stage stopped in town first and then went on to the fort.[63]

Once established at Fort Elliott, Reynolds naturally looked to extend his line south, and in March 1878 he got a subcontract to carry the mail to Fort Bascom. He immediately brought in new stock and established three stage stations on the new route. On this assignment the stage did not travel around the clock but spent the night at one of the road ranches; it took about six days to make the trip. Sometime within the next two years, the route was extended to Las Vegas, with P. G. heading the Pan Handle & Las Vegas Mail and Express Line, usually referred to simply as Reynolds' line or the Pan Handle Stage Line. It was the longest and most taxing of his routes and he eventually made his son George the "prime operator." While he ran it, however, P. G. made his customary periodic tours; a trip in 1880 took him away from home from April 25 to June 8.[64]

As the stagecoach era drew to a close, P. G. increased rather than retrenched his operations. When he bought Cal Ferguson's line to Tascosa in 1886, he also acquired new stock, set up new stations and stables, and improved the express service. During the next two years he acquired a number of routes east of Dodge City, including those from Kinsley to Coldwater, Pratt to Greensburg, Kingman to Pratt, and Dodge City to Kiowa. He sublet some of these to his son George and to others, including H. W. Frazier, who drove the stage between Dodge City and Greensburg via Ashland, and to M. L. Munn, who carried the mail between Dodge City and Appleton.[65]

The stage business was by then on its last legs, for the more competitive railroads had been extended into the Region; still, new and competing stage lines were organized. These late additions must have understood that theirs was to be a short, transitional venture. Others, at least, saw what was happening. In 1887 the editor of the *Appleton Era* noted: "Four stages of P. G. Reynolds' lines, each stage with four horses or mules, passed the night in Appleton Saturday. The iron horse knocked the wadding out of their business in Kiowa and Pratt Counties. They were going west into newer country."[66] Reynolds also established lines southwest and north of Dodge City. In 1887 he had one that went to Granada and Two Buttes, Colorado. It served some of the inland Kansas towns that never quite made it and were abandoned in the exodus of the early 1890s and some of the newer competing towns, including Garden City, Scott City, Leoti, Santa Fe, Fargo Springs, Hartland, Ulysses, Hugoton, Syracuse, Woodsdale, and Horace.[67]

At this time, in the evening of his life and that of stagecoaches generally, P. G. and Henry Tisdale put together the Southwestern Stage Company. The partnership had more rolling stock and more employees than any of P. G.'s previous ventures. According to the *Dodge City Times*, the partners had "received from Washington the award of all the stage-line mail contracts of western Kansas. The contracts sum up to $250,000 per year." When a special issue of the *Dodge City Globe Live Stock Journal* described major businesses in the town, Southwestern Stage Company was listed:

SOUTHWESTERN STAGE CO.

Tisdale & Reynolds.

Thirty years ago this old and reliable company started their stages from Kansas City, and plyed them to different points in the then wild west, and as the iron horse kept moving more and more toward the sitting sun, we find this company keeping to the front until they permanently located in Dodge City, where they are making the following points: Dodge City to Englewood, Dodge City to Ashland, Garden City to Leoti, Garden City to Fargo Springs, Hartland to Hugoton, Syracuse to Horace, Granada, Colo., to Minnepolis, Colo. Mr. Tisdale resides in Lawrence, Kas., where he is well and favorably known for his many good qualities. Mr. P. G. Reynolds lives in this city and personally superintends the business. He is a native of New York, has been in Kansas thirty years, thirteen of which he has resided in this city. They have now in use one hundred fifty head of horses. Aside from their large stage business, they own the city bus and transfer line, which does ample service for our hotels, plying between the Rock Island and Santa Fe railroads. Messrs Tisdale and Reynolds are prompt and reliable in all their business transactions and have through these important qualifications laid the foundation of a successful business career.[68]

The broadening of the Southwestern Stage Company's operation was a sign of the Dodge City–Panhandle Region's disintegration. Other towns besides Dodge were becoming centers to which people of the Panhandle area looked for goods and markets. In Kansas, Liberal and Garden City became rivals for the Tascosa trade, and Meade was carving out a small section of Oklahoma as its own. Everywhere the railroads were changing trade habits and bringing markets closer. Reynolds and Tisdale were merely picking up remnants of old stage lines going out of business and spreading their service to areas not yet served by new railheads. The stagecoach wagon-road economy was slowly suffocating, and Reynolds was capitalizing, very successfully, on its last gasp.

P. G. never stopped trying to make his lines better. The most extensive improvements came in the last two years of operation and included better stock, more comfortable vehicles, quicker delivery, better connections, fewer delays, more deliveries, and improved passenger accommodations. If the handwriting was on the wall, he refused to reduce service or turn to other endeavors. In 1888, P. G. controlled more routes, more mail contracts with more equipment, horses, and employees and with more trouble than at any time in his career. One of the few lawsuits he is known to have was filed in the summer of 1886, when he brought action against the proprietor of the infamous Cattle King Hotel in Englewood, who had embezzled money from Southwestern Stage Company while acting as Reynolds' agent.[69]

On the surface, Reynolds never seemed more prosperous. He was also dying. And so was the wagon-road economy. Individual wagons still hauled freight to towns without railroads and a few stages continued delivering mail to post offices and passengers in remote and disintegrating towns. Stages still rolled into Beaver from Englewood in 1898 and the coach from Meade continued south on a daily basis for many years, but these were oddities, anachronisms held over from another age. By the end of 1888 the railroads had eroded the business once owned exclusively by the wagon and the stagecoach so much that the end was easily predictable.

P. G. had been in failing health since the spring of 1887, and as a concession to his condition he and Mrs. Reynolds checked into one of the hotels at Geuda Springs in Sumner County that May. Geuda Springs was a popular spa for Kansans, who found the water to contain certain minerals that were said to have amazing curative powers, especially for people suffering from dropsy. (Later in 1887 brother Milton W. was to purchase the *Geuda Springs Herald* and use it as a platform for advocating the opening of Oklahoma Territory to settlement.) The town had about six hundred residents, several hotels for visiting bathers, a drugstore, a bank, a blacksmith shop, and a Frisco depot. Health seekers could drink or bathe in the waters of several springs, each purported to have different medicinal qualities. If the waters did not cure, the peace and tranquility of the place at least brought rest and relaxation. For P. G., it was not enough; there was yet another debilitating winter and more visits to local doctors and distant specialists. On June 14, 1888, he returned from Kansas City, where he had been under treatment "for dropsy and similar problems." It was his last trip. He died July 14 at his home on Second Avenue in Dodge City.[70]

P. G. Reynolds and the stagecoach passed from the scene together. True, son George continued operating the stage lines for a brief time, but the last hookup was clearly at hand. Transportation of the mail was being turned over to the railroads, if not with celerity, certainty, and security at least with dispatch, definiteness, and assurance. But while they lasted, the contributions of the southern stage lines were particularly important. Like the freighters, the mail contractors helped bring to the undeveloped Dodge City–Panhandle Region "a good, producing population" and did much to sustain the people once they had settled there. Assured communication was essential to the economy and the personal lives of the men and women who were the Region's pioneers. Philander Gillette Reynolds' role in the transitional period is rarely mentioned, even in the local histories of the Region, but his presence was significant. The ultimate success of the mail-stage lines and the old bull wagons can be measured in the rapidity with which the railroad laid down a network of tracks to serve the expanded population and made freighters and mail contractors, the entrepreneurs of the road, obsolete.

8. Stage Drivers: The Men in the Box

"FROM the earliest days of stagecoaching," writes Ralph Moody, "the drivers, particularly the more colorful and dashing, were regarded by Americans with much the same idolatry as that of the Romans for their chariot racers."[1] Sitting high in the box, as the driver's seat was called, and wielding a whip that made a cracking good sound, with four spirited horses at his command and beneath him a swaying coach laden with mailbags and travelers anxious to make an end of their journey, the stagecoach driver on a Dodge City–Panhandle Region trail surely must have felt some of the allure and excitement of his role. But a Roman charioteer on the order of Ben Hur he was not. Glamorous he was not. After sweltering all day in dust kicked up by the team or freezing in near-zero cold on the windswept prairie, he had no illusions of grandeur. An understanding of the importance and necessity of his job might remain, but it was clear to him that it was only a job, and a tough one at that.

Far less is known of stage drivers in the Dodge City–Panhandle Region than of other wagon-road users. Of those who left records of their lives, none reeked or even hinted of glamour. The one authentic desperado in the lot, Henry Newton Brown, certainly belied the role while in Kansas and the Panhandle. There were rumors of past association with Billy the Kid, but in Tascosa he built a solid reputation as a worthy citizen working on the right side of the law. In Kansas, until the May morning he and Assistant

Marshal Ben Wheeler obtained the Caldwell mayor's permission to be absent for a few days and headed west out of town, Brown was a model of law-enforcing propriety. He looked and acted the part of a fearless marshal, and the people of Caldwell were reminded: "He neither drank, smoked, chewed nor gambled." His fellow townsmen found him cool, courageous, and gentlemanly. He was a "quiet and obstrusive" man who arrested troublemakers with dispatch, shot only those who resisted, and minded his own business when not looking after the peace and security of the town. His neighbors took him on picnics; appointed him marshal three times; lavished gifts on him, including "an elegant gold-mounted and handsomely-engraved" Winchester; and rejoiced in his marriage. Understandably, the stunned citizens of Caldwell could not believe that Brown was shot down by a mob after he and Wheeler had been party to a bungled bank robbery.[2]

The stage drivers, particularly P. G. Reynolds' drivers, came nearer—but only nearer—to the hard-drinking, tobacco-spewing, tough-minded eccentrics of Hollywood vintage film. Fred Tracy found one such driver on his way to Englewood, Kansas in 1885. "The driver wore a walrus mustache," he recalled, "big white hat and high heel boots. He possessed an extensive vocabulary of profanity. About his first remark was about the heavy rain and that probably that God Damn Mulberry Creek would be up and we would not be able to cross." Ben Steed on the Fort Elliott line was so profane that the ranch women dreaded to meet the mail stage. But for each driver resembling the tough image, there were many more pedestrian souls doing a good job for modest pay. About the only safe generalizations applicable to all drivers were these: they were generally young men in their twenties or early thirties; they were new to the West; and, like their freighting compatriots, they remained on the job only long enough to find something better to do.[3]

Driving stage was not the easy way to wealth. Pay for all drivers was at or near the level of that for a day laborer. In the ranks of civilian employees, the army paid ambulance drivers, "teamsters for public transportation," and laborers the same thirty-five dollars a month; clerks made one hundred dollars, and even a house painter or sailmaker who repaired wagon covers and tents made more than twice as much as a driver. Consequently, the turnover of drivers was high. The fact that most missed the census takers indicates something of their transient nature. In an age when every farm boy had handled teams of horses since the day he was old enough to stumble down a furrow behind a plow, most young men moving west had the skills to qualify as a stage driver. P. G. had no trouble finding replacements when his drivers moved on to greener pastures, which they did literally as well as figuratively, since most eventually became either ranchers or farmers.[4]

The driver's major qualification was that of reinsman, that is, knowing how to handle horses, oxen, or mules. About the only article of dress the drivers had in common was their gloves or gauntlets, which had to be thin enough for the driver to communicate and respond to the team through the leather ribbons in his hands. Reins, not the whip, gave the driver authority the team recognized. But in the parlance of the day, a good reinsman also had to have good horse sense, which required far more than just the ability to maneuver a team. A good reinsman knew his animals and all their quirks of character. It was horse sense that P. G. Reynolds' driver was displaying when he told Orrin Burright that sometimes when the ponies were racing across the flats they thought they were running away, and since they were making good time, he just let them think they were. A capable driver knew when to command and when to give a horse its head. On the plains, with wheels in the ruts of the trail and no other wagon in sight, the driver had little to do but contemplate the wonders of nature. Many a driver saved his own skin and that of his passengers in a storm by letting the horses find their own way to shelter.[5]

It was at best a lonely job, made even lonelier by the absence of the box's other occupant as seen in the typical drama. Although the stages traversed Indian country and ran through the panhandles of Oklahoma and Texas, which outlaws frequented, there was no regularly assigned man riding shotgun. Outfits belonging to men like P. G. Reynolds and Cal Ferguson were working stages that carried mail, passengers, and an odd assortment of freight; rarely was valuable cargo assigned to a route. There were no gold mines in the territory. The shotgun belongs to Colorado and California—especially Hollywood.

Since Reynolds dominated the stage business in the Region, his drivers may stand as representative of the lot. Although his operation was uniquely his own and his personality and the circumstance of his routes were different from those of other owners, the overall conditions of employment were roughly the same.

After observing the self-confident and sometimes eccentric behavior of many western stage drivers, an English traveler observed: "The stage driver is inferior to no one in the Republic. Even the President, were he on board, must submit to his higher authority." There was, however, a higher authority that even the most confident driver recognized: all drove the stage by sufferance of the boss. The relationship between employee and employer might vary from owner to owner, but ultimate authority rested with the man who could hire and fire. P. G.'s management style apparently was benevolent but firm, perhaps even fatherly. One of his obituaries noted that "while his business threw him with the roughest classes of the frontier so that he was almost constantly associated with them yet he never engaged with them in wickedness, never . . . lowered his manhood by condescending to their level. His life is a standing argument against the error that 'In order to command the rougher classes we must become rough like them.'" The operative word is *command*. There never was any doubt about who was boss. Although a deliberate, soft-spoken man, P. G. was very much in charge. He demanded from his drivers close attention to business, promptness, and full effort, but no more than he expected from himself. The three Reynoldses, father and sons, drove more miles on their line than any of the hired drivers, but even the unrelated employees were frequently treated as part of the family. The Census of 1880 shows three drivers, Ben Haywood, A. McAllister, and Eddie Clapp, living at the Reynolds residence.[6]

On the trail away from Dodge City headquarters the drivers were given considerable discretion. With Reynolds busy back in Dodge or driving some other route, the driver did have the kind of authority that had impressed the English traveler. It was ultimately the driver's decision whether the stage ran. On a number of occasions Ben Haywood delayed starting or stopped on the trail to wait out a bad turn in the weather. Interrupting a schedule obviously called for some skill in dealing with people. Ideally, the driver acted with a reasonable amount of tact but with enough forcefulness to maintain control.

David Nevin has pointed out: "The driver also had to have sound judgment and a capacity for quick decisions. When a blinding snowstorm suddenly obliterated the road ahead, when a stream was running too full to ford, when a horse went lame at night, it was the driver who decided on the spot what should be done." Reynolds' drivers had that authority, but it was not always used wisely. Tom Wilson's decision to leave the safety of a station in the middle of a blizzard that had already dumped twelve inches of snow on the trail was not only foolish but fatal. Correct decisions depended upon more than a level head and an absence of bravado. Equally important was sound knowledge of the country, the road, and the danger spots. J. J. Long, who drove for Reynolds from Fort Supply to Fort Elliott, said that after a year he "knew the road so well we would not lose the trail even in a blinding snowstorm." It was Ben Haywood's knowledge of the Dodge City–Fort Supply route that told him he was in danger when he heard the horses splash in water where no water was supposed to be. P. G. had no choice but to rely on the common sense of his drivers, and he gave them considerable latitude, which went further than judgment calls on schedules. To get the mail through, drivers could do whatever was necessary, even replacing a balky horse and buying another with the promise that P. G. Reynolds would pay the owner.[7]

Any stage line, but certainly P. G.'s, was more than just a conveyor of passengers and mail, and the stage driver was more than just the man in white duster who kept the coach in the ruts from one station to the next. For people in the inland towns and ranches, the stage was the major link with the outside world and, furthermore, the most current connection. The stage brought intimate letters of personal hope and sadness and newspapers telling of world events, but, just as welcome, the driver brought the latest gossip and news he had picked up along the trail. Judge O. W. Williams explained: "We had left Tascosa and crossed the Canadian River . . . when we were overtaken by the little buckboard carrying mail. . . . The driver, of course, stopped to swap news with us, according to time honored custom." Dodge City heard of A. G. Springer's killing from one of P. G.'s drivers. Reynolds himself brought the news that former Dodge City policeman Joe Mason had killed Ed Ryan in Sweetwater, Texas. Dick Bussell explained that he "got to talking" to some soldiers and drivers, who said there were lots of buffalo on the Canadian; he followed the trail down and collected two hundred hides. The *Kiowa Herald* reported as "reliable information" that P. G. Reynolds said the Kansas Railroad was laying track at a rate of one mile per day and the division town would be located at Fort Supply and Mobeetie. P. T. Lieneman remembered that it was the stage driver who told the people of Fort Supply that the prairie fire threatening the post had burned a broad swath clear to Fort Elliott. The news and information the driver gave was far more current and just as accurate as that the newspapers carried and, consequently, was eagerly sought.[8]

The driver was also something of an errand boy, occasionally a proxy agent, and at times a substitute for the Yankee peddler. As a result the arrival of the coach was always considered a major event, and the driver was generally a popular figure. P. G., who frequently drove the line, was a particularly welcome visitor in town, and the newspapers noted his presence and that of his drivers with warmth and pleasure:

The smiling face of P. G. Reynolds was around again.[9]
The polite stage drivers who go over the line between here and Dodge have done us considerable favors, which have been appreciated.[10]
P. G. Reynolds, the mail contractor, was down at this end last week, paying his drivers and making everyone happy with his good natured face.[11]

The driver's role as errand boy could bring disaster. Kenneth McCloud, a driver for P. G. on the Sidney line, was asked by a Hodgeman county farmer to bring cartridges from Dodge City. On his next trip, McCloud explained to the farmer that he could not find the right size. There followed an altercation in which McCloud, loudly cursed for not trying hard enough to find the cartridges, had to use his whip to fend off his attacker. It was a brief quarrel, and McCloud drove on. He was soon overtaken by three men, including Will Haun, the son of the man who had berated him. The *Dodge City Kansas Cowboy* told the story:

They overtook the mail about half way through Horse Thief Canyon, leveled their muskets, ordered him to stop by saying, "halt, you s—— of a b———, or I will bore a hole through you; you struck my father with a whip." The passengers were ordered to get out at the point of the muskets, among them was a lady of very nervous temperament and subject to heart disease. She was so overcome with excitement as to require careful handling. Will then ordered his man to take the whip and whale the mail man, which he did. Then Will took the whip and gave him three good floggings at different times, and further stated that he had a notion to kill him anyway, and leveled the gun on him. This was a cowardly act, and the cowards finally let him pass after threatening him with death, if he did not apologize to the old gentleman for the accidental touch of the whip.

LATER—H. B. Bell, the deputy U.S. marshal has arrested Bill, and the old gentleman for stopping the U.S. mail and lodged them in the Dodge City jail. Bill told Bell that if it had not been for the lady passengers present he would have made the carrier strip naked in order to flogg the skin from his body.[12]

Good Samaritans frequently have found the trail full of ingratitude.

Part of the driver's errand-boy role was a result of the stage line's express business. In the Far West, gold shipments figure prominently in the literature of the stagecoach. Plains freight was of a more prosaic nature. The front and back boots of the Concord stage could be packed tight with express and baggage, and sometimes parcels were stuffed under and around the passengers' feet. As was true of other stage operators, P. G. served as the agent for several express companies. When he took over Cal Ferguson's line on the Jones and Plummer Trail, he made certain that the newspaper informed the public that his agent at Meade, J. D. Kelley, was also serving and making connections with Adams Express Co. and Wells, Fargo & Co. "It will be conducted," he assured the reader, "the same as an express office on the railroad."[13]

Freight rates on the stage line fluctuated considerably over the years and were much higher than those of oxen or mule freighters. Although it varied from time to time, ox freight generally was about a penny a pound from Dodge City to almost any destination in the Panhandle, costing less than a fourth of what the coach express charge would have been. A trunk sent by Reynolds stage cost four dollars per hundred miles. A more interesting comparison of costs was made when the cowboys at a rendezvous camp near Fort Supply decided to get married en masse. After consultation with a matrimonial paper, arrangements were made to bring the women to Dodge City, from whence the cowboys agreed to get them to Fort Supply. "P. G. Reynolds," wrote Bill Jones, one of the romantic cowboys, "wanted ten dollars apiece to bring our women [with their baggage] to us. Ben Nichols said he would deliver the goods with a mule train for five dollars a head, and as the preacher was a Methodist, he would let him ride free." The women came by mule freight.[14]

If the sender were willing to pay the cost, no item seemed too prosaic or exotic to be carried. The Hardesty brothers in the Oklahoma Panhandle frequently had frozen oysters delivered by stage. Reminiscing in her later years, Mrs. Warren W. Wetsel, who claimed to be the only woman in Potter County at one time, remembered with delight the oysters, still frozen, that were delivered by stage to Tascosa for the parties her father gave. A road-ranch mistress who abhorred laundering sent her dirty clothes twenty-five miles by stage to the nearest washerwoman. Liquor wholesaler George M. Hoover of Dodge City frequently sent consignments of liquor by stage, especially to Fort Supply and Fort Elliott.[15]

If the cargo were important enough to warrant the charge, the rear boot could handle a fairly large consignment. Although it was unusual, P. G. did manage some livestock, and on at least one occasion he did so with unfortunate results. The problem was a pig:

A week ago last Friday, Mr. P. G. Reynolds, the stage man had a thoroughbred Poland-China boar pig consigned to him from the east, to be taken by stage to Meade Center; the crate containing the pig was fastened on the hind boot of the stage. A short distance out a slat was broken off, and when near the vicinity of the Prairie View Stock Farm of William Tilghman, the pig jumped out, and was not missed until the stage reached Mulberry, 12 miles south of this city. Inquiry was made for the missing pig, but no trace of it could be found until about a week after, when he learned from Mr. Tilghman that a stray boar pig turned up at his place, which he did not like to have mix up with his thorough bred Berkshire hogs, and that he turned in and altered it, as he did not consider it a prize pig, or anything as good as he had. This at once accounted for Reynold's missing pig, which was claimed by the owner to be a thoroughbred.[16]

Because it was the only public conveyance in many communities, there were few transportation requirements that the stagecoach did not fulfill. On occasion it even served as an ambulance. When a man was too ill to sit a saddle, he could count on the stage to get him to a doctor. Mose Hayes, owner of the old Springer Ranch, explained the folly of waiting for a physician. When his brother-in-law became ill with small pox, a neighbor, Frank Bigger, rode night and day to get to Fort Dodge. He sent back a doctor with the post ambulance, but by the time the doctor arrived, the patient was dead, and by the time the rest of the sick family reached Dodge City, one of the children had died. When Mose felt the pox coming on, he caught the mail hack to Fort Supply and the stage from there. We crawled into bed at the Dodge House "burning up with fever," but he survived. A bullwhacker known only as "the big Dutchman" was not so fortunate. He fell under a wagon, which crushed both thighs. P. G. offered the services of his coach to bring the man to the doctor, but eventually they had to give up moving him because of his critical condition. He did not survive.[17]

"By the 1860s, the stagecoach reigned as the most popular means of carrying people, mail and valuables across the West," writes David Nevin. Including people in the list makes *popular* too strong a word. Riding a stage was favored only in the sense that it might be the preferred alternative to walking or riding a horse. For people traveling south out of Dodge City who were not astride a horse, there was little choice. The stagecoach was *the* public conveyance. Although there were striking differences between P. G. Reynolds' lines and those of Ben Holladay or John Butterfield, all shared certain problems, dangers, and hardships. Where the Butterfield and Holladay lines were big operations with networks connecting passengers with the civilized niceties of large cities, Reynolds operated a working line off the beaten path of commerce. None was as romantic as they were popularly pictured, none made travel a pleasure, and none escaped the discomforts and dangers of the trail. Demas Barns wrote of post-Civil War travel in the West: "The conditions of one man's running stages to make money, while another seeks to ride in them for pleasure, are not in harmony to produce comfort." Most passengers would happily have settled for safety and certainty, realizing that comfort was at best only a relative possibility.[18]

For a P. G. Reynolds stage, danger was almost a daily companion. The long distances, the severity and unpredictability of the climate, and the scabrous terrain were ever present hazards, but the more publicized perils of Indians and outlaws were nearly nonexistent. Some of Reynolds' drivers believed the line had a special immunity from Indian attacks. It is true that in 1878, during Dull Knife's Raid, the Northern Cheyennes passed directly in front of one of P. G.'s coaches and did not molest it; they did, however, steal horses belonging to another of P. G.'s drivers. In the early days at least, Reynolds had the privilege of requesting a military escort on the Camp Supply Trail, a service he rarely used. It was not unusual, however, for a detachment from the fort, of the army's own volition, to ride down the trail to see why a coach was delayed.[19]

As for outlaws, Dick Bussell observed in commenting on P. G.'s long proprietorship of the mail line from Dodge to Supply and on to Mobeetie and Tascosa: "I never heard of that stage being held up." If true, it was a remarkable record, considering the lawlessness of the times and the isolation of the trail. Part of the explanation lies in the nature of the operation. P. G. was always careful and efficient, preparing as thoroughly as possible for any emergency, but the record probably was due more to the nature of passengers and cargo. Although Sid Reynolds remembered unnamed well-known persons traveling on the line, the clientele consisted mostly of grangers, working cowhands, and soldiers—none noted for carrying large quantities of cash. The strongbox was not the main feature or major attraction of the Reynolds line, and only rarely did drivers carry large sums of cash. When W. M. D. Lee bought the improvements of a number of small operators in the Panhandle, he needed thirty-five thousand dollars in currency to make on-the-spot payments. Marion Armstrong, one of P. G.'s drivers, put the money in an inconspicuous gunnysack and carried it openly on his hack. So rarely was such a valuable shipment made that no one suspected Armstrong of delivering more than family letters.[20]

The drivers were prepared for trouble if it came. Ben Haywood, assigned to the Fort Dodge–Camp Supply stage, carried both a rifle and a pistol for protection. On one of his trips, as he emerged from a deep cut in the trail, a man dashed out and grabbed the reins

George A. Reynolds's son, Sidney Rex, noted his father's identifications on this widely circulated photograph of the Dull Knife Raid captives. Courtesy Rex Reynolds, Niles, Michigan.

of his lead horse. Ben reached for his rifle and shouted at his team; the bandit dropped the reins and ran. This episode was as near a robbery as Ben was to experience. George Reynolds carried a revolver on the same run but did not have to use it in self-defense. It was handy when the dogs in town annoyed the horses. George "would simply pull out his six gun and shoot the dog right on the street. Apparently this was acceptable behavior even though it appalled the ladies in church."[21]

A more serious robbery attempt was experienced by driver W. A. Davis near Dodge City. Shortly after the Tascosa stage picked up passengers at the Defree ranch, trouble began. The *Fowler Graphic* told the story:

Grant Wells and wife got aboard the stage, while a younger brother of his, on a broncho, was following the stage. Soon after leaving the ranch, three men on horseback were seen approaching from toward Dodge at a rapid gait. As they approached, one of them, seemingly the leader, shouted to Davis, "Open up them mail bags, I want to see what's inside." They were riding around the stage with considerable demonstration, and when in the rear of it, one of them dismounted and jumped upon the broncho, (behind the younger Wells) and began spurring him, and pulling Wells' hair, slapping his face and otherwise abusing him. Grant Wells seeing this, alighted from the stage and told him to desist; that his brother was sick. One of the other two [Robert E. Robbins] then said, "I'm a wolf and this is my time to howl," drawing his revolver from his pocket—Wells drew his at the same time and received a shot upon the muzzle of his gun. The ball split, one fragment entering his shoulder and the other his hand. Wells first shot struck his assailant in the forehead the ball passing through his brain causing almost instant death. The remainder of the assaulting party then rode rapidly away, not staying to care for their companion. The stage then proceeded to Dodge with the wounded man. The corpse was also taken to Dodge City, by T. C. Dugan.

The incident was given wide coverage as an example of Dodge City lawlessness, with New York's *National Police Gazette* carrying the story alongside a quarterpage sketch of an artist's conception of what happened. The story writer was most impressed with the accuracy of Wells' "well-directed arm shot," especially since he was wounded.[22]

By all odds the biggest danger to driver and passengers alike was the weather, not hostile Indians and armed desperadoes. Summer heat was exhausting and uncomfortable, but it did not kill; a severe blizzard on the open plains could cost life and limb. Winter travel was unpredictably dangerous, particularly on the east-west trail between Tascosa and Fort Supply, which was the most treacherous of all the routes. Even routine winter travel was demanding, but generally it was considered a part of the day's work. Unless they were unusually severe, with high winds and driving snow, storms merely added to the unpleasantness of travel and rarely halted mail delivery.

John Butterfield preached: "Remember, boys, nothing on God's earth must stop the U.S. Mail." The credo was echoed by all other mail contractors. Austin Barnes, the first contractor on the Tascosa–Fort Supply line, warned his riders that there was a four thousand dollar forfeit for any mail delivery not completed. His directions were brutally simple: "Put that mail through on time or kill every horse trying." Kid Dobbs did just that on two trips in the winter of 1880. When P. G. took over the route, he was under the same restraint. Although he converted the line to mule-drawn hacks, which made it possible to carry passengers, his paramount consideration continued to be getting the mail through on time.[23]

This commitment was tested severely in January 1881 when a long and severe storm hit the Fort Elliott area, killing two men in separate parties on the Jones and Plummer Trail. Marion Armstrong had been driving the Fort Elliot–Tascosa line that winter and had been plagued by bad weather and heavy snows. P. G. made it a practice to cover all his routes personally in troublesome times, and on one of his trips he met Armstrong on the trail, hours behind schedule. Reynolds "roared" at him, according to Armstrong, and when the driver attempted to explain that he had broken through the ice and had taken half a day to thaw out, Reynolds became even more abusive. Armstrong demanded his pay and quit on the spot. P. G. paid up and finished the delivery, disregarding Armstrong's parting warning that the trail across the prairie must be marked before someone unaccustomed to the land took over the route. True to Armstrong's predictions, the next driver, John Cannington, became lost in a storm. He wandered for three days before reaching his destination, but by then his feet were so badly frozen that they had to be amputated.[24]

When the January storm hit, the trail was still unmarked. Tom Wilson, the new driver, was carrying two passengers when he left the North Fork station in the middle of a raging blizzard. Wilson judged the snow to be twelve inches deep when he started out. It was a fatal decision, but he was acting under pressure to see the mail through. About halfway to Dixon Creek, the buckboard became stuck in the snow. All efforts to free it proved futile, and eventually the mules broke the tongue on the hack. Using the north wind as a guide, the three men tried to make it to the next station, alternately walking and riding. After three days of aimless plodding, William Higgins, one of the passengers representing a New York business firm, was so badly frozen that he could not continue. That night they rested, huddled under a buffalo robe and tarpaulin, only to discover in the morning that the mules had wandered off.

Leaving Higgins wrapped in the buffalo robe and tarpaulin, the other two followed a fireguard to East Amarillo Creek, where the second passenger gave out. Wilson continued alone and was spotted the following day by a rancher who was hauling driftwood. He was taken to LX Ranch headquarters while the rancher, Jack Daughtery, searched for the other two men. The second passenger was found dead, but Higgins' body was never recovered. Wilson was taken to Fort Elliott but died shortly thereafter; he had made a tremendous effort, walking in severe cold more than forty miles without food. The buckboard and mailbags were recovered and the mail was delivered.[25]

Wilson was not the only Reynolds driver on that route to die with his frozen boots on. In the Blizzard of '86, one of P. G.'s coaches came into Fort Supply with the driver sitting frozen to death in the box. The passengers inside were unaware of the tragedy until they reached their destination and the driver failed to move from his seat.[26]

It is generally conceded that the worst nineteenth-century storm Kansas and the Panhandle experienced was the Blizzard of '86. For people who came to the Great Plains before the winter of 1885–86, the one common experience that held them apart from the Johnny-come-latelys was surviving the blizzard, which began New Year's Day. During the night, the temperature plummeted to twenty degrees below zero and the wind whipped the fine, dry snow into house-high drifts. The snow continued for three days, but its cessation was scarcely noticeable because the wind continued to fill the air with dry, suffocating flakes and the unrelenting temperature remained. Another flurry blew in with renewed intensity on the fifth day and continued for some time. It was this blizzard that killed the Fort Supply driver, but not all were as unfortunate. After being marooned on the Santa Fe train coming into Dodge City, E. D. Smith waded waist-deep snow to town and waited three more dull days for the stage to leave for Meade. While he waited, two frozen corpses were brought in from the trail, and another man was so badly frozen he was not expected to recover. Not until January 6 did the hack with four horses make it through with much difficulty, the horses being changed at several road ranches. The January blizzard of the previous winter was a near match for the 1886 storm. That year, the Fort Supply stage was caught two miles south of Appleton; it wandered from the trail, but luckily the horses stumbled into a haystack, which fed and sheltered them. The driver, who was alone, took refuge in an abandoned dugout, where he remained forty-eight hours without food or water. The stage finally made it into Dodge at sundown on the fourth day. [27]

Typically, a driver would simply hole up at the nearest shelter if the weather turned too severe, in spite of the demand that the mail must go through. However, blizzards occasionally came on with little warning. Ben Haywood told of being caught in one such blinding snowstorm. He found that by angling back and forth across the ruts he could feel beneath him the trail that he could no longer see. Common sense called for less heroic and more cautious action:

On a return trip to Dodge City from Camp Supply, he [Haywood] was caught in one of the terrible storms that came up in a flash on the High Plains. He decided the best thing for him to do was to pull up under one of the bluffs on Bluff Creek and wait.

There was an excitable, nervous fellow on the stage. When he found out that they were camped under the bluff with the blizzard howling and the world turned white, the passenger got down on his knees and begged the Lord to deliver him and repented of all his sins.

When Haywood pulled out with the coach and came near Dodge City, he stopped the vehicle. Out tumbled the praying passenger and thanked the Lord for his deliverance, and vowed in a loud voice that he would never come back to this part of the country again. [28]

The delay cost seven hours, but before sunup the next morning the stage, mail, and passengers arrived safely in Dodge City.

On the Dodge City–Fort Supply Trail and on much of the Jones and Plummer Trail, the ruts were deep enough that the drivers

P. G. Reynolds advertising copy. This and similar prints of a team and coach appeared in a number of newspapers in the Region. Reproduced from History of Miami and Roberts Counties (n.p., 1976).

could let their animals have their head at times when they could not see the trail. J. Wright Mooar pointed out that much of the trail was "just like an old river bed," cut deep and wide by wind and water erosion. All this changed in the level river bottoms and on the upland flats, where there was less chance that deep gorges would be cut in the sod. Most drivers prided themselves on being able to drive the trail blindfolded, and undoubtedly they did doze off in the afternoon sun and on the all-night runs. The teams' instincts in snowstorms were also fairly reliable. J. Wright Mooar described the merits of a mule that was leading a long line of freight wagons:

Everything stopped, and Levi Richardson come back down the line and said he believed his mules had froze. His mule left the road and had quit, and he couldn't make her go. I remember John Mooar [J. Wright Mooar's brother] walked up to him and put his hand up there and breathed that way, and pulled the ice and glaciers off of him, and he could see by the time he'd been walking along and hadn't seen when they left the road. Pat Baker was driving the second team, and he says, "I'll make her go." Pat went up there and whipped her with a black snake, and she wouldn't budge out of her tracks, and Pat went around and took her by the near-bit and went around to get the off-leader by the bit, and he run his shoulder against the door of the house he was hunting. She went right up and put her nose against the door and stood there. There wasn't a man in the train that didn't feel like kissing that old mule. [29]

In descending order of danger after the blizzards were the creeks and rivers that had to be forded. Quicksand was a potential danger after any flood, particularly at the Canadian and Cimarron crossings. Said Dave Bowers of Buck Creek, Texas: "Our worst dread . . . was the Canadian River which was frequently up and there was always danger of quicksand." Tom Judy remembered his father's describing the loss of a Lee and Reynolds wagon at the Cimarron crossing on the Jones and Plummer Trail. As the wagon slowly sank, the horses were cut loose. The driver was still considerably shaken when he was safe on the riverbank. "As I looked back," he said, "I would see the wagon sinking and then the tongue folded straight up and went under." One driver, realizing the peril of quicksand after a flood, occasionally required passengers to wade across a swollen stream behind the coach so that they could turn back if it started to sink. P. G. lost one of his best teams when a driver tried to ford Commission Creek in Texas after a flood. The *Ford County Globe* sharply criticized the federal government for demanding such hazardous duty "simply to be on time with the mail."[30] Even without quicksand a flooding river was far too treacherous to take lightly, even if one were well acquainted with the crossing. Reginald Aldridge explained that it normally took forty hours, traveling day and night, to get from his ranch to Dodge City on the Reynolds stage line. "But when there has been much rain and the rivers are swollen," he said, "it may take much longer." He cited as an example a return trip from Dodge:

. . . we found the Cimarron River, though not very deep, so boggy, after heavy rains, that the driver was afraid to cross, and we had to lie there for twenty-four hours, getting our meals at the nearest stage-ranch. The stage of the previous day was for the same reason detained there, and before we crossed a third had arrived on the scene. Finally one vehicle was got across, while the passengers—our combined forces amounting to about eight—were obliged to take off their trousers and boots and wade. On the other side we were all crammed into one machine intended for five, and, by dint of getting down and walking whenever we struck a bad bit of road, we reached Beaver Creek, which runs by Supply. It was dark when we arrived there, and, as the creek was so swollen that it could be crossed only by boat, our driver told us that we must camp on the bank and wait for daylight. We accordingly stretched ourself on the ground with such blankets as we had brought with us, while innumerable hungry mosquitoes preyed on our supperless carcasses. However, we managed to snatch a little sleep, and the next morning were ferried across the creek. We remained at Supply all day, and started again at 7 P.M., two vehicles being now allowed us, and arrived at the ranch about ten the next morning, without further adventure, just forty-eight hours after time.[31]

Strangers, accustomed to schedules' being met, were frequently less understanding when the driver decided to pull up and let nature take its course. On a night so dark that he could not see the lead horses, Ben Haywood heard his team splash in the water. He wheeled them around and got up on the flat, where he could see the Cimarron on a rampage and spreading far beyond its banks. When he decided to wait the flood out, a passenger bellowed that he had to be in Fort Supply that night. Ben calmly told him: "If you have to be there, go ahead and swim, that's the only way you'll make it." By sunup the flooding had receded considerably, but it was midmorning before Ben felt it was safe to ford the river.[32]

Accidents caused by equipment failure, harness breaking, and renitent animals were a part of any operation. Generally, the quality of P. G.'s stock on the Dodge City–Fort Supply and the Dodge City–Tascosa lines was excellent, but the same cannot be said of the early days for the lower leg of the Region. Nevin observed that the farther west the overland stages went, the poorer the breeding and quality of stock. For P. G., the farther south the lines went, the poorer the stock. "Passengers would watch in barely concealed terror," Nevin reports, "as squealing, kicking, biting mustangs— obviously barely broken—were forced into harness. . . . teams started off so violently that novice travelers inside the coach assumed they were victims of a runaway. Mark Twain noted that with a team of mustangs 'the coach shot out of the station as if it had issued from a cannon.'" P. G.'s southern line sometimes reflected comparable chaos. The harnessing of mules at Mobeetie was roughing it as certainly as if Mark Twain had been there. One incredulous passenger wrote: "They had four head of these little wild Spanish mules. They had to throw them down, hogtie them, then harness them, and everybody would get in. Then they would be turned loose, and would run until they ran themselves down."[33]

Orrin Burright found the drivers amazingly complacent about the recklessness of their teams:

All the driver had to do was to keep the four-mule team on the road and they did the rest. It didn't make any difference, so the driver said, whether the mules were running away or not. Sometimes they thought they were running away—and he let them think so, just as long as he kept them under control and in the road. He didn't care how fast they ran for the road across Finney and Meade counties was as level as a floor and there was no danger of the stage tipping over or upsetting.[34]

Not infrequently a passenger had to become a part of the operation to get a stage or mail hack through. Pushing the coach out of a boggy place was not unusual. Making a trip to Dodge City, Mose Hayes found himself on a hack with the opposite problem Twain and Burright confronted: the lead horse balked at the first steep hill and refused to budge. Hayes had to get out and ride the horse, spurring him on with personal attention. The first freighters they met were offered the horse in exchange for one of theirs, with the driver's promise that P. G. would pay the difference. "Ours don't go north," the driver explained, "but can go back south fine." Passengers on the road between Bluff Creek and Bear Creek on a very dark and snowy night were unharmed when a gust of wind blew the stage over. They scrambled out, pulled and heaved until they had the coach right side up. After driving a few more miles, the driver decided it was too risky to continue and stopped until daylight. The only damage to the stage was a broken lamp, and one of the passengers suffered "a loss of a bottle of good whiskey."[35]

As P. G. built up his operation with his own barn, stables, and horses, the conditions on the southen route improved. Still, under the best of circumstances, there were bound to be accidents. Reynolds, himself, was knocked unconscious when a rearing horse struck him on the head. Harness breaks usually caused only a few minutes' delay as repairs were made by the driver; a major accident might detain the coach for hours. One of the reins guiding a double-team hitch driven by P. G. and his son broke just as the stage started out of Dodge City. It was raining "like Halifax" at the time, according to the *Dodge City Kansas Cowboy*, and the team became frightened and ran away. At the corner of Front and Bridge streets the team made a tight circle, upsetting the stage. The horse ran from the wreck and got tangled up in Colonel R. J. Hardesty's buggy in front of the Dodge House. One of the passengers, the wife of Captain Gilman of Fort Supply, was injured. Departure was delayed two days. The Greensburg stage received far more damage when it was blown off the road and lost the entire top. The driver jumped free, and after he and the passengers righted the coach, they were on their way, with little disruption of the schedule.[36]

An unusual delay of the mail occurred on the Dodge City–Fort Supply line, representing an early-day hazard of plains travel that was not to be experienced at a later date. Old Cactus describes the incident:

Buffalo are getting on the rampage. Since Captain [Writ] Davis has cleaned out the horse thieves, they have turned from their quiet grazing propositions to that of horse thieving. Only last Friday they stole Mr. P. G. Reynolds' two mail horses, harness and necessary appendages, and made an attempt to steal the mail and vehicle, and evidently would have stolen the driver, but he was too sleepy to be moved off. The circumstances are about this: On Friday last the mail hack stopped at Buffalo Springs to feed and dine. While thus resting a herd of buffalo came along and gobbled up the mail horses, and away they went at a 2:40 gait. By the time the driver woke up to a realization of his condition, his locomotion power was gone—gone beyond recovery, and he sat down, philosophically, devising some plan to get back his hack, but for the space of 24 hours he could devise no favorable plan. Meanwhile, the commanding officer at Camp Supply, owing to the non-arrival of the mail, sent out a detachment . . . with instructions to go on until definite information was obtained of the fate of the mail. Sergt. Hart did go on to Buffalo Spring, where he met the driver serenely seated on his wagon tongue. . . . With lariats, saddle stirrups, halter straps and the like, harness were constructed, and in due time the U.S. mail was on its way southward at an eight mile per hour rate, drawn by two fierce cavalry prancing steeds. The heterogeneous outfit arrived at Supply about 6:30 p.m. on Saturday evenings. . . .[37]

The good-natured acceptance of hardships and misfortunes was an essential characteristic of the stage drivers. The patience they learned to practice in their daily routine and the humor with which they accepted delays, accidents, and dangers were to be important resources when they moved into other frontier activities.

The names of only a few drivers have survived; fewer still left enough of a trace in history to indicate what kind of men they were. Following the careers of a few of these early plainsmen who did leave a mark on the land demonstrates the extent and nature of the contributions they made as permanent settlers. Their introduction to the Region came on the trails, and their experiences as drivers helped determine the kind of imprint they were to leave on future communities. Since they are representative, if not typical, of the earliest residents, an understanding of their character and background sheds light on the development of the Region. Their lives as drivers required a certain toughness and unsophisticated directness. Perhaps they were even a part of the "roughest classes" to which the Reynolds' obituary referred. However, the record of the majority of those who for a short while drove stage in the Dodge City–Panhandle Region would not place them on the wild side.

Ben Haywood was one such driver. He fit the images of neither glamour nor wickedness, being in fact a God-fearing, churchy man who brought to Kansas a full measure of Protestant ethic from New England. He was a character, perhaps even eccentric; he fit no other stereotype. Benjamin Franklin Haywood was born in 1844. He was about thirty-one when he began working for P. G. Reynolds after coming to Kansas from Maine by way of the logging camps of Alpena in northern Michigan. He was an expert axman, having grown to manhood on the banks of the Penobscot River in the heart of Maine's timber country. The year he was eleven and beginning to get the knack of a solid ax stroke, 181,809,000 feet of logs were floated down the river from his hometown. Ben was also proficient with teams of oxen and horses, an equally important skill in bringing trees to the mills. In Alpena, after leaving the logging camps, he delivered mail on foot through the Michigan timber, following a tree-blazed trail that required one night each way sleeping in the open—good training for Reynolds' stage line. [38]

While in Alpena, Haywood read a newspaper advertisement for mule skinners to help take a group of settlers from Boston to Lawrence, Kansas. He applied for the job and got it. Once he had safely delivered his cargo, he was attracted by the stories of opportunity in the booming town of Dodge City, so he moved west once more. His first job in Ford County was that of teamster moving freight for the army from Fort Dodge to Camp Supply. This brought him to the attention of P. G. Reynolds. Ben began driving for P. G. in 1877 and continued for at least three years, one of the longer associations by a Reynolds driver. While he was driving for Reynolds, he took a tree claim on the line between Ford and Meade counties; his brother joined him and they homesteaded adjoining quarters. [39]

Ben was a religious man. He did not smoke, drink, or swear. His most violent oaths were "Gal-Bust-It" and "By-Garrie." He never lost his Down East brogue, and if his speech lacked the fire-and-brimstone profanity of the stereotypical driver, it was all the more striking for its quaintness and originality. He was a poet of sorts and a great declaimer, as distinguished from a mere speaker. In his seventieth year he was called upon to favor a retiring editor with one of his pieces: "Uncle Ben Haywood got a hearty encore on 'Western Kansas' after reciting a portion of the well known poem,

*Benjamin Franklin Haywood, 1844–1918, stage driver,
lumberman, and farmer, circa 1915. Courtesy C. Robert
Haywood, Topeka, Kansas.*

'The Long-horned Texan Steer.' When it comes to pulling off a
stunt of that kind, Uncle Ben is there with the goods." By then Ben
had accumulated some nine hundred acres of farm and pasture
land, a fairly large herd of cattle, and a number of horses. Having
homesteaded early and taken a tree claim, he was inordinately

proud of his maturing grove. Other timber claims, his brother's just down the road a mile, for instance, became a profitable source of fuel and fence posts and a serviceable shelter for cattle.[40]

Ben's grove became something quite different. Photographs taken some twenty-five years after the first planting, sometime around the turn of the century, showed the mature growth. The black locusts were in full bloom, and the stifling fragrance of the honey-blossom pendants on a sultry day seem to exude from the old prints. Uncle Ben's Grove, through which Crooked Creek meandered, became something of a public establishment for neighboring communities, serving as the setting for picnics, church conventions, ball games, patriotic celebrations, and baptisms. No one was tolerated in the grove who used profanity or had tipped a bottle.[41]

The best description of the grove in its prime came from the pen of I. J. Stanton, editor of the *Fowler Gazette*. In the company of a number of friends, he had driven out to it on a Sunday outing. After remarking on the beauty of the grove, planted, cut, and trimmed to resemble the layout of the World's Fair, Stanton wrote: "As we passed out of the grove . . . Mr. Haywood decorated our machine with locust leaves and bid us adeau as we left the shade."[42]

The wreath of honey locust bears the distinctive touch of Ben the poet. While it is true that not even in his poet's eyes did the isolated stand of trees measure up to the forests of his youth, it was timber. Nor should it be thought that the grove was all show and nostalgia; Haywood was still Yankee enough to appreciate the economic fact that a good, straight locust tree could produce fence posts and telephone poles worth three to five dollars apiece. But a significant part of his enterprise lay in recapturing a sense of his earlier home. There was the comforting sound of wind in the trees, the sensation of being in the sheltering depths of the woods, and a knowledge that the plains of Kansas would never be a barren, treeless land again.

Because he spoke with a strange New England accent, remained a bachelor, was tight with a dollar, and pursued his own independent and implacably logical ways, Ben was considered something of an eccentric. But he did much to strengthen the community as he experimented with new crops, imported blooded stock, supported the church, and charmed the local literary societies. From his stage days with P. G. Reynolds to his death on November 29, 1918, he came to understand and admire the West. He found total fulfillment in his commitment to the land and gave unstintingly of his time in developing it. [43]

Two others who rode for P. G. in the Panhandle became men of local distinction. Marion Armstrong was one of Tascosa's first peace officers, and John J. Long was Beaver's first banker and lifelong merchant. Neither served for more than a few months as a driver and would not have been remembered if that had been the extent of his contribution to the settling of the West.

Marion Armstrong worked for Reynolds during the bitter-cold winter of 1880–81 on the toughest line Reynolds ran, catering to some of the toughest customers in the Panhandle. He had no prior experience, but then the job required more of character and endurance than craft, and Armstrong had that. His father had moved to Wise County, Texas in 1857 when Marion was a year old. Life in North Texas was difficult, made more so by the senior Armstrong's staunch Union convictions during the Civil War. Marion grew to manhood there, married, and started a family. By 1878 he was, in his own words, "down and out." [44]

After discussing several possible locations for a fresh start, Marion and his brother, Sam, decided to move to Arizona by way of the Texas Panhandle. Traveling in a covered wagon across unsettled, totally unfamiliar country, they encountered more than the usual run of hardships. As they approached Mobeetie, with its comforting assurance of food, shelter, and human companionship, they began to reconsider their objective and agreed to settle in the new town. But the rowdy element dominating life there soon made it clear to the Armstrongs that a garrison town was no place to bring up a family. Although they were travel weary and their money was gone, they returned to their first plan, which took on the commitment of a family compact, and moved on toward Arizona. Crossing the Canadian River proved a disaster when their wagon bogged down in quicksand. Forced to backtrack to an abandoned sheep camp they had passed on their way to the river and considering the exhausted condition of their animals and themselves, they had little choice but to spend the winter there. When one of the horses died, they gave up their compact to go on to Arizona and decided to accept the first opportunity that knocked.

An offer from Rack Capland to maintain stage stands on the Red Deer Creek and White Deer Creek crossings seemed fortuitous after their hapless journey. With great hopes that he had at last found a home, Marion "dug a dugout house in eighteen days." In his words:

> I was twenty-three years old when I landed in my dugout house with my wife and two babies, my oldest boy Thomas, three years old, my youngest, Melvin, six weeks old. If it had not been for the excitement, I believe we would have died of pure loneliness, but quite a good many people passed that way. A Pueblo Indian that worked for a cow outfit down about where Canadian City now stands, came up and stayed all night with us. He and I went up the creek about a mile and killed a buffalo out of a small herd that had drifted in to water so we had plenty to eat the rest of the winter.[45]

When Capland went broke and abandoned the mail route, Armstrong "borrowed" one of the contractor's mules to replace his dead one and moved on. This time they made it to the LX Ranch, where Marion found work and the family settled into a rock dugout on Bonita Creek. "Bonita Creek," Armstrong wrote, "was at that time, as its name implies, a beautiful creek with willow and cottonwood trees, beaver dams, and hay meadows. And there were lots of wild turkeys. After I broke my shotgun I caught them by running them on horseback. Just below the mouth of the creek there were some big cottonwood trees where they roosted by the hundreds." It was not, however, a paradise. The Armstrongs felt the terrible isolation and were frequently frightened by overly curious or, for all they knew, hostile Indians.

When P. G. Reynolds took over the contract for the "Lightning Express–Daily Mail," Armstrong moved to "East Tascosa," on August 10, 1879 to man the new mail route. Marion's run was from Tascosa to Dixon Creek and sometimes on to Mobeetie, a total of one hundred twenty-five miles. For a time he rode the line on horseback or drove a hack, sharing duties and confidences with Henry Newton Brown. The quarrel with P. G. that led to Armstrong's immediate resignation left him with a wife and two children to feed and "broke flat . . . not knowing where my next job was." At least he was paid. One of P. G.'s virtues was to keep his obligations clear. Armstrong worked for a time for W. M. D. Lee before being elected Tascosa's first constable and justice of the peace. Serving as peace officer in Tascosa was not as hazardous or as stimulating as being marshal of Dodge City, but it was not without its moments of excitement. He was there the afternoon Tascosa dug the second grave on its Boot Hill. His close friend, Sheriff Cape Willingham, who had worked at LX Ranch with him and had moved to Tascosa at the same time the Armstrongs went there, appointed Henry Brown deputy while Marion was serving as constable. A group of cowboys from an outfit trailing a herd north were hooraying the town when Willingham demanded their guns. Fred Leigh, the apparent leader of the crew, defied the sheriff and rode down the street. Willingham and Armstrong, both unarmed, ran to get their weapons and caught Leigh as he swung out of his saddle in front of a saloon. Aiming his shotgun at Leigh, the sheriff demanded that he turn over his pistol. Instead of obeying, Leigh remounted his horse and reached for his gun. It was a fatal mistake. The charge from both barrels of the sheriff's gun blasted him off his horse. He was dead when he hit the ground. Brown, Armstrong, Henry Kimball, J. E. McMasters, and Ira Rinehart immediately backed the sheriff. The dead cowboy's friends rode out of town, leaving the burying of Leigh to the townfolk. It was a turning point in Tascosa's history. In Frederick Bechdolt's words: "When the smoke of Cape Willingham's shotgun cleared away . . . a new situation was revealed; the law had come to Tascosa; one conformed or faced the larger consequences."[46]

Armstrong's contributions to Tascosa were generally far less dramatic. The family contributed to the civilizing of the town by working actively for county status for Oldham county, singing in the church choir, sewing up pistol-whipped cowboys, and burying the dead with Christian services. Like most men of energy on the plains, Armstrong tried ranching when cattle became profitable. Times turned against him, and after five years of drought he found ranching "ran pretty low." At one point he sued the XIT Ranch because the Texas ticks brought in by its South Texas cattle decimated the small herds around Tascosa. It was a losing effort. In 1892 he moved to Oklahoma Territory, settled on the Washita River, built a house, and "broke some land." Things didn't seem to improve much. Life was as hard in Oklahoma as it had been in Texas.

Armstrong was a teetotaler and a Methodist who stood for a personal code of staunch integrity and high moral principles. When his wife became ill, he worried about finding money to pay for treatment. "We'll just do without the doctor and medicine," she said. "They never done me any good anyway." "So," Marion wrote, "we just made up our minds to do without them and have done so ever since." The same kind of rugged perseverance marked his later life when the depredations of "bad men—red and white," strongly suggested they ought to quit the country. Marion wrote: "This was a thing that I had never done, having been raised on the frontier. We could hardly expect to quit. The more I talked the more determined I became to carry on." His life was one of trial and tribulation, with few material rewards, yet he and his family can be counted among those stalwart citizens, "hardened on the frontier, who knew all of its evils and hardships and yet stood for the advancement of law and civilization." [47]

Like Ben Haywood, J. J. Long came to P. G. Reynolds' service with an abundance of practical experience as a teamster, except that in his case it was on the frontier. In other respects he was typical. He was young, twenty-five years of age, and he remained on the job only briefly before seeking more lucrative and exciting employment.

J. J. ("Johnnie") Long was born in Pennsylvania on November 2, 1851, the oldest of several children. When he was thirteen, his father died, leaving him as the main support for mother and children. The next year, the family moved to Kansas. When he was twenty-one, he was employed by the U.S. Army at Fort Leavenworth as a teamster and was sent to Fort Dodge, where he joined George A. Custer's punitive expedition to the Yellowstone in 1873, driving a four-mule hitch more than one thousand five hundred miles. The following year, he participated in the Red River War. As in the previous expedition, Long drove a team of mules as part of a large supply-wagon train. The outcome of the campaign depended upon the army's bringing constant pressure on the scattered but highly mobile Indian forces, who knew the terrain thoroughly. Without supplies for men and horses, the army could not remain in the field. With each engagement carrying the troops farther and farther from their bases at Fort Sill and Camp Supply, the ability of the supply trains to reach rendezvous points was crucial.[48]

Heading the first expedition, which formed at Fort Dodge but quickly moved to Camp Supply, was Brevet General Nelson A. Miles, colonel of the Fifty Infantry. What Miles lacked in tact and social graces, he made up in "vaulting ambition." He understood that on the frontier the only path to rank and fame lay in killing Indians, and he resolved to do just that. Miles's troops were part of a five-pronged attack converging on the headwaters of the Red, the army being determined to chastize the Indians and drive them back to the reservation. Miles and his scouts engaged the hostiles at various points and finally met a major contingent at Tulé Canyon on the edge of the Stakes Plains. The skirmish involved some four hundred Indians, who were convincingly routed. Miles's troops pursued the scattered bands into that barren expanse of land known as Llano Estacado. The Indians covered their retreat by burning the prairie and scattering all game before them. Miles was more than a match for this kind of warfare, and he drove his troops to the point of exhaustion in order to keep pressure on the warriors.[49]

With his supplies nearly depleted, Miles sent the supply-wagon train, under the command of Captain Wyllys Lyman, back to Oasis Creek, where a supply depot was supposed to be located. Lyman found no depot and hurried on toward Commission Creek, where he met the tardy civilian supply train. As it moved south as quickly as possible to rendezvous with Miles, the train was attacked on September 9, 1874 by some four hundred Kiowas and Comanches. The resulting fight, known as the Battle of Lyman's Wagon Train, "was the most prolonged Indian battle in Panhandle history and one of the most violent." It began as a running fight, with the train under sporadic fire from the Indians, who, however, kept considerable distance between themselves and the troopers' guns. The dozen cavalrymen escorting the train were able to keep the hostiles at long range for some eighteen or twenty miles. After the train, with considerable difficulty, had successfully negotiated the steep ravines of Gageby Creek, the Indians rushed the wagons en masse. Lyman had no choice but to stand and fight. To young Long it seemed they were being attacked by a multitude. "As they made the first rush," he wrote, "the soldiers fired into them and they dropped back. There were over four hundred of them, but it seemed to me there were one thousand." After the first repulse, the Kiowas and Comanches settled into a siege that lasted until September 14, with the issue always in doubt. The teamsters fought alongside the troopers and suffered their fair share of casualties.[50]

Long's remembrance of the siege was one of personal distress and individual bravery:

> We parked the wagons up close for a protection, but by the time we had the strings drawn up forty mules had been killed and wounded. We had thirty-six mule teams and about seventy soldiers besides the cavalry, about a hundred in all. We took our spades and dug trenches that night and we stayed in them in the day time. We had no water and had to lie there all the day in the sun. We could make no fire to cook, but we had plenty of bacon and hardtack. By the second night we had gotten pretty desperate, not having had any water at all. One of the boys happened to be in his wagon and opening boxes of canned tomatoes. In those days the canned "tomatoes" were mostly juice, so we dumped them out and everybody drank the juice and likely that was the only thing that saved us. At this time I was twenty-three years old. (1874). We saw the Indians had begun to leave, and Smalsky, [William F. Schmalsle] a scout, slipped out of camp at twelve or one o'clock and made a run through the Indian lines and went back to Fort Supply for help.

Schmalsle's daring, Lyman's initiative, and the Indians' lack of persistence saved the train from further damage. Shortly after the Indians left, Miles command made contact. His troops were as delighted to see the supply train as Lyman's men were to find them. Lyman's civilian scout J. J. Marshall reported: "The men were out of rations and the sight of the supply train had the effect to revive their drooping spirits wonderfully."[51]

Although far from meeting Miles's early boast that he would sweep the Indians before him like a housewife's broom, the strategy of the campaign was beginning to pay off. The Indians, unaware of his presence, were being driven toward Colonel Ranald S. Mackenzie's force. Mackenzie was less ambitious than Miles, but his troops had been given such harsh and raw discipline that they responded to his aggressive pursuit of the Indians with courage and tenacity. Learning of a large encampment of Indians in Palo Duro

Canyon, Mackenzie attacked and destroyed the base, killing more than a thousand horses in the process. Without food, lodging, and horses, the Indians had little choice but to retreat and try to lose the troops in the vastness of the Staked Plains. Mackenzie relentlessly pursued the scattered bands from water hole to water hole across the open prairie with persistence equal to that of Miles. The summer-long drought that had plagued the military operation turned into a nightmare of torrential rains in the fall and unseasonably early snow and ice storms as winter came on in late November and December. The wrinkled-hand chase, so called because the skin of the men in the field was always soaked, brought intense misery to the troops and even more suffering to the harassed Indians. Captain Robert G. Carter's log entry for December 16 indicates something of the troops' hardships:

Remained in camp, rain last night and snow this day. The storm lasted three days and the command suffered greatly. Some of the horses were frozen to death, due to their weak condition. Many men were nearly barefoot. . . . The wagons, after a terrible trip over the soaked prairie, reached the command this day (15th) at dark, with supplies and forage for the half-frozen and starving horses. [52]

The supply wagons were kept in motion, some going back empty for supplies and others returning loaded.

The physical demand of this type of warfare was far more taxing on both Indians and troopers than the occasional skirmish. In Long's words:

We had been nine days on three days' rations, and had not been able to get any buffalo meat because the Indians had run the buffalo away from us. We made no more campaigns but just did a little scouting after this. Before Christmas we went back to Adobe Walls and started back to Antelope Creek. Christmas Eve it has rained a little and begun to snow, so we laid over Christmas day and the next day we went on by the Palo Duro. We struck the Indians in what was their winter camp, I suppose, and they pulled out down the Red River and across Greer County and went in south to the Wichita Mountains. We went after them, though it was in zero weather. That winter was very disagreeable. We had to walk, for we would have frozen on the mules. One time we had to walk forty miles before we could find a place to camp.

The Palo Duro engagement and the sweep that followed ended the Red River War.[53]

Long made one more major expedition in 1878: against the Utes in Colorado. In between these two ventures, he hauled cottonwood logs for constructing corrals and buildings at Fort Elliott. For a year, including the winter of 1876–77, he drove a four-mule team on the mail line between Camp Supply and Fort Elliott. After his Indian Wars experience, a coach and four might appear anticlimatic. It was not. His army experience on the open plains, particularly learning to cope with the elements, proved useful and necessary training for the new job. As he explained it:

We took three days to go and three days to return, camping the first night on the Canadian, the next night on Wolf Creek, and reaching camp Supply the third night. We made about thirty-three miles a day out on the prairie, and knew the road so well we would not lose the trail even in blinding snowstorms. We had our worst place in crossing the Canadian when it was frozen over. We would have to get out and cut the ice before we could cross, then we would have to build a fire to dry out our frozen clothing. I had two buffalo robes, and we would sit on one with the fur side up and put the other over us and sit there fairly well protected until we were ready to go on. We made the round trip every week. . . .[54]

His association with Fort Elliott led him to his next job: bartender at the Mint Saloon in Mobeetie. The saloon business in the wide-open barracks town was a lucrative one. After accumulating some capital, Long joined in a partnership in a nearby mercantile store. Mobeetie became his lifelong home, and there followed a succession of newer stores and other enterprises. In his first store he had set up a bank merely by holding money in his vault and making personal loans as a matter of convenience for his customers. Eventually, this practice expanded into the First State Bank of Mobeetie, with J. J. as its first president. He operated a store in Miami and built and operated the first cotton gin in that part of the Panhandle. Long married Mary Richardson, daughter of a pioneer buffalo hunter, and raised a family in the town. His greatest service, next to encouraging farmers to plant cotton, was rendered in 1898 when a tornado destroyed much of Mobeetie. Largely through his influence, some of the people stayed to rebuild. Unfortunately, it was a lost cause because the town continued to dwindle. Long remained steadfast, however, until his death in 1925, four years before the Panhandle and Santa Fe Railroad built a line two miles north, which spelled the old town's demise.[55]

Long was quiet and unassuming by nature and kept his own counsel. As Wheeler County's first treasurer, he continued in that capacity for years. A friend wrote that although Long was a faithful Republican, "during his entire tenure of office there probably was not three people in the county who knew his politics." He rarely talked of his early exploits but did much to preserve the memory of pioneer days. He was, as F. Newton Reynolds put it, "one of the physical landmarks of Old Mobeetie." A close friend of Billy Dixon since the days of the Red River War, Mrs. Olive Dixon, Billy's wife, paid Long her highest tribute: "An earlier generation had its Colonial heroes; the present has its plainsmen."[56]

As important but minor cogs in the wagon-road economy, these three representative men—Haywood, Armstrong, and Long—made their major contributions to the Region after their stage-driving days. All three had come to the prairie as young men without material resources and with limited education. Driving the coach was only a temporary job while they explored other possibilities. Although each found a different opportunity, all stayed through the transitional period. One of the important byproducts of the stagecoach operation was its direct contribution to the positive settlement of the Region with men who stayed to develop the land as permanent settlers.

There were, of course, negative contributors, people who did not conform to the pattern of stable respectability represented by the three Reynolds drivers. What did the lynched Henry Newton Brown, the notorious bad man, contribute, save the negative example of his taking off? Maybe only a small crumb—but still something of a frontier morality play to be discussed and analyzed in bar and parlor alike. The law-abiding citizens of Caldwell felt pity for his bride and took some consolation in Brown's instant death, which spared him the degradation of hanging. The *Caldwell Journal* spelled out the moral of the tale in the closing lines of the editor's account of the startling news from Medicine Lodge:

FINALE.

There was another heavy sound,
A hush and then a groan,
And darkness swept across the sky,
The work of death was done.

The tragic death of the robbers has already been told. That it was just, all know; that was a terrible penalty for their crime, visited on them by the iron hand of judge lynch, all admit. There have been cases before where it was surely justifiable and there will be others to come. The near relations which two of the principals bore to the citizens of this city made it doubly horrible. They had made many warm friends in this city, and while here had made two as good officers as the city has ever had. They had been given credit for honor and bravery, and while here no man can say, and say truthfully, that they had not been worthy this trust. That they have brought disgrace on the city, no one can help; and that they met their just deserts, all rejoice. But let the mantle of charity fall over their memory, and like the tear of the repentant sinner which the peri brought to the gates of heaven, let it obliterate them as it did the sins of the penitent, blot them out from existence, and let them be judged by the Higher Court where we are taught to believe that all shall receive justice. Let them fall into the past as beings that are gone and forgotten, and while the dark cloud that obscures the final ending is rent by a few rays of golden light, let no rude hand be stretched passionately forth to close forever from sight those redeeming glimmerings.[57]

Since little is known of most of the other short-term drivers, it is difficult to assess their total contribution. Other than maintaining schedules and filling the contractual agreements of the stage lines, as important as these tasks were, the ordinary work a day stage driver left few marks on the history of the Region. If the drivers were heroes, they are largely unsung. For a brief time they made the wheels of one essential part of the wagon-road economy turn with regularity and efficiency. As was true of other men performing necessary but mundane jobs, the drivers helped in transforming the raw prairie into settled and productive communities.

9. Way Stations and the People Who Ran Them: Guideposts Marking the Trails

THE landmarks used in describing trails were either the creeks and river crossings or the way stations. Occasionally, natural land formations, such as Mount Jesus or Devil's Gap on the Military Road, were mentioned as points of reference, but the way stations were the more familiar and accepted guideposts for identifying routes and marking distances. As they developed in the 1870s and 1880s in the Dodge City–Panhandle Region, way stations were variously called stage stations or stands, inns, road ranches,[1] way stations, posts, stores, and, in one instance, stockades. Each term described a slightly different function, although all performed a number of common services. Stations varied widely in size and operational style. Some were owned by stage companies, but most were independently established with the expectation of making a profit, that is, a living, for the owners. If the record of rapid operator turnover is any indication, it would appear that few succeeded in accomplishing that objective. It is, of course, impossible to account for all the stations on the trails at this late date. They came into existence with little public notice and were abandoned with even less. Caterers to the stage coach and freighters on the prairie trails were no more permanent than good restaurants on a modern highway, but while they existed they were an important part of the transportational system, contributing to the settlement and stability of the Region.

In spite of their diversity, way stations shared certain common characteristics. First, few were established exclusively to capture the trade generated by the trails, and fewer still were built by the stage companies. This is apparently somewhat unusual in the trail system in the West, although it was typical of the early post roads in the East. Most of the western stage companies outside the Region established their own stations or purchased facilities already established in military forts, towns, and cities along the route and staffed them with company agents. The most notable exception to the rule was Ben Holladay, who cared little for passenger comfort and did not own or supervise any way stations. John Butterfield; Russell, Majors and Waddell; and the Leavenworth and Pike's Peak Express, on the other hand, built and operated with their own agents stage stations that were spaced to correspond with one day's travel or the relay change of teams. The stage lines in Texas depended heavily on military forts, building their own facilities within protection of the walls. Of the twelve stops on the Jackass Line between San Diego and San Antonio, eight were forts. Independent owners who established stations on other trails without the support of the stage lines built them specifically to service the stage business. Donald F. Danker found the proprietors of road ranches in neighboring Nebraska "a hardy and brave group" who moved far in advance of settlement for the specific purpose of capturing the "profit from overland trade."[2]

On the trails in the Dodge City–Panhandle Region, the location of way stations was in many instances accidental. There were few independent operators, such as Matt Hutchinson, who determined a road ranch's location in cooperation with stage owners. Joe Plummer and Ed Jones were unique in that they staked a trail to their trading post, a trail later used by other freighters and stage lines. Most station operators, however, simply found themselves at a convenient river or creek crossing or about the right distance from another road ranch on the trail. The Cators at Zulu, the first Hutchinson road ranch in Meade County, and O. D. Lemert at Crooked Creek just happened to settle where the freighters or stages needed service or at a usable crossing. Since distances between stops for the stage or freighters varied from fifteen to forty miles, luck or simple availability seemed to determine where some road ranches would become operative. The Cators, Jim Springer on the Canadian, and Jack Hardesty on the Tascosa Trail are examples of being about the right distance from the nearest competitors or being an established landmark on the trail.

The second condition on the Region's trails was that few road ranches could survive on trail business alone; some diversification was required. The Hutchinson brothers on the Jones and Plummer Trail pursued a variety of enterprises ranging from sugar manufacturing to sheep raising. The operator at Little Blue Station in Moore County, Texas was that county's first farmer. Silas Maley also tried farming on the Bluff Creek bottoms, as did John and George Gerlach on the Canadian. Jim Springer sold whiskey and expertly extracted cash from card-playing troopers at Fort Elliott.

On the other hand, it was not advisable to attempt to couple the station with some major activity, such as ranching. When an over ambitious operator attempted to continue two or more major enterprises, one of two things happened: the other enterprise suffered or the road-ranch service was abandoned. This was a hard lesson for most owners to learn because they first saw the way station as an opportunity to gain a little ready cash while continuing their major interest, whatever that might be. After the brief buffalo-hunting phase, the most attractive side line for station operators was the cattle business. Typical of those who attempted ranching were Hoodoo Brown, who went broke, and Dave Mackey at Odee and Mose Hayes at the Springer Ranch, who gave up catering to travelers to concentrate on cattle. Jim Cator continued multiple operations, including ranching, longer than most, but even he was unable to develop the large herds that his neighbors acquired as long as he maintained a way station.

The third requirement for way-station success was some connection with a mail contractor as postmaster, stage attendant, or innkeeper for stage passengers. While it is true that an astonishing number of freight wagons rumbled over the trails and each year the number of nonmilitary travelers increased, the purchases these itinerants made would not have sustained a road-ranch family. Such income from food and forage was too erratic and inconsequential to guarantee a profit. Freighters generally carried their own provisions, as did the stage drivers. "I carried most of my grub with me" is not an unusual entry in travel accounts and journals. The mail contractor's business was certain; whether triweekly or daily, the income could be depended upon, come fair weather or foul. Whatever added goods and services were sold to travelers, freighters, or incoming settlers became pure gravy, to use a western term, or marginal efficient profits, to use an economic one. The life of a station that was dependent on local sales and did not cater to mail contractors was usually brief; few were able to locate at points suitable to serve the early buffalo hunters, then the cattlemen, and still later the grangers. Way stations in towns were faced with the same problem of meeting the changing needs of a varied clientele. Of the three towns created by the buffalo trade in the Panhandle, only Beaver survived to serve both ranchers and farmers later.

Finally, the survival of all way stations, as was also true of towns, was ultimately determined by the railroads. P. G. Reynolds' stables and agent at Appleton were forced to move down the road a mile and a half to newly platted Minneola when the Rock Island bypassed the first town. When the Chicago, Nebraska, Kansas and Southwestern Railroad failed to materialize in Wilburn, Kansas, the Hutchinson Road Ranche was doomed. In the Dodge City–Panhandle Region, the railroad was king and dictator.

In theory, at least, the stage stations were there to look after the comfort of passengers and ensure the efficient operation of the stage line. Most did, although they were rarely a gourmand's delight or a fastidious sleeper's idea of cozy comfort. Sleeping accommodations were cramped, and the variety of food limited. Few were praised, as was the Hutchinson Road Ranche, for the quality of meals or known, as was the Springer Ranch for Mrs. Mose Hayes' berry pies. Neither were the road ranches as squalid and dirty as those described on Ben Holladay's line, although Old Pete's Place at Bluff Creek and Dugan's Store on the Mulberry were vermin ridden and unattractive. The cost was also far more reasonable; where a Holladay passenger could expect to be charged one dollar and fifty cents for his dinner and Bayard Taylor complained that he paid "a square price of one dollar" for "less than a square meal" in Colorado, P. G. Reynolds advertised meals on his line at fifty cents.[3]

The danger to life and limb of the passenger, according to David

Nevin, "was real enough; and so was the damage done to digestive tracts by Western food."[4] Some of the personal accounts of way-station conditions in the Dodge City–Panhandle Region would support Nevin's contention. Easterners, such as Frank Healy's mother, found stage travel very unpleasant:

> I made the journey . . . as far as Dodge. There I was met by Harry Chaffin, a young man from near Boston but one of the so-called "cowboys." He accompanied me to the ranch, an eighty-mile drive. The first day we drove in a stage to Meade, Kansas. Literally there wasn't a single thing to be seen but stretches of prairie. No homes for miles and miles. We took dinner at Fowler and I can see now the table as it looked—boiled eggs cold, bread, no butter, mush and more flies than I would ever have believed could have been bred if I hadn't seen them. A red faced one-armed man shook over the table a stick to which had been tied strips of pink paper. It all made an indelible impression on my mind, which was wide open just waiting for impressions.[5]

Orrin Burright, who worked for the Chain C's Ranch, recalled the discomfort of a stop at the Mulberry crossing just south of Dodge City. It was an important roach ranch, not only because of the possible difficulty of crossing the creek, but also because the Adobe Walls Trail branched off from the Jones and Plummer Trail there and the facilities were used by many freighters and trail-herd cowboys. A. H. Dugan, Ham Bell's father-in-law, ran Dugan's Store with a tight fist. According to Burright, he "had a gyp deal going," since he charged ten cents a bucket for water regardless of how much was used. But it was a lunch of cheese and soda crackers inside the store that brought Burright's group to grief. They sat on an old sofa to eat and spent a little extra time there to give the horses a rest before continuing on down the trail:

> During the afternoon I had begun to feel just like I felt when I slid down a strawstack as a child . . . I literally itched all over as though I had wheat beards under my clothes. It got so bad neither of us could sleep so we got up early the next morning and made a thorough investigation by first rolling down our socks. It didn't take us long to find out the trouble. But it surprised us—it was something I had heard about but I hadn't experienced, although I had heard the cowhands talk about it, and of course, my father had known the sensation when he was in the army. Graybacks were operating on us!
> . . . We had 'em! So we sat down before breakfast and took a hunt. We

Freighting outfit, early 1880s, headed for the C.C.C. ranch in Beaver County, Oklahoma. Taken in front of Charley Sumers store in Liberal, Kansas. On the back of the photograph is written: "Note the Peeler on the wheeler mule and the old gray mare tied to the rear wagon. This old mare was staked out at night with bell on. The mules were turned loose but would never stray far from the bell mare." Courtesy Arthur N. Howe, Maize, Kansas.

picked off 81 of them. Some of these cowhands had told us that they had
so many of them that they knew graybacks didn't have to be married
to have large families because if just one was left to prowl on a man
there would be more lice. Since we got 81 of them, I guess we got them
all. . . .[6]

Others had similar experiences. Mrs. W. W. Owens told of her first encounter with fleas on the trip to her new home in the Panhandle:

The next day we drove 30 miles to the Cimmarron. There was a man
running an Inn in two rooms. Another traveler was spending the night
there. We had the room where the cook stove was—also the fleas—
millions of them—the first fleas I had ever met in my life. When we went
into the house the Innkeeper spread a blanket on the floor, I thought for
warmth, but it was to keep the fleas off of us. We went to bed, but not for
long as the fleas nearly ate us up. We had made a bed on the table for the
baby. About four o'clock we shook our blankets, rolled up our bedding and
woke the man telling him we had to get an early start.[7]

Newcomers, especially those accustomed to eastern hotels and
cafés, found the road ranches disappointing. Fred Tracy, fresh from
Illinois on his first coach ride, didn't recognize one when he saw it.
He recalled his naïveté with considerable amusement:

I said "what will we do for dinner" and he [the stage driver] replied that
we would eat at the Mulberry Ranch. . . . I thought a ranch would be a big
white building with a porch all the way around and some cowboys loafing
on the porch. Great was my surprise when I asked one of the freighters
where the Mulberry Ranch was and he pointed to a sod building a short
distance away. I walked up to the house and found it to consist of two
rooms, both with dirt floors. In one room a woman was cooking dinner and
in the other room some stakes had been driven into the dirt floor and
boards laid on top to form a crude bar. There was a table with four chairs
around it and on the shelf behind the bar were several bottles of whiskey.

The accommodation the next night in the town of Appleton, although called a hotel, was no more elegant than the Mulberry
soddy:

The hotel was a two-story frame building perhaps twenty feet wide,
with weather-boarding on the outside and the naked studding showing on
the inside. On the upper floor some sheets or other curtains had been
stretched across, dividing the space into a number of rooms. Another
storm came up that night and the building just weaved and groaned. I expected it to fall down any minute so I didn't sleep much.[8]

Oliver Nelson was nineteen in 1885 when he was put in charge of a station in Indian Territory called Buzzard's Roost. His pride in converting the dirt-floored cabin to a livable habitation reveals how crude and uncomfortable the station must have been for previous passengers, as well as how odd it must have looked to sophisticated travelers, even after Nelson had completed his redecoration:

My job was to keep house and have meals for the drivers and passengers. I cleaned up the cabin—which needed it bad. It had three rooms, strung end to end, each with an outside door in the east. The north one had the cook stove. It had a west door, which was seldom used; so I fastened it shut, drove in several nails, and hung up some extra ovens and things and covered them with bran sacks. We ate in the middle room, and my cot was in one corner. (Everything was homemade; there was no furniture out there). The south room was the "parlor" where passengers waited and people came after their mail; also the driver slept there. It was about twenty feet long; had a weak ridge pole propped by a post in the center—later two side props were put in about three feet each way from the center prop.

When winter came, the frame room was about as cold inside as out. But I caulked up the cracks with anything I could get, and calcimined with bran sacks, then papered on that with newspapers. I got a good many advertising pictures through the mail, so I placed the choice ones in groups on the wall. Besides this the company had printed orders tacked up all around. It looked quite neat. Ladies passing through would ask where my wife was. I would tell them, "I'm alone." Then they would say, "Oh, the family has just moved out?" "No." "Well, who fixed this place up?"[9]

Whether they had newspapered walls or were flea infested soddies, the way stations were not modeled after the Dodge House. There was no model. Each was in its own way an interesting combination of improvisation and raw efficiency, and yet each was, in a real measure, a reflection of the Region. Located by chance or by geographic convenience for the needs of a mail contractor and not passengers, the stations served until the railroads replaced them and the stage lines with more orderly accommodations.

A brief sampling of specific stations and their operators—case studies, if you will—confirms these generalizations. Each station has its own story of its owner's success or failure, success being more than matched by failure. None failed more completely than Madison P. ("Matt") and Sallie Doores Hutchinson.

Madison Philips ("Matt") Hutchinson (1858–?), road rancher on the Jones and Plummer Trail and hotel owner at Wilburn, Kansas. Courtesy C. Robert Haywood, Topeka, Kansas.

Matt Hutchinson was the son of Elijah Hutchinson of Crab Orchard, Kentucky. Crab Orchard held two historical distinctions: it was a tourist center because of the purported health benefits of its chalybeate spring, and it was an early and important way station on the old Wilderness Road. There is no evidence that the Hutchinsons had ever been connected with either, which might have inclined them to become road ranchers. Since 1812 the family had been farmers of some prominence in the area.[10]

In 1879 the economic pressures of limited land and a rapidly expanding clan, forced Elijah to seek new opportunities. That year, with even more careful planning than the elder Cator had given, the oldest Hutchinson son was sent to Kansas to explore the possibilities of land there. He apparently surveyed sites in both eastern and western Kansas before finding land to his liking in Meade County. Returning to Kentucky, he brought back the patriarch to confirm his judgment. In March 1880 the family moved west. At that point it consisted of three married sons (Humphrey, Willie, and Matt), their families, and Martha, the youngest child, an unmarried daughter who joined them a few months later. With them was a longtime hired hand, Bill McCollough, who was one of the first, if not the first, black men to reside in that part of Kansas. All the Hutchinsons took homesteads north of present-day Fowler on the edge of the sand hills near Crooked Creek and on or near the Jones and Plummer Trail. Elijah's homestead was the family headquarters.[11]

Although they eventually engaged in a variety of ventures—freighting, hauling bones, farming, and sugar-cane refining—their major business was raising sheep. Since the trail passed near his sod house, Elijah turned it into a road ranch. A buffalo head was mounted on the barn and became the identifying symbol for the ranch. The contact with freighters and travelers dispelled the loneliness, which could be oppressive on the prairie, and there was even an occasional flair of excitement. For instance, a somewhat inebriated and lovelorn traveler found the husband away from a claim just south of Dodge City and made "certain indecent and insulting proposals" to the lady of the house. When the husband returned and found out about it, he pursued the cad and caught him at the Hutchinson Road Ranche, where he "administered an old fashioned pounding, much to the delight and edification of all assembled."[12]

Elijah's homestead seemed a fortuitous choice, with easy access to water, varied soil, and the immediate commercial opportunity of serving drovers and travelers. Homesteaders were to find that the major obstacle in establishing a claim and surviving was the need for immediate income to tide them over the first year until crops could be produced. The road ranch provided such support with limited but certain funds. The move from the restrictions of Kentucky seemed to be paying off, but the early rewards were transitory. Within a few months, Elijah's health broke; in the words of his obituary, "the flower upon the prairie had scarcely wilted" before he was stricken with "a languishing disease." He remained incapacitated until his death in early fall 1887. But long before the father was buried the family had split into independent operating units that continually made the wrong decisions when choices were presented. Not the least of these was Matt and Sallie Hutchinson's decision to continue operating a road ranch.[13]

With the platting and settlement of Fowler in 1884, the original road ranch was poorly located, being too close to the new and rapidly growing trade center. At that point, Matt made the first of several unfortunate decisions; rather than move to Fowler, he relocated the road ranch some eight miles north of Elijah's homestead, labeling it the M. P. Hutchinson Road Ranche. For the moment it was a good choice, being "midway between Fowler and Dodge on the trail from Dodge to Tascosa, Texas." Matt worked out an arrangement with Cal Ferguson, the stage operator, to use the M. P. Hutchinson Road Ranche as his first stop after leaving Dodge. Therefore, the essential for success, the connection to the mail and stage business, was made. It was a cardinal requirement, but it did not necessarily ensure success.

The establishment of Wilburn in February 1885 made the new location no more satisfactory than Elijah's old place had been. Since each move was costly, Matt held out against pressures to change. As late as July 1886 he was reassuring the people of Fowler that he would not move to the new rival, Wilburn, and that Ferguson would continue to use his road ranch as the only stop between Dodge City and Fowler. He even went to the expense of advertising the road ranch, putting an announcement in the Wilburn newspaper to call attention to the operation. This was nearly one of a kind. Only one other road ranch in the area ever formally advertised its availability:

Ho Travelers.
For the best
Accommodation
for yourselves & teams, stop at
M. P. Hutchinson's
Road Ranche
Mid-way between FOWLER *&*
DODGE, *on the trail*
from Dodge to
Tascosa Ter.
TERMS MODERATE[14]

All his protestations of remaining out of Wilburn went for naught when P. G. Reynolds became involved. In April 1886 a fire in a house next to Ferguson's stable ignited the whole block, and much of his stock, coaches, and feed was lost. P. G. bought the remaining assets and took over the mail route on the Jones and Plummer Trail. The new stage proprietor offered an even better arrangement for Matt, provided Matt moved his facilities to Wilburn. If he would build a hotel and livery there, P. G. agreed to make Wilburn his first station out of Dodge City and to use it as a meal stop rather than Fowler, where the noon meal had been served in the past. It seemed too good a deal to pass up. On August 18, 1886, Matt took over the Wilburn House, a newly erected hotel, and advertised "Good Board and Lodging at a Reasonable Price"—to be exact, room and board for one dollar and fifty cents a day. Selling the old road ranch for nine hundred dollars, Matt and Sallie began enlarging the Wilburn House in anticipation of a growing business. Matt believed that managing the booming town's only hotel and restaurant would give him the diversification his old road ranch had lacked. It was now truly a joint effort, with Sallie handling more and more of the business. The Hutchinsons were a welcome addition to Wilburn, and the newspaper editor, who took up lodging at the Wilburn House, spoke glowingly of Sallie's cooking and found her husband to be "a jolly fellow."[15]

P. G.'s decision to provide his passengers with a meal and rest in Wilburn brought into the operation Matt's brother, Willie Hutchinson, and others in the community. Although he was a trustee for Fowler Township, Willie agreed to supply the livery part of the Reynolds agreement and began construction of a large livery and feed storage barn in November 1886. Local farmers were contracted to supply hay for the stage horses. P. G.'s stage was making a major contribution to the prosperity of Wilburn.[16]

Midwinter doldrums apparently set in, or perhaps Matt's weakness for drink got out of hand; at any rate, in December he was off to Colorado in search of a tree claim, while Sallie remained at the Wilburn House as proprietress and cook. In spring the Hutchinsons sold the hotel to Peter Kilts, who took over the management. P. G. must have assumed that his contract with the Hutchinsons was ended, for he began building his own stables. The other Hutchinson brother was left regretting his change of allegiance from

Fowler. Although it was not then apparent, all three—Matt, Willie and P. G.—had backed the wrong town. In the summer of 1887, Wilburn reached its peak. The city government was in full force, business was brisk, and new settlers were filling the surrounding claims.[17]

The dream of metropolitan grandeur expressed by the *Wilburn Argus* editor ended on January 31, 1888 when the Rock Island Railroad reached Fowler. Although Wilburn did not disappear overnight, it gradually faded as businesses moved, sometimes literally hauling buildings across the prairie to neighboring farms or to Fowler. The available train service for mail and passengers in Fowler minimized the need for a daily stage or hotel in that part of Ford County. The railroad once again dictated who would survive; Wilburn and P. G.'s stage line were among the casualties.[18]

A somewhat more successful venture was that of George W. ("Hoodoo") Brown in Meade County, Kansas, although he, too, left the business owing money. Brown came by his odd nickname, which was universally used to distinguish him from the dozens of other Browns, secondhand. Hyman G. Neill (sometimes O'Neill) used the name *Hoodo Brown* as one of his aliases. Neill was described by the Parsons, Kansas press as being "in the western wilds for many years, and for a long time was one of the worst class of low gamblers. A recital of the many terrible affairs with which he has been connected in this country would make a whole book of horribles." George W. Brown was tagged with the moniker just as thousands of little boys who had the surname *James* were known until adulthood, and sometimes forever, as Jesse. Two Hoodoo Browns on the frontier at the same time was bound to cause confusion. Even the old-timers got them mixed; for instance, J. Phelps White, who worked for the Littlefield outfit in the Panhandle, reported years later that George W. was the same as Neill. George W. Brown did not need to borrow adventures or rugged characteristics because his own life was exciting enough. Although as a road rancher he was in the path of Dull Knife's Raid, broke a leg in a fall from a horse, survived the western Kansas elements, and was involved in killing a man on his own, his life at the way station seems almost anticlimactic.[19]

George W. Brown was born in Newton County, Missouri in

1847. After moving to Barry County, his father was forced to take the family to Illinois because of the threats he received as a Union man. When war came, young George, seventeen, joined the Union Army in December 1863 as a member of Company E, Third Regiment, Illinois Cavalry, bringing his own horse to battle. He saw considerable action, spent time in the army hospital, and at the end of the war fought Indians in Dakota. He was mustered out at Fort Snelling, Minnesota on October 18, 1865. In 1868 he began drifting west, working for Joseph G. McCoy at Abilene, freighting with ox teams, trail-herding cattle into Colorado, serving as an army scout, cutting timber for railroad ties, buying buffalo hides. He ended that phase of his career hunting buffalo, first to supply meat for army posts and later for the hides. Somewhere in all this activity he found time to marry Sallie Lemon in 1867 and to operate a saloon in Granada and another at Dodge City, where, he said, the Arkansas River made it as handy to cut his whiskey with water as for the Texas men to water their cattle before selling them. He believed the first killing in a Dodge City saloon was in his place. By 1879, about all that was left in the way of plains ventures that Brown had not tried were road ranching, cattle ranching, farming, and managing a store. During the next eleven years, he did all of them.[20]

His account of how he got into road ranching is unusual in that he saw commercial possibilities in an established trail and let his experience with freighting determine where he would set up his store:

One time while I was freighting I fell in with another old freighter by the name of Lewis. He and I traveled together till I got to Dodge City. Two nights before the night we got to Dodge City we camped on Crooked Creek at a place called "The Wells," about half a mile north of the salt well, but the salt well was not there at that time. . . . the night Lewis and I camped there was a bitter cold night, and we had nothing much to burn, and we suffered considerable from the cold. I said to Mr. Lewis, "It's a wonder that someone has not a road ranch here." I thought over that considerable and made up my mind to start one there myself. So I hired a man, went down there and built a sod house for my storehouse. Then I built another one for my family. Then I went down to George S. Emerson's store in Dodge City and told him I had a ranch built down at the Wells on the Jones and Plummer Trail and I'd like to get a bill of goods, but I had no money. George says, "Buy as many as you want and pay me when you can." Mr. Emerson knew what I wanted better than I knew myself, as he had been furnishing the other road ranches with their goods on the road that ran by Ashland to Camp Supply. I moved with my family sometime in August, 1880. [21]

Brown's road ranch has been described by several contemporaries who used it. The *Dodge City Ford County Globe* noted its establishment by briefly indicating that "food and lodging can be had for man or beast." On the other hand, a visit there was excitement and a break from the loneliness of the prairie for Carrie Schmoker Anshutz, whose parents homesteaded in Meade County in April 1879:

> Once every two weeks we drove to the settlement for the mail and those were red letter days for me. There were no roads. We drove across the valley to the Jones and Plummer Trail to the "Hoodoo" Brown Road Ranch then just built, two low sod buildings, one for a dwelling and the other for a store in which groceries, whiskey and tobacco were kept. [22]

Sheriff George T. Hinkle of Dodge City found it a refuge but little more, certainly not to be anticipated as Carrie Schmoker had. "We made 41 miles to Hoodo Brown's by 5 p.m.," he said. "Brown's is the metropolis of Meade County, its inhabitants consist of Mr. and Mrs. B., a crazy Dutch man and a hobbled bull calf." Hinkle and his traveling companion, George Anderson, pitched a tent near Hoodoo's soddy. When the snow changed to a blizzard, they moved to a half-completed adobe, and before the night was over they were huddled inside Brown's chicken house. [23]

Brown maintained a well-stocked store, offering flour, meal, bacon, dried fruits, gunpowder, guns, rope, harness, saddles, ox yokes, canned goods, spices, tobacco, sugar, tea, and, above all, liquor. George Hoover's retail establishment sold Brown whiskey by the barrel, beer by the case, and even a few gallons of wine. J. Philip White may have confused the two Hoodoos, but he did remember clearly that there were women (Mrs. Brown and her girls) and whiskey at the store. Brown also built corrals for oxen, mules, and horses. His customers were the mail contractors and freighters on the Jones and Plummer Trail and the cattlemen who occasionally brought a herd through or were traveling to Dodge on business. One such traveler recalled, with gratitude, Brown's service to him. Boss Neff, one of the Panhandle's earliest ranchers, discovered "a bunch of cattle" for sale at a very reasonable price when he stopped at Odee Station, but he didn't have the necessary fifty dollars to pay for them. The only man he knew in the country was Hoodoo, and he didn't know him very well. However, he rode on up the trail to Brown's road ranch and told Hoodoo of his problem. Brown gave him the money with no more security than the traditional handshake. "I returned the money," Neff recalled, "together with plenty of interest."[24]

On at least one occasion Hoodoo abandoned his road ranch and ran for cover. When Dull Knife and the Beautiful People made their desperate run for life and freedom across Kansas, Brown heard they had left the reservation and were headed for Meade County. He immediately moved his family to Dodge in spite of the jeers from some of his neighbors. The wisdom of his move was acknowledged later when three persons were killed in the vicinity, but, as he explained, he was more concerned about his family's safety than his own. With the Browns safe in town, Hoodoo took a wagon and for the modest sum of seven dollars went back down the Jones and Plummer Trail alone to the vicinity of Wilburn to pick up the body of John F. Tuttle's black cook, who had been killed and scalped. After the raid, Kansas settlers remained uneasy. The adjutant general of Kansas announced that he would distribute guns to any citizen militia that was organized. Meade County, particularly the Ohioians at Pearlette, took advantage of the offer. Under the captaincy of R. A. Milligan, who had Civil War service, Hoodoo and A. J. ("Captain") French were elected lieutenants. The militia's one and only drill ended in a ridiculous shambles. Later someone anonymously sent Milligan a tin sword and a paper cocked hat; he did not recall the defenders.[25]

Life on Crooked Creek was basically good to the Browns. It is true there were ups and downs, but according to his own account Hoodoo was doing well. Far from being dull, although isolated, new people were constantly stopping at the station, and there was time for an occasional nostalgic buffalo hunt. In November 1885, Hoodoo organized a small party of local people who had come to the plains after the buffalo disappeared. They found a few scruffy stragglers, which they killed with much enthusiasm and bored friend and stranger alike in the retelling. Hoodoo's last hunt was in the fall of 1886; it turned out to be a shabby travesty of the old glory days. Brown's family seemed to be prospering also. In July 1879, Mrs. Brown gave birth to twins. The family eventually moved from the soddy into far better living quarters in Meade Center. But tragedy, too, was to be a part of their lives: the only permanent mark Hoodoo left on the land is Graceland Cemetery, which he deeded to the Meade community and in which he buried his youngest daughter, Grace.[26]

Brown killed a man at his road ranch shortly before he left Kansas. It happened at night, and the circumstances are unclear. Brown claimed he was being ambushed by cattle thieves; local ranchers felt it was a grudge assassination of an employee to whom Brown owed money. Although the killing seemed not to affect Hoodoo's good reputation in Kansas, it did hang over his head until he was tried in Kingfisher, Oklahoma in 1890.[27]

Sometime in 1885 the mail contractor stopped using Brown's place as a stage station. The Meade Center Townsite Company purchased a site for a new town on July 9, 1885, about two miles west of Brown's ranch, and the town was officially platted March 24, 1886; however, the town was booming before these official actions were taken. One of the earliest campaigns of the civic-minded and aggressive newspaper editor, H. Wiltz Brown, was to have the route of the Jones and Plummer Trail shifted so that it would run down Meade Center's main street. The editor announced on May 6, 1886 that through the "good work of the PRESS-DEMOCRAT" the trail had been turned to pass through the town.[28]

Undoubtedly Hoodoo had realized earlier that the new town would take over his road-ranch functions. His had been a restless life, and it was a hard habit to break. In February 1886 he bought a section of land on the Canadian River in Texas, and in June he opened a clothing store on South Douglas Avenue in Beaver. Then, in partnership with H. Chaney, he bought a drugstore in Meade Center and decided to remain there. With new settlers arriving almost daily during the winter of 1886–87, Hoodoo began building Meade Center's first hotel. But in spite of his past connections with the stage line, it was not to be headquarters for P. G. Reynolds' operation.[29]

The Meade County boom was brief, the decline immediate and

devastating. Brown probably overextended his resources, counting on the high land prices as a cushion in case of need, but land values were the first to feel the decline. By 1890 the whole of western Kansas was in panic. In 1888, Meade County had a population of 4,561; this figure sank to 1,831 in 1891 and did not equal the 1888 population again until 1909. When Brown was forced to sell to cover his obligations, it was at 1890s prices. He moved to Oklahoma and spent his declining years there. Mrs. Brown died in 1902, and Hoodoo ended his days at the National Home for Disabled Soldiers in Leavenworth, Kansas.[30]

It might appear that Hoodoo was guilty of overdiversification, which dissipated his energies and capital, but he failed primarily because of location, the competition of the townsite speculators, and the decline of land prices. Much of his diversification came after he ceased to be a road rancher. Although Brown failed to establish himself in Kansas or keep the road ranch going until the end of the stagecoach era as others had done, he provided an important service through the early and toughest years of the frontier. His own declining years were marked by hardship, the delayed murder trial, and illness. The borrowed nickname seems to have been well chosen.

By far the most securely fortified way station on any of the trails was that built by A. G. ("Jim") Springer on Boggy Creek where it empties into the Canadian River. Springer had come west from New England and started ranching on the Arkansas River just across the bridge from Dodge City. In 1874 or 1875 he moved to the Panhandle and built a trading post for the buffalo hunters. It was well supplied, meeting most of the hunters' needs, from underwear to ammunition, as well as the recreational interests of soldiers at Fort Elliott, who came to play cards and drink whiskey. Springer's ranch was a favorite hangout for the black troops, who found themselves less than warmly received in Mobeetie.[31]

Springer planned to build a five-room house, comfortable enough for a New England sweetheart he hoped to marry, but because of its isolated site and his own extreme fear of Indian attacks, he constructed what the soldiers called Fort Sitting Bull. John Cook, who traded with Springer on a number of occasions, described the station:

It was built on the blockhouse, stockade, Indian frontier plan. It faced south towards the river. A square pit six by six feet and six feet deep had been dug inside the building. Then from it, leading south, was a trench running outside fifty feet, where was dug a circular pit ten feet in diameter and five feet deep. this and the trench were cribbed over and the dirt tamped down over it. The circular pit was portholed all around. Also, from the pit inside the blockhouse there was a trench running to the corral and stable. The stockade being loopholed made the whole place so impregnable that a few cool, determined men could make it impossible for the allied tribes to take it without artillery.[32]

In spite of his precautions, or perhaps because of them, Springer remained edgy and in February 1877 he shot a lone Indian who came too close to his fort without giving proper warning.[33]

As a host looking after the comforts of travelers on the trail, Springer apparently left much to be desired. Bill Jones's assessment was: "Jim Springer was like a porcupine—he always traveled with his rough side out." He was dour, tightfisted, and taciturn, but in a crisis he came through. Jones told of breaking through the ice on the creek a mile from Springer's ranch; by the time he staggered into the saloon, he was near death. Springer spent the night reviving Jones and never charged him a cent.[34]

Springer brought some Spanish longhorn cattle with him from Dodge, and as the buffalo thinned out he added to his herd, making him the first cattleman in the Panhandle. He made at least one drive to Dodge City and his herd grew and prospered, but his business was primarily that of trader, storekeeper, and road rancher. In fact, he probably made more money and spent more time selling whiskey to black troops than he did with any of his other activities. When the mail route was extended from Fort Elliott to Mobeetie, Springer's ranch became a major rest and meal stop on the stage line. It was named the Boggy Station on October 9, 1878, and Springer was designated as its postmaster.[35]

With three buinesses, each doing well, Springer soon accumulated considerable property in the form of cash, bonds, and cattle; his cattle alone were worth about twelve thousand dollars. Diversification was paying handsome dividends. Unfortunately, Springer was never to marry his eastern sweetheart, nor did he live long enough to enjoy the fruits of his labor. His death came unexpectedly, adding to the shock felt by those people of the Region who believed that he, above all others, was safe and secure in his fort.

Springer and his hired hand, Tom Leadbetter, were playing poker with some enlisted men from Camp Supply, who had camped overnight on their way to Fort Elliott, when his term at Springer Ranch came to an end. The story of what happened is somewhat garbled, but one version that seems to be as accurate as any other was reported immediately in the *Dodge City Times*:

> It seems that the Sergeant [Patrick Kerrigan] of the escort and Springer were playing cards, when a dispute arose between them. Springer drew a revolver and struck the Sergeant over the head; the Sergeant showed resistance, when Springer shot at the Sergeant and grazed the top of his head. Some other soldiers that were in the ranch, ran out to get their guns, when the report was raised that four men were approaching on horseback; the corporal ordered the escort to fall into line; and it was reported to be Paymaster, Major [A. J.] Broadhead. He thinking they were robbers, ordered the men to fire should they approach. Some way the volley was fired into the ranch, with the result as stated.
>
> It was not altogether clear as yet, why the volley was fired into the ranch; but when further particulars are received, some plausible cause may be given.

The inquest found that Springer had fired first and that Leadbetter was in the act of restraining Springer when he was killed accidentally. The soldiers were exonerated from any blame, as they were judged to have acted "purely in self-defense."[36]

Springer's brother came from Delaware to settle the estate, selling the holdings to two Dodge City men, John F. Tuttle and Frank ("Bud") Chapman. The post office was discontinued after Springer's death, and when it was reestablished in the fall of 1879, it was under the name of Springer Ranch with Tuttle as the postmaster. The way station and ranch, regardless of who owned or operated them, continued to be referred to as Springer Ranch. However, Tuttle was primarily a cattle rancher, not a way-station operator, and he left his mark in history by staking a new cattle trail to Dodge City.

The partnership between Tuttle and Chapman was a brief one, lasting only until the spring of 1879. According to Mose Hayes, the future owner of the ranch, the break was over the affection of a woman. On one of his trips to Dodge, Tuttle rode back to the ranch in the mail coach with an attractive lady. The stage became lost in a blizzard, and the two, along with the driver, spent a miserable night huddled together in the coach. Tuttle persuaded the lady to come keep house at the ranch. The partners fell to quarreling over her affections, and Tuttle bought Chapman out to get rid of him. The lady, however, found Tuttle's foreman more interesting company than either of the feuding partners. It was now Tuttle's turn to be ousted. When Tom Raines, the foreman, threatened to kill him, Tuttle decided he had had enough. By then he had had one hired man killed in a gunfight on the trail and his cook had been scalped by the Cheyennes. Tuttle was not interested in the way-station business and undoubtedly would have turned that part of his operation over to someone else if he had not thought it the better part of wisdom and valor to give up the entire venture. So he sold the place to Aldridge and Rhodes, a half-American, half-English concern. Rhodes was the son of a Philadelphia textile-mill owner, and Reginald Aldridge was an Englishman who previously had been in partnership in a ranch near Denver. Rhodes rarely came to the Panhandle spread, although he was appointed postmaster, but Aldridge spent his summers in Texas, going home to England for the winters. The partners hired Mose Hayes to manage the ranch, which he eventually purchased.[37]

Mrs. Hayes, "a stocky, black-eyed girl," when she married Mose, was mistress of the Springer Ranch post office and, according to Laura V. Hamner, "mother to the whole cow country." The way station became more than just a post office and rest stop for the stage as it was brightened by Mrs. Hayes's presence. There a cowboy could have his shirt patched, find delight in sumptuous desserts, receive the best of care when ill, and, above all, bask in the friendly presence of that prairie rarity, a woman. Her husband said of Mrs. Hayes: "She always had a smile for a boy, always got him a good meal if he was hungry." In fact, she gave away so many free meals that the transients "were eating more than Mose could haul in with his wages." But there was a solution. Oliver Nelson, one of the free-loaders, tells it:

Before long the boys began bringing in flour, beef, coffee, and sugar—everything that could be used and more than was needed. At Christmas they brought several turkeys, and everyone went to Mose's cabin for a big time. It was kept up that way till new grass came, without a murmur from Mrs. Hayes. Then the boys registered a brand in her name, and when the spring roundup started, they slapped it on every maverick they run into. Mose already had a little bunch and went into the company that spring, and the misses turned in 250 head.[38]

When a smallpox epidemic hit Ed Brainard's neighborhood, the good people of Mobeetie asked its victims to stay out of town. But when Brainard knocked on Mrs. Hayes's door, her first words were, "Come in the house." Ed refused to bring the contagion in, but Mrs. Hayes fed him and did what she could to help get the sick to Fort Dodge, where medical assistance could be had.[39]

The mail route was changed in February 1883, and the post office was discontinued. The road ranch days were over, although the ranch continued to prosper. While it operated, its well-supplied security was a blessing to traveler and operator alike. It is ironic that Springer, one of the most successful in developing multiple operations, for all his precautions against external dangers, was the only road rancher to be killed and buried at the way-station site.

Owners and their families were not the only way-station attendants. Although they were usually a family enterprise, a two-man partnership, or a one-man operation, a number of way stations had hired hands to do chores, and occasionally a neighbor girl was paid to help out in the kitchen. The lady John Tuttle persuaded to become a housekeeper at Springer Ranch was unusual, if not unique. Arabelle Sewell, who cooked and waited tables at Odee, was one of the few women living at a way station who was not a member of the family. Generally a hired cook was a man. Old Cactus, a sort of Regional gourmand, noted the culinary abilities of the cooks employed on the old Military Road as newsworthy items. Jim Springer's hired hand, who apparently signed on as part of the deal when Springer purchased Dillard Fant's cattle, soon became more than a cowboy and included among his duties bartending, cooking, and poker playing.

Such hired hands, the road-ranch boss, and even the stage drivers were called Jack, regardless of what their mothers had named them. Just as all white men were John to the Indians and all Pullman

porters were George at a later time, the station hands answered to
Jack. It was not a sign of disrespect, just a form of easy familiarity.
No one underestimated their importance.

A typical Jack was James R. Quinn, who worked for H. A. Busing
during the summer and fall of 1887. Quinn's parents had a claim
near the Cimarron road ranch, and young Quinn found the job of
caring for the stage stock better than no job at all, but nonetheless
boring. "About 10 o'clock each morning," he wrote, "I would run
the horses in from the pasture, feed, curry and harness them so all
would be ready when the coach came in to make the change. I
would then unharness, water and feed the tired team. This was my
daily routine."[40]

The men P. G. Reynolds hired to look after the on-man hack stations on the Fort Supply–Tascosa run had more exacting responsibilities and were rarely bored. Between Fort Supply and Fort
Elliott, there were normally two such stops, and the Lightning Express—Daily Mail Route required four additional stops to make
Tascosa. Stations on the first half were fairly substantial; those on
the second had only the barest of necessities.

Bill Jones spent several lonely months in one of the hack stops.
Bill was born in Missouri, but his father moved the family to southern Kansas in 1872. Four yeas later, as a very green and suscep-
tible boy, Jones struck out on his own, arriving in Dodge City at the
peak of its buffalo-hunting days. He hired out skinning buffalo at
twenty-five cents a hide and made what he considered a small fortune, only to squander it within a few weeks on the delights of Dodge
City. He next found a job as a night herder for an ox freighter on
the trail between Sweetwater and Dodge City. When that job was
finished, he accepted the first and nearest position offered: way-
station attendant, looking after one of the isolated hack stops. His
statement is as succinct and clear an enumeration of duties as can
be found:

> My work was to look after one of the stage stations. I rode to the sta-
> tion on the buckboard, as the wagon or buggy was called in which they
> hauled the mail and passengers. I found the station consisted of a picket
> house, about sixteen feet square, well fixed for a man to camp in, a corral
> and a stable for six or eight mules, and plenty of grass for the stock.
> All I had to do was to look after the mules, see that the Indians did not

P. G. Reynolds coaches at Hartland in 1887. Courtesy Kansas State Historical Museum.

run them off, and have them ready for the stage driver when he came along. As he came along only twice a week, I had plenty of time to cook, eat, sleep, and play my old fiddle, besides keeping a lookout for Indians.[41]

Bill's stay was not dull, but it ended abruptly with more excitement than he cared for. Five Indians invaded his house one evening and forced him to play his fiddle. Every time he stopped, they insisted: "Heap good, play more." He played all evening and all night, with the quality of his music deteriorating considerably. "An old-fashioned cane mill," he said, "would have sounded good by comparison to the music I was making." Finally, after becoming completely exhausted, he fainted. He awoke to find two dead Indians outside the house and the others gone. He never knew what had happened, nor did he stay around to find out. "I resigned my commission right on the spot and lit out for Dodge," he said. After working at a variety of jobs, including a stint with Lee and Reynolds, he went on to become a prosperous rancher in Paradise Valley.[42]

The way stations and their attendants, such as Bill Jones, Hoodoo Brown, and Mrs. Hayes, made stage travel bearable. To a stage-sick passenger, the pause at even the grubbiest road ranch was a welcome relief from the swaying and jolting confinement of a stifling coach. Passengers suffering from the heat and dust of summer or the cold and wind of winter found the shade or warmth of the adobe building a calming comfort. To women passengers, the sight of twin privies standing off a short distance from the ranch house must have been an even more comforting sign of the return to civilization than the station house itself. Whether it was shade, cool water, steady ground, or a solid meal, each stop held some special pleasure or assurance.

The contribution of the way station, however, was more than the fleeting convenience of an oasis in an otherwise barren land. In many areas, way stations represented the first commercial enterprise. The variety of their stock of goods determined what the local people consumed. Jim Springer's brand of whiskey was the Fort Elliott troopers' brand of whiskey. Jim Cator's choice of canned goods became the buffalo hunter's bill of fare. Even though the proprietor's market had a limited geographical extent, the monopoly was none the less real. As post office, restaurant, hotel, general store, livery barn, recreation center, travel agency, and, on occasion, bank, the way station served as town and commercial center for people in the vicinity. Little wonder that Carrie Schmoker found Hoodoo Brown's sorry soddy a source of excitement. Calling Brown's place "the metropolis of Meade County" was more reality and prophecy than satire. Although the railroads were the ultimate arbiter of townsites, some way stations did influence locations. Appleton, Kansas shuffled down the road a mile and a half to meet the demands of King Rock Island; still, it was the way station that had gathered the original cluster of families who made the new Minneola an instant town.

For a time, way stations served as anchors to the freighting trails and did much to make life and travel on the prairie tolerable. They were an integral part of the wagon-road economy that stimulated settlement and social stability. In the end, many of way-station operators and their families became part of that settlement and lent their character and strength to the kind of society the Region developed.

10. End of the Trail

Scarce any trace remaining, vestige, gray,
Or marked lines along old trails,
To points where herds once moved—the day
Now night the sunset fails. —H. H. Halsell[1]

WHILE the talk of new rail lines and new track was no more than rumor and gossip, the people served by the wagon trails believed the old ruts would give one more service. "It is our observation," wrote the editor of the *Meade County Globe*, "that railways usually follow water courses and the greater trails of the country. If this holds good in Meade County we are doubly blessed, as the placid waters of Crooked Creek bubble up by our door, and the great trail from Dodge City to Tascosa, via Fowler and Meade Center, is a feasible route." The Fowler editor ran the same story, suggesting that the Atchison, Topeka and Santa Fe would find that in following the old trail "few cuts and fills" would be required, and, furthermore, "the public domain south of us could be crossed without additional legislation, and the Panhandle of Texas, which is rapidly settling up, would furnish immense traffic." Citizens in both Meade and Fowler believed their chances of acquiring rail connections were especially good because the north-south line to Mobeetie would "not deviate far from the old Jones & Plummer trail."

Wilburn, north of Fowler, gambled and lost on the prospect that the Chicago, Nebraska, Kansas and Southwestern Railroad would

run a line from White Cloud, Nebraska to "some point in Texas."
Wilburn folks believed the line would follow the Jones and Plummer,
at least through Ford and Meade counties. The citizens of Bloom,
fifteen miles east of Wilburn, were as strongly convinced that the
same Chicago, Nebraska, Kansas and Southwestern would make
its north-south line follow the old Dodge City–Fort Supply route.
The conviction was shared with the town boomers in Ashland, who
also supported the platting of Deep Hole as the logical first depot
south of their town.[2]

The long-standing north-south orientation was so firmly fixed in
the minds of people who knew the Region that they could not imag-
ine it would not prevail when the railroads began seriously surveying lines. If there was to be a continuation of the existing patterns,
the logic of following either the Military Road or the Jones and
Plummer Trail was clear. Furthermore, people living in the hinter-
land believed Dodge City would continue to dominate the transportation facilities. The Meade editor thought the disruption of Dodge
City's monopoly of trade in the area would be ruinous to Dodge
merchants. He suggested that even the threat of diverting some of
the trade away from town would bring "irreparable injury." If Meade
merchants were to support even a wagon road leading directly into
Cimarron, Kansas, the Dodge merchants would make concessions
to prevent the loss of trade. Dodge City, as "the great distribution
point for all this section of country for miles and miles to the
south," was so dependent on that trade that it would do all it could
to keep it. The powerful merchants of Dodge City, with their long-
time connections with railroad officials and politicians, would fight
even harder to preserve their north-south trade when the railroads
came. Under the circumstances, many residents of the Region believed that the old trails, which had helped maintain the configuration of the Region, would continue to serve as "guide and compass"
for the new transportation system.[3]

This final service was not to be. The small improvements, cuts
and fills, made on the prairie trails over the years were insignificant
when compared with the requirements of grading for tracks. Any
following of the old trails by the new tracks would be accidental and
inconsequential. By the time the rail lines reached the Region, the
pattern of east-west tracks had been set by facilities beyond the

borders of Kansas, Oklahoma, and Texas. When the tracks were finally laid, the trails were completely ignored.

In a remarkably short time the economy based on wagon transportation, with its network of roads, freighting wagons, accommodations, and stagecoach lines, came to an end. The railroads killed the industry. Obviously, animals and wagons did not disappear overnight, however, with but a few anachronistic exceptions the long-distance hauling ended within a half-dozen years after the rail lines cut through the Region. Wagons remained as local carriers only. P. G. Reynolds' old stage barn at Ashland was converted to a transfer and bus business, and Perry Monroe and Frank Cavender, who had managed one of Reynolds' stage lines north of Dodge, moved into town to operate it. Theirs was a symbolic shift; from a stage line covering a one-hundred-mile run to short hauls to the train depot.[4]

Local business sustained the wagon freighters for a time. Until the end of World War I, they continued to be an essential part of the transportation system as they moved goods from railroad yards and depots to stores, ranches, and farms. Early cooperation extended even to trains' stopping at any point along the track if there was a large consignment to be unloaded. Gradually, this inefficient custom of flagging down the train or unloading at any place other than the designated stop was ended. Boxcars continued to be spotted on special tracks far enough apart to allow the freighter to maneuver his teams between them. This new role of the teamsters was far less important to the customer than it had been, and it was far less profitable. However, until the railroads increased their network of local lines and motor trucks replaced wagons, freighters were an essential auxiliary to the new system. It was, nevertheless, a new system with new priorities and functions. The old wagon-road economy was no more.

The discarding of the old system was complete by 1890, and the Region as a recognized operational unit was destroyed. Within ten years after the arrival of the first locomotive in Panhandle City and Meade, the orientation of commercial and political life had been altered completely. The fortunes of individuals and communities also were changed drastically. Mobeetie, Tascosa, Appleton, and Wilburn suffered immediate or slow death; the recently established trail towns of Ashland and Meade experienced rapid growth and county-seat importance. New towns with new names—Canadian, Panhandle City, Miami, and Minneola—appeared overnight along the new arteries of commerce.

Not only did the face of the Region change, but the old attitude of "salutary statehouse neglect" of remote and inconsequential areas ended. Jim Lane's outpost settlement became, clearly, Beaver, *Oklahoma*; the trail town that grew up next to Hoodoo Brown's soddy received its political authorization from Topeka; and Tascosa, which had filled the governmental needs of nine counties, repeatedly lost county jurisdictions until the final vote in 1915 sent the last county records to Vega. The casual blessing of state officials changed to close, or at least closer, supervision. [5]

Dodge City, the unofficial capital of the Region, appeared to have just weathered its third economic transition. The town had moved, more or less gracefully and successfully, through the buffalo-hide prosperity and decline, to the cattle-town bonanza and decline, into the land rush of homesteading farmers. Each new change had left the town in a stronger financial position. Through it all, one important source of profit had not been affected; Dodge had retained its preeminence as a supplier and market for the Region, which eased the transitions from one economic phase to the next. The latest loss of the cattle-trail business had not been the disaster many had predicted. Even Samuel ("Sam") Prouty, the last editorial champion of Dodge City as a cattleman's town, conceded that the farmers had brought with them "success and prosperity" for the town and all of Western Kansas, which was now "blooming and booming." An envious neighboring editor agreed, writing in 1888: "Dodge is rapidly assuming metropolitan airs. In addition to waterworks and electric lights, posts have been placed at street corners, on which are nailed boards bearing names of the streets and avenues." It had become the stable town that Nick Klaine, Prouty's old adversary, had envisioned and worked for: free of gamblers, courtesans, outlaws, and hell-bent cowboys. Even in far-off Topeka the press noticed that there were "silent but irresistible forces at work to regenerate Dodge City." [6]

At the peak of this new prosperity, Dodge was hit hard by an economic depression that hung on for a dozen years. This time there was no wagon-road business to fall back on. Robert Wright, a merchant who had prospered in each of the previous economic phases and had relied heavily on the wagon roads, referred to the new times as "The Great Decline." It was more than a period of local adjustments to new conditions. The nation was gradually slipping into the Panic of 1893, and Western Kansas led the way. The land boom was over; drought and falling prices staggered the new agricultural developments, settlers stopped coming, and established homesteaders began leaving.[7]

With Meade County, Dodge's nearest county to the south and a fair representative of surrounding counties, losing more than 70 percent of its population between 1888 and 1895, merchants in Dodge City would have suffered even if the wagon-road economy had remained. Order-of-sale notices spread across the newspapers, replacing the previous notices of final proof of claim. Of the banks in Dodge City chartered before 1886, all closed during the next five years. Extensive utility and street improvements begun in 1886 brought on a financial crisis in 1891 when the town could not meet its scrip obligations in either interest or principal payments. Before the dreary decade was over, city officials had refused to acknowledge their own scrip and had admitted that they did not know the total amount of the town's indebtedness.[8]

Other towns in the Region suffered even more than Dodge City. Small towns like Fowler and Bloom, recently booming with optimism, ceased to exist as organized entities. Losing most of their businesses and residents, they remained stagnant, without town government and with limited facilities, until well after the turn of the century. One lesson was clear: railroads did not necessarily mean prosperity.

The fortunes of individuals were to be as affected and as checkered as those of the towns. Some men had enough capital in reserve to ride out the economic crisis and still be in a position to take advantage of changed circumstances that came with the new century. Dodge Citians A. J. Anthony, George Hoover, and Robert Wright were stung by the depressed times but remained solvent and quickly recouped their losses once prosperity returned. They had been forced to dip deep into their reserves, and Wright confessed that he had "seven thousand acres . . . sold under the hammer, at less than fifty cents per acre; and some for less than that price." Most of the earlier leaders in the Region did not fare so well. Charles Rath was cornered in Mobeetie and lost everything; J. J. Long saw his town blow away during a tornado in 1894, and with it much of his wealth; Hoodoo Brown was forced to sell ("give my place away, almost") at deflated prices, and he moved steadily downhill until he died. Most of the men who were familiar figures on the old trails simply hunkered down, tightened their belts, and survived. Red Clarke, George Reighard, Oliver Nelson, and Ed Jones tended their small farms and, as Nelson expressed it, went "under cultivation, stayed there, and prospered." After a lifetime of adventure, Billy Dixon settled into his cabin on Turkey Track Ranch and collected his $750 a year for carrying mail from Zulu to his post office.[9]

A few lucky ones were able to capitalize on other people's misfortunes. Adam Schmidt, who had depended on the freighting trade for his blacksmith clientele, adapted to the changing economy and eventually was able to purchase the finest stone home in Dodge City. Old bachelor Ben Haywood, former stage driver, resisted all efforts of the community and newspaper editors to find him a bride and picked up quarter sections of land sold for a song by homesteaders returning east "to the wife's folks." Colonel Jack Hardesty was not only able to retain his cattle empire, he added to it land that cost only a fraction of what it was selling for ten years earlier. Many believed that the truly lucky ones were those who left the Region for more prosperous climates, and they cited as prime examples Bat Masterson, in his new journalistic career in the east, and W. M. D. Lee, in the heady world of high finance.

It would be wrong, of course, to attribute all or even most of the woes and windfalls to the demise of the wagon-road economy. Declining prices; the end of cattle trading in Dodge City; the financial pressures of the Santa Fe Railroad, which curtailed divisional facilities in Dodge City—all hit at about the same time the railroads intervened between Dodge City and the rest of the Region. Nationally, the Panic of 1893 saw some 15,242 commercial houses fail and seventy-four railroads declare bankruptcy. Dodge City was not the only town in which banks closed. Of the 158 national banks that suspended operations in 1893, 153 were in the West and South. It

The Last Hook-Up is the title of this photograph of the last time a Reynolds coach was driven over the trails. Pictured in front of P. G.'s home at 801 Second Avenue, Dodge City, are George Reynolds and driver Tom Goodwin. The lead team's names were Tom and Jerry. Courtesy Rex Reynolds, Niles, Michigan.

was a time of trouble, Coxey's Army, the Pullman Strike, Mary Elizabeth Lease's oratory, and the rise of the Populist party. In 1890 corn sold for as little as ten cents a bushel in Kansas, and interest rates reached an unrealistic 15 percent. By 1889, 60 percent of all farms in Kansas were under mortgage, and between that year and 1893, more than 11,000 farm mortgages were foreclosed. [10]

As one of many conditions adversely affecting the Region, the timing of the railroads' interruption of the wagon-road economy could not have been worse. The disruption of old economic patterns in the middle of a national crisis only added to the burden that towns and individuals were forced to bear. Small wonder that men looked back on the raw prairie years of the slow-moving coaches and wagons with nostalgia and yearning for the good old days. There was more to their nostalgia than a remembrance of more prosperous times. With the passing of the old system there went the sense of community and personal concern that had permeated the Region.

There had been a remarkable intermingling of the lives of people who had depended on the trails. In spite of the distances between settlements and outposts—between the Staked Plains, Fort Supply, and Dodge City—the people of the Region felt they were neighbors, and in fact they did know each other personally, even if their home bases were miles apart. An old freighter like Ed Jones knew not only merchants (Robert Wright, Jim Lane, and Henry M. Beverley), but also ranchers (Deacon W. H. Bates, Joe Morgan, and Charles Goodnight), buffalo hunters (J. Wesley Mooar, Billy Dixon, and George Reighard), and army officers (Frank D. Baldwin and Nelson A. Miles). When Bat Masterson rode into Ed Jones's road ranch in search of outlaws, he was greeted as a friend who had once shared a buffalo camp. When Red Clarke, who was with Masterson in that posse, traded real estate with Frank Trask, the deal was closed with a handshake between men who had shared other buffalo-camp fires with six men who were to serve as Dodge City peace officers. There must have been a dozen freighters who remained in the Region until 1890 who had driven army wagons with George Reighard, Charles Rath, and J. J. Long. The intertwining of lives and friendships was almost endless.

Such close relationships not only made business transactions comfortable but led to easy cooperative efforts and mutual assistance. When the people around Camp Supply, more than a hundred miles south of Dodge City, needed to stir the Post Office Department to consider more frequent and regular mail delivery, the citizens of Dodge signed the petition with as much enthusiasm as the post sutler at Supply. The army had no difficulty in organizing a company of scouts at Fort Dodge to avenge the death of Tommy Wallace in the Texas Panhandle. All who enlisted had known Wallace personally. Members of the Dodge City Cattle Growers Association, which maintained headquarters in Robert Wright's store, were as interested in keeping diseased cattle out of Colonel Hardesty's herd in the Public Land Strip as they were to prevent them from coming into Ford County. Their efforts blocked state legislation that would have included the upper Panhandle of Texas and Indian Territory in the Texas cattle embargo. Hoodoo Brown, who lived on the Kansas border, undertook the dangerous mission of retrieving the scalped body of a hired hand of a Texas Panhandle cattleman out of compassion and a sense of responsibility. Such actions generated a Region quickly vanished, to be replaced by localized or state loyalties. The system of slow transportation had brought the distances closer, at least in personal terms, than the more rapid transit by rail.

The economy was to recover, rebounding under the imperialistic administration of William McKinley. Prices of ranch and farm products regained their previous levels and moved on to new highs. Land prices adjusted to more realistic levels, and settlers returned to take up abandoned homesteads. But the Dodge City–Panhandle Region, with its keen sense of community, would never return. The future of the land lay in new directions.

The new directions were to be strongly influenced by that "good producing population" that had used the trails and wagon-road economy to establish a permanent base. When an undeveloped area experiences intensive settlement, the specific characteristics of the first group to establish a viable, permanent, self-perpetuating society are "of crucial significance for the later social and cultural geography of the area, no matter how tiny the initial band of settlers may have been." This principle of the Doctrine of First Effective Settlement is analogous to that of imprinting in very young animals.

The lasting contributions of a few hundred initial permanent settlers can have more impact on later cultural developments than those of the many waves of subsequent immigrants. In our national history the few thousand colonists who arrived before 1700 have had more to do with our cultural heritage than the hordes of immigrants who passed through Ellis Island between 1890 and 1920.[11]

The same imprinting is recognizable when the void of an unsettled territory on the frontier is quickly filled with settlers. The Dodge City–Panhandle Region was one such empty area that was substantially populated within a two-decade period. The cowboys, buffalo hunters, and soldiers who preceded the settlers left little permanent cultural baggage. They explored, cleared the land of settlement barriers, and advertised its potential, but they could not perpetuate either their economic base or their life-style.

In the wake of these ephemeral transients came the farmers, ranchers, and townspeople who intended to settle down and develop a lasting society of their own choosing. As settlers, they brought with them concepts of moral values, personal virtues, and cultural styles they hoped to transfer to the new communities. These were refinements, they believed, of the imperfect models of their old homes. The kind of society they expected to fashion was not to be a replica of their old setting, and it certainly was not to emulate the kind of life the hide towns and cow towns had spawned. Frank Mathews, the *Wilburn Argus* editor, testified that he found his new community "a moral town," contrasting favorably with old Dodge City by the "conspicuous absence . . . of the dram shop, gaming hall and their votaries." Observed Mathews: "The western rough has returned to the frontier, and the snob of the east has not yet arrived." What Wilburnites wanted was "stability, tranquility, and opportunity." The new settlers sponsored schools, churches and literary societies while they were still living in dugouts and experimenting with sod corn. If former Maine logger and former Kansas stage driver Ben Haywood's rendition of "The Long-horned Texan Steer" failed to meet the artistic standards of Edwin Booth's Shakespearean season of 1881, it nevertheless paid tribute to elegance of expression and style, albeit tempered by western standards and themes. A. Bennett of the *Pearlette Call* and Nick Klaine of the *Dodge City Times* might not compare favorably with contemporaries Ambrose Bierce or Thomas Bailey Aldrich, but they nevertheless used the power of the press to advance learning, Culture (with a capital *C*), and a better, more refined community.[12]

The imprinting of these early settlers was to survive the breakup of the Region. What evolved from the early wagon-road economy would continue to adjust to local peculiarities, the hardening of governmental boundaries, economic innovations and specializations, new modes of transportation, and cultural mutations caused by successive waves of immigrants. Just as the trails south were to be cut by more viable transportation lines with new east-west orientation, so, too, were the old cultural patterns altered by new orientations and what passed for progress. The sense of community vanished quickly in the Region after 1890, but the force of the initial cultural imprinting remained as an indelible base for the three-stage area. The trails south that had served as the skeletal support of that early unity and the lasting cultural heritage passed from the scene with scarcely a trace. Only dim reminders and memory remained.

Willa Cather wrote for all trails and trail voyagers. Returning after a lifetime, Cather's pioneer walks over the land he had once known and stumbles upon the grass-covered ruts of the trail his family followed to the prairie and the place where they had spent their first night on their land:

Everywhere else it had been ploughed under when the highways were surveyed; this half-mile or so within the pasture fence was all that was left of that old road which used to run like a wild thing across the open prairie, clinging to the high places. . . .

I had only to close my eyes to hear the rumbling of the wagons in the dark, and to be again overcome by that obliterating strangeness. The feelings of that night were so near that I could reach out and touch them with my hand. I had the sense of coming home to myself, and of having found out what a little circle man's experience is. For Ántonia and for me, this had been the road of Destiny; had taken us to those early accidents of fortune which predetermined for us all that we can ever be. Now I understood that the same road was to bring us together again. Whatever we had missed, we possessed together the precious, the incommunicable past.[13]

Notes

Chapter 1. The Dodge City–Panhandle Region

1. *Pioneer Stories of Meade County*, comp. County Council of Women's Clubs, Meade County, Kansas, p. 177.

2. Merrill Jensen, ed., *Regionalism in America*, p. 408. See also Howard W. Odum and Harry Estill Moore, *American Regionalism: A Cultural-Historical Approach to National Integration*.

3. *Dodge City Times*, December 28, 1878.

4. Ibid., May 3, 1883; Hervey E. Chesley, *Trails Travelled; Tales Told*, ed. Byron Price, p. 48.

5. *Dodge City Ford County Globe*, January 15, 1878; *Dodge City Times*, December 20, October 25, 1883.

6. "Report and Map of the Route from Fort Smith, Arkansas, to Santa Fe, New Mexico, Made by Lieutenant Simpson," pp. 2, 22–23.

7. W. Turrentine Jackson, *Wagon Roads West*, pp. viii, 327.

8. Wilbur Zelinsky, *The Cultural Geography of the United States*.

9. For a discussion of the cattle king's role as compared with that of the cowboy, see Lewis Atherton, *The Cattle Kings*, p. xi.

Chapter 2. The Dodge City–Fort Supply Trail

1. D. E. Newsom, *Kicking Bird and the Birth of Oklahoma*, pp. 35–47; *St. Louis Missouri Democrat*, October 25, 1867, story under byline of Henry M. Stanley; Robert W. Richmond, *Kansas: A Land of Contrasts*, pp. 90–92.

2. Dee Brown, *Bury My Heart at Wounded Knee*, p. 62; Marvin Garfield, "Defense of Kansas Frontier, 1868–1869," *Kansas Historical Quarterly* 1 (November 1932): 454–55.

3. George Armstrong Custer, *My Life on the Plains*, p. 210; Robert C.

Carriker, *Fort Supply, Indian Territory: Frontier Outpost on the Plains*, p. 16.

4. Custer, *Life on the Plains*, pp. 210-11.

5. Carriker, *Fort Supply*, p. 19; A. L. Runyon, "A. L. Runyon's Letters from the Nineteenth Kansas Regiment," *Kansas Historical Quarterly* 9 (February 1940): 70-71

6. Carriker, *Fort Supply*, p. 39.

7. "Runyon's Letters," p. 71. Runyon was the father of Damon Runyon, the well-known recorder of the characters and mores of New York's Broadway.

8. Richard T. Jacobs, "Military Reminiscences of Captain Richard T. Jacobs," *Chronicles of Oklahoma* 2 (March 1924): 29.

9. Father Boniface Verheyen, "A Missionary's Trip Through Southern Kansas in 1876," *The Abbey News*, 13 (March 1940): 11-12; *Dodge City Times*, August 25, 1877.

10. Carriker, *Fort Supply*, pp. 44, 57-58. Deep Hole was located on Sec. 36, Twp. 34, R. 23. "Kansas Post Offices," Manuscript Department, Kansas State Historical Society, Topeka; India H. Simmons, "Southwest History Corner," *Dodge City Daily Globe*, March 26, 1937.

11. Frances Marie Antoinette Roe, *Army Letters from an Officer's Wife, 1871-1888*, pp. 86-87.

12. Roe, *Army Letters*, p. 89.

13. Jacobs, "Military Reminiscences," p. 31. The Northern Redoubt was located on Sec. 16, Twp. 32, R. 23.

14. Post Adjutant, Camp Supply, to V. A. Goddard, June 15, 1872, quoted in Carriker, *Fort Supply*, p. 70.

15. Robert M. Wright, *Dodge City: The Cowboy Capital and the Great Southwest*, pp. 43-44.

16. Carriker, *Fort Supply*, p. 89; *Dodge City Messenger*, June 25, 1874.

17. Carriker, *Fort Supply*, pp. 83-84; Robert K. DeArment, *Bat Masterson: The Man and the Legend*, p. 54; Harry E. Chrisman, *Lost Trails of the Cimarron*, p. 104.

18. Ethel Etrick Watkins, *Annie: Child of the Prairie*, p. 34.

19. Ashland Clark County Clipper, July 2, 1885, January 7, 1886; *Dodge City Times*, August 12, 1883.

20. *Dodge City Times*, June 1, 1878.

21. Ibid., August 25, 1877.

22. "Old Clark County Ranch Figured in Early History," *Dodge City Daily Globe*, February 23, 1935.

23. *Dodge City Times*, March 9, 22, 1878; *Dodge City Messenger*, June 25, March 9, 1878.

24. Among others on the Salt Fork that winter were Bat and Ed Masterson, Wyatt Earp, Tom Nixon, Dave Morrow, Neal Brown, Fred Sughrue,

and Charlie Trask. *Dodge City Messenger*, August 4, 11, 1877, June 1, 8, 1878; *Dodge City Ford County Globe*, June 11, 1878; De Arment, *Bat Masterson*, p. 17; *Dodge City Times*, June 15, 1878.

25. "Clark County Ranch," *Dodge City Daily Globe*, February 23, 1935.

26. Ibid.; *Dodge City Times*, January 18, 1883; Billy McGinty, *The Old West*, p. 38; Jay S. Andrews, *History of Bloom, Kansas*, p. 82.

27. *Dodge City Times*, August 25, 1877.

28. Ibid.; *Dodge City Ford County Globe*, March 13, 1883.

29. Klaine was located on NW ¼, Sec. 1, Twp. 33, R. 23. John A. Walden, "Pioneer Postoffices," *Ashland Creek County Clipper*, November 2, 1939.

30. Verheyen, "A Missionary's Trip Through Southern Kansas," p. 12; *Dodge City Ford County Globe*, February 28, 1979; *Dodge City Times*, March 9, 1878; "Kansas Post Offices."

31. *Dodge City Times*, July 7, 1877; John A. Walden, "Mosquitoes Got Scalps in Last Indian Scare," *Dodge City Daily Globe*, January 27, 1940.

32. Federal Census of 1880, Clark County, Kansas; *Dodge City Times*, August 4, September 22, 1877; John J. Callison, *Bill Jones of Paradise Valley, Oklahoma*, pp. 47–49; *Dodge City Ford County Globe*, February 5, 1878, September 8, 1877.

33. De Arment, *Bat Masterson*, pp. 92–93; Nyle H. Miller and Joseph W. Snell, *Great Gunfighters of the Kansas Cowtowns, 1867–1886*, p. 204; *Dodge City Times*, August 11, 1877.

34. *Dodge City Times*, September 22, 1877.

35. Ibid., August 25, 1877.

36. Carl Julius Adolph Hunnius, "Survey of the Staked Plains and Headwaters of Red River."

37. *Ashland Clark County Clipper*, September 10, 1885.

38. *Englewood Clark County Chief*, June 10, 1887; Walden, "Mosquitoes Got Scalps," *Dodge City Daily Globe*, January 27, 1940.

39. *Ashland Clark County Clipper*, January 1, 8, 1885; *Topeka Daily Capital*, June 15, 1886; Verheyen, "A Missionary's Trip Through Southern Kansas," p. 12. Glenn's place was located on NW ¼, Sec. 12, Twp. 33, R. 23.

40. *Ashland Clark County Clipper*, October 9, 1884.

41. Ibid., March 19, 1885, January 21, July 15, 1886; Ella Wallingford Mendenhall, "Livery Barns," *Ashland Clark County Clipper*, July 2, 1942; *Topeka Daily Capital*, July 6, 1958.

42. *Ashland Clark County Clipper*, August 13, September 10, 1885; *Appleton Era*, January 7, March 5, August 12, 1886; *Dodge City Globe Live Stock Journal*, August 11, 1885, March 2, 1886.

43. Andrews, *History of Bloom*, passim.

Chapter 3. The Fort Elliott Extension and the Mobeetie-Tascosa Trail

1. Jimmy M. Skaggs, *The Cattle-Trailing Industry*, pp. 90–91; Interview, Mrs. I. T. Strickland by Herbert Rogers, September 13, 1937, Indian-Pioneer History, XLV: 467. *Dodge City Globe Live Stock Journal*, November 4, 1884.

2. Interview, Sam Manning by Linnaeus B. Ranck, November 5, 1937. Indian-Pioneer History, CVIII: 62–65.

3. Oliver Nelson, *The Cowman's Southwest*, ed. Angie Debo, pp. 252–53.

4. Manning by Ranck, November 5, 1937, p. 63.

5. Carriker, *Fort Supply*, p. 146; Hunnius, "Survey"; Nelson, *Cowman's Southwest*, p. 253.

6. *Dodge City Times*, September 1, 1878.

7. James L. Haley, *The Buffalo War*, pp. 145–46, 193–94; *A History of Lipscomb County*, comp. Lipscomb County Historical Survey, p. 18.

8. F. Stanley, *Rodeo Town: Canadian, Texas*.

9. Nelson, *Cowman's Southwest*, p. 255.

10. Ibid., p. 259.

11. Ibid., p. 260.

12. Ibid., pp. 282–83.

13. Carriker, *Fort Supply*, p. 147. The crossing was at Needmore Spring as identified by Gunnar Brune, *Springs of Texas*, I: 227. The road ranch there had trouble keeping supplies and the owners were constantly writing their Dodge City contractor: "We need more bacon, potatoes, etc." Their repeated orders gave the creek its name.

14. Brune, *Springs of Texas*, I: 227; Glyndon M. Riley, "The History of Hemphill County," p. 19.

15. Hunnius, "Survey"; James M. Oswald, "History of Fort Elliott," *Panhandle-Plains Historical Review* 32(1959), p. 33.

16. Oswald, "History of Fort Elliott," pp. 38–39; "Fort Elliott, Texas," Records of the War Department, Office of the Quartermaster General, Reservation File, Indian-Pioneer History, Oklahoma Historical Society, Oklahoma City.

17. *Fort Griffin Echo*, April 12, 1879.

18. Interview, R. ("Dick") Bussell by J. Evetts Haley, July 19, 1926, June 8, 1934.

19. J. Evetts Haley, *Charles Goodnight: Cowman and Plainsman*, p. 358; Acting Assistant Quartermaster to the Quartermaster General, 1879, quoted in Oswald, "History of Fort Elliott," p. 19.

20. Oswald, "History of Fort Elliott," pp. 53–54.

21. Interview, Garrett H. ("Kid") Dobbs by John L. McCarty, October 20, 1942, John L. McCarty Papers.

22. Interview, S. P. Reynolds by J. Evetts Haley, July 18, 1934; Laura V. Hamner, "Free Grass."

23. M. H. Loy to J. Evetts Haley, November 1, 1929; Riley, "History of Hemphill County," p. 6; Brune, *Springs of Texas*, I: 19.

24. O. H. Loyd, "Oldham County Texas: An Authentic Historical Brief of Old Tascosa and Oldham County."

25. See Willie Newbury Lewis, *Between Sun and Sod*, for a discussion of Clarendon's business orientation.

Chapter 4. The Jones and Plummer Trail

1. The 1900 Census, Woodward, Oklahoma indicated the date of birth as 1851; the 1880 Census, Ford County, Kansas indicates 1855. The date cited (1852) was the one given by the family at the time of his death. Genealogical information collected by Bill Jones, Bill Jones to C. Robert Haywood, July 29, 1983; Bill Jones to William C. Greggs, April 9, 1981; Interview, Alma Jones by J. Evetts Haley, December 13, 1936. The early-life details appear in stories of Ed Jones's death in the *Oklahoma City Daily Oklahoman*, June 5, 1935; *Woodward Daily Press*, June 4, 1935; *Woodward County Journal*, June 6, 1935.

2. Coila Sieber, "Trail Maker"; Henry H. Raymond, "Diary of a Dodge City Buffalo Hunter, 1872–1873," ed. Joseph W. Snell, *Kansas Historical Quarterly*, 31 (Winter 1965): 390; County Organization Census, Ford County Kansas, October 21, 1872; John R. Cook, *The Border and the Buffalo: An Untold Story of the Southwest Plains*, ed. Milo Milton Quaife, p. 257; *Oklahoma City Daily Oklahoman*, June 3, 1935.

3. C. E. ("Ed") Jones to L. F. Sheffy, December 31, 1929. The powderburn description was given by Ed's sister, Gertrude Polak. Jones to Haywood, July 29, 1983; Interview, J. Wright Mooar to J. Evetts Haley, July 28, 1937; Stanley Vestal, *Queen of Cowtowns: Dodge City*, pp. 200–201.

4. De Arment, *Bat Masterson*, pp. 28, 33.

5. Ed Jones remembered the caravan in terms of teams: "I organized 100 teams and went to Adobe Walls." Jones to Sheffy, December 31, 1929; Wayne Gard, *The Great Buffalo Hunt*, pp. 137–40; Mooar to Haley, July 28, 1937; Rathjen, *Texas Panhandle Frontier*, p. 158.

6. Frederick W. Rathjen, *Texas Panhandle Frontier*, pp. 156–57; Brown, *Bury My Heart at Wounded Knee*, p. 265.

7. Deposition of James Lanton, January 28, 1896, Indian Depredation Case No. 4593. Ida Ellen Rath, *The Rath Trail*, p. 121.

8. Raymond, "Diary," p. 362, passim. The account of the Red Deer Creek slaughter is a composite of two interviews of J. Wright Mooar by J. Evetts Haley on July 28, 1937 and March 2–4, 1936. The words here are Mooar's. The two accounts are remarkably alike, considering the time lapse between interviews. There are only minor discrepancies, such as the time of day Plummer returned and whether he crossed the creek.

9. Olive K. Dixon, *Life of "Billy" Dixon*, p. 190. An account of the Frank Maddox survey party's action by William Benjamin Munson varies somewhat from Mooar's statement, but both agree in general. Many of the Indians in the raid were identified when they were prisoners at Fort Marion, Florida. Richard Henry Pratt, *Battlefield and Classroom*, ed. Robert M. Utley, pp. 137–43; E. C. Lefebre to John D. Miles, June 14, 1874; W. B. Munson to Laura V. Hamner, June 29, 1921.

10. Early reports of the attack on Adobe Walls included Joe Plummer among the defenders. However, he was not mentioned as one of the twenty-eight by any of the other people there. See the *Leavenworth Daily Commercial* of July 26, 1874, for mention in the earliest report.

11. J. Wright Mooar, "Buffalo Days as Told to James Winford Hunt," *Holland's: The Magazine of the South*, 52 (February 1933): 44; Mooar by Haley, July 28, 1937.

12. Mooar by Haley, July 28, 1937; Henry Raymond to Sadie Raymond, June 28, 1874.

13. G. Derek West, "The Battle of Adobe Walls (1874)," *Panhandle-Plains Historical Review*, 36 (1963): 31.

14. *Pioneer Days in the Southwest: Thrilling Descriptions of Buffalo Hunting, Indian Fighting and Massacres, Cowboy Life and Home Building*, pp. 65–85.

15. Campbell had been associated with J. Wright Mooar's crew when they hunted on the South Canadian and was well known to both Jones and Plummer. Gard, *The Great Buffalo Hunt*, p. 146.

16. Frank D. Baldwin Diary.

17. Ibid.; Frank D. Baldwin, "Baldwin's Report, August 20, 1874."

18. Interview, Mose Hayes by J. Evetts Haley, June 10, 1930.

19. Jones to Sheffy, December 31, 1929. Obviously, others transported more hides than did Jones. See Charles Rath's record in Chapter 6.

20. Hamner, "Free Grass."

21. Miller and Snell, *Great Gunfighters*, pp. 208–17; De Arment, *Bat Masterson*, pp. 87–94.

22. Walter Prescott Webb, *The Great Plains*, p. 229.

23. *Dodge City Times*, June 29, 1978; *Dodge City Ford County Globe*, July 16, 1978; Jones to Sheffy, December 31, 1929; Hank Reeves, "Chuck Wagon Gossip." Interview, Ed Brainard by J. Evetts Haley, June 17, 1937;

Laura V. Hamner, *Short Grass and Longhorns*, pp. 66–74; Pauline Durrett Robertson and R. L. Robertson, *Panhandle Pilgrimage*, p. 276.

24. Heinie Schmidt, *Ashes of My Campfire*, p. 63.

25. Watkins, *Annie*, p. 36; *Pioneer Stories of Meade County*, pp. 236–37.

26. Interview, Mr. and Mrs. Tom A. Judy by C. Robert Haywood, July 6, 1982; *Dodge City Times*, November 26, 1882; Frank S. Sullivan, *A History of Meade County, Kansas*, p. 34; *Pioneer Stories of Meade County*, p. 122.

27. *Fowler City Graphic*, July 2, 16, 1885.

28. *Meade County Press-Democrat*, April 30, May 14, June 25, July 16, 1887; *Fowler News*, November 8, 1979.

29. Chrisman, *Lost Trails*, p. 40; John L. McCarty, *Maverick Town: The Story of Old Tascosa*, p. 188; L. L. Beardsley, "Early History," in *A History of Beaver County, Cimarron Territory*, II: 23. Tom Judy, who has lived on the Cimarron for more than sixty years, indicated that the character of the river was altered drastically by the flood of 1914. The course is no longer as smooth and the grass is neither as lush nor as uniform as it was before the flood. Judy interviewed by Haywood, July 6, 1982; Dixon, *Life of "Billy" Dixon*, p. 288.

30. José Ynocencio Romero, "Spanish Sheepmen on the Canadian at Old Tascosa," edited by Ernest R. Archambeau, *Panhandle-Plains Historical Review* 19 (1946): 65.

31. Nelson, *Cowman's Southwest*, p. 294.

32. *Fowler City Graphic*, May 4, 1889.

33. Berenice Loyd Jackson, "Jones and Plummer Cattle Trail," *Beaver Herald-Democrat*, July 24, 1980.

34. Oscar A. Kinchen, "The Squatters in No Man's Land," *Chronicles of Oklahoma* 26 (1948): 389; Fred Carter Tracy, "Personal Memoirs of Fred Carter Tracy, Beaver, Oklahoma," p. 180.

35. Tracy, "Personal Memoirs," p. 131; E. H. Brainard, equally knowledgeable, added a few details but agreed in general with Hayes's description. From the Jones and Plummer place on Wolf Creek, Brainard said, the route went south across the west prong of that stream and continued south between the two prongs, crossing Horse Creek just north of the Canadian, which it paralleled for about four miles before crossing. From the Canadian it angled southeast across Red Deer Creek, turned south to the Washita near Section 59 and from there continued to the Hemphill County line about eight miles from the southwest corner to reach its terminus at Mobeetie. E. H. Brainard to G. M. Riley, December 30, 1937, quoted in Riley, "The History of Hemphill County."

36. For examples of pencil-drawn maps, see those submitted to the Kansas State Historical Society by M. W. Anshutz of Nye, Kansas in 1939; see also A. N. Howe, "Early Ranches," in *A History of Beaver*

County, II: 445. The southern-section description is now cast in bronze—immortalized along Texas highways. The markers read:

> JONES AND PLUMMER TRAIL
> ESTABLISHED ABOUT 1874, WHEN USED BY THE
> FREIGHTING FIRM OF ED JONES AND JOE PLUMMER
> TO HAUL TONS OF BUFFALO HIDES
> FROM THEIR GENERAL STORE IN LIPSCOMB
> COUNTY TO DODGE CITY, KANSAS
>
> ALSO IN ITS EARLY DAYS, THIS TRAIL
> CARRIED CRUCIAL SUPPLIES
> TO GENERALS NELSON MILES AND
> PHILIP SHERIDAN DURING THEIR
> FAMOUS 1874 INDIAN CAMPAIGN.

37. Hayes by Haley, June 10, 1930.
38. Capitola Gerlach, "Gerlach's Store"; Federal Census of 1900, Hemphill County; O. R. McMordie to J. Evetts Haley, July 19, 1926; Interview, George Gerlach by Olive K. Dixon, November 9, 1922.
39. Gerlach, "Gerlach's Store."
40. Judys by Haywood, July 6, 1982. There is no doubt about Temple Houston's respect for the Canadian. In one of the fluid meetings at end of court, Judge Charles G. Landes proved to Houston's satisfaction that the Canadian was three hundred feet deep. The subsurface water met with the bottom of the river at flood tide, the judge said. Since the flood swept away the bridge, which was on pilings extending three hundred feet below the riverbed, the river had to be at least as deep as the piling. Houston, who had seen the bridge go, accepted the judge's contention. Charles G. Landis, "Forty-seven Years in Potter County"; Charles N. Gould, *The Geology and Water Resources of the Eastern Portion of the Panhandle of Texas*, pp. 42–43.
41. L. F. Sheffy, "Old Mobeetie: The Capital of the Panhandle," *West Texas Historical Association Year Book* 6 (July 1930): 3.
42. *Dodge City Ford County Globe*, August 6, 1878; *Dodge City Globe Live Stock Journal*, November 3, 1885; Frederic R. Young, *Dodge City: Up Through a Century in Story and Pictures*, p. 56; *Dodge City Times*, October 6, 1881; *Tascosa Pioneer*, June 9, October 20, 1886; Alvin Ricker, "Tascosa," *Oklahoma City Daily Oklahoman*, October 26, 1930.
43. Young, *Dodge City*, pp. 31–35; *Dodge City Ford County Globe*, June 24, 1887.
44. The site was SE¼ and SW¼, Sec. 34, Twp. 29, r. 26. *Wilburn Argus*, April 16, 1886; *Dodge City High Plains Journal*, May 6, 1961, p. 14.

45. *Wilburn Argus*, April 23, 1886.

46. Corporation Charters, Records Compiled by the Secretary of State, Kansas; *Fowler City Advocate*, July 9, 1885; *Wilburn Argus*, June 23, 1887.

47. *Wilburn Argus*, December 29, 1887; *Fowler Gazette*, September 15, 1911.

48. Bertha Mendenhall, "History of Fowler," in *Pioneer Stories of Meade County*, p. 83; letter to the Fowler postmaster from Perry J. Wilden, September 10, 1933, *Fowler News*, September 21, 1933.

49. *Pioneer Stories of Meade County*, p. 130; Sullivan, *History of Meade County*, pp. 17, 34.

50. Meade was located on SW¼, Sec. 2, NE¼, Sec. 10 and NW-¼, Sec. 11 of Twp. 32, R. 29. *Topeka Capital*, July 21, 1885; Sullivan, *History of Meade County*, pp. 28–29, 38; *Meade County Press-Democrat*, March 11, May 6, 1886; *Topeka Commonwealth*, October 6, 1885.

51. *Topeka Capital*, July 3, 1888.

52. M. W. Anshutz to George Root, August 11, 1939.

53. Hayes by Haley, June 10, 1930; Jack Potter to G. A. Root, March 19, 1926; Chrisman, *Lost Trails*, pp. 240–43; Orrin Ulysses Burright, *The Sun Rides High*, p. 90.

54. Wayne Gard, *The Chisholm Trail*, p. 255.

55. Austin E. and Alta S. Fife, *Cowboy and Western Songs*, p. 300.

56. *Dodge City Times*, March 15, 22, 1879; Addison, Bennett, "Meade County in 1879, Personal Recollections by A. Bennett, For the Graphic," *Fowler City Graphic*, September 17, 1885.

57. *Dodge City Ford County Globe*, July 13, 1880. *Dodge City Times*, July 6, 1878; H. S. Tennant, "The Two Cattle Trails," *Chronicles of Oklahoma* 14 (March 1936): 12. He was probably confused with "the gentleman outlaw," Henry Plummer, who fell victim to Wyoming vigilantes.

58. *Woodward Daily Press*, June 4, 1935; Sieber, "Trail Maker."

59. Haley, *Buffalo War*, p. 32.

60. *Oklahoma City Daily Oklahoman*, June 5, 1935. *Woodward Daily Press*, June 4, 1935.

61. *Dodge City Times*, January 15, 1881; Jim Herron, *Fifty Years on the Owl Hoot Trail*, ed. Harry E. Chrisman, p. 120. George W. Brown, "Kansas Indian Wars," *Collections of the Kansas State Historical Society, 1926–1928* 17 (1928): 135; Nettie M. Younger, *The History of My Pioneer Mother*, p. 2; *Pioneer Stories of Meade County*, passim; Sheffy, "Old Mobeetie," p. 67; *Dodge City Globe Live Stock Journal*, November 16, 1886; C. Robert Haywood, "Pearlette: A Mutual Aid Colony," *Kansas Historical Quarterly* 49 (Autumn 1976): 270.

Chapter 5. The Dodge City–Tascosa Trail

1. *Dodge City Times*, October 6, 1881; *Tascosa Pioneer*, June 9, October 20, 1886; Ricker, "Tascosa," *Oklahoma City Daily Oklahoman*, October 26, 1930.
2. J. Evetts Haley, *The XIT Ranch of Texas*, pp. 229–30.
3. Chrisman, *Lost Trails*, pp. 83 ff.
4. A long, detailed account of his life was given at the time of Hardesty's death in the *Dodge City Globe-Republican*, May 5, 1910.
5. Chrisman, *Lost Trails*, pp. 85–86.
6. *Ashland Clark County Clipper*, October 16, 1884.
7. Chrisman, *Lost Trails*, pp. 89–92.
8. Interview, Harry Ingerton by J. Evetts Haley, June 27, 1937; Myrna Tyron Thomas, *The Windswept Land: A History of Moore County, Texas*, p. 23; Ernest Archambeau to C. Robert Haywood, September 21, 1983.
9. Cator Family Papers; Ernest Cabe, Jr., "A Sketch of the Life of James Hamilton Cator," *Panhandle-Plains Historical Review* VI (1933): 13–23; Dotty Jones, *A Search for Opportunity: A History of Hansford County*, pp. 6–9.
10. Angie Debo, "An English View of the Wild West," *Panhandle-Plains Historical Review* 6 (1933): 22–44.
11. Deposition of James H. Cator, October 11, 1892, Indian Depredation Case No. 4601.
12. Interview, Billy R. Harrison by C. Robert Haywood, June 11, 1982. Harrison, curator of anthropology at the Panhandle-Plains Historical Museum, directed the excavation of the site in November 1981; Ingerton by Haley, June 27, 1937; Wright, Beverly & Co. Business Records, 1879–1887.
13. Cabe, "Sketch of James Cator," p. 20.
14. Philip J. Rasch, "Zulu in Hansford County"; *Dodge City Times*, February 22, 1883; Margaret Locke Kirk, "The Story of a Gentle Lady Who Pioneered the Panhandle in 1882."
15. Paul Knaplund, *The British Empire, 1815–1939*, pp. 430–31; Kirk, "A Gentle Lady"; Debo, "An English View of the Wild West," p. 37.
16. Kirk, "A Gentle Lady."
17. The Little Blue Station was eleven miles west and a half-mile south of present-day Dumas near U.S. 152. A highway marker stands about a half-mile north of the site. Interview, Woods Coffe, Jr. by C. Robert Haywood, July 20, 1983; Fred Squyres to C. Robert Haywood, August 2, 1983.
18. Interview, A. H. Webster by J. Evetts Haley, April 9, 1927; Interview, Lew Haile by Boone McClure, March 11, 1959; Brune, *Springs of Texas*, I: 318.

19. Romero, "Spanish Sheepmen," p. 64; O. H. Loyd, "Short Description of Oldham County, Texas"; John Arnot, "Tascosa Trail."

20. *Offers for Carrying the Mail*, House Executive Documents, 46th Cong. 2d sess., 1879–80, p. 1373; *Dodge City Times*, December 27, 1883, August 8, 1885; Romero, "Spanish Sheepmen," p. 65. Romero's detailed description of place-names on the trail are of little value because of changed designations. For instance, there is no record of Indio and India creeks. Loyd, "Description of Oldham County."

21. Demps Forest & Co. to Jim Cator, Cator Family Papers.

22. *Dodge City Times*, March 15, 22, 1879; *Fowler City Graphic*, September 17, 1885; "Kansas Post Offices."

23. *Dodge City Times*, May 17, 1883, Tracy, "Personal Memoirs."

24. *Dodge City Times*, December 13, 1883.

25. *Fowler City Graphic*, September 17, 1885; *Tascosa Pioneer*, August 12, 1886; *Dodge City Times*, February 22, 1883.

26. *Dodge City Globe Live Stock Journal*, November 3, 1885; *Fowler City Graphic*, July 2, October 29, 1885; *Wilburn Argus*, July 9, 1885.

27. *Wilburn Argus*, July 9, August 16, September 3, 1886; *Meade County Telegram*, July 2, August 12, 1886; *Dodge City Globe Live Stock Journal*, April 20, 1886.

28. *Meade County Press-Democrat*, July 1, August 5, 1886; *Wilburn Argus*, September 3, October 8, 1886; *History of Beaver County*, II: 15.

29. *Tascosa Pioneer*, September 29, 1886.

30. Ibid., February 11, 1888.

31. Cator Family Papers; *Tascosa Pioneer*, September 29, 1886; *Meade Globe*, March 12, 1886; John Arnot, "My Recollections of Tascosa Before and After the Coming of Law," *Panhandle-Plains Historical Review* 6 (1933): 74–75; *Beaver Herald-Democrat*, January 1, 1896.

32. *Oklahoma City Daily Oklahoman*, October 26, 1930.

Chapter 6. Freighting

1. Not all historians saw the teamsters as stereotypes. Wrote one: "The men who engaged in high plains wagon-freighting were as varied a group as the American frontier ever threw together in one course of endeavor." Henry Pickering Walker, *The Wagonmaster: High Plains Freighting from the Earliest Days of the Santa Fe Trail to 1880*, p. 67.

2. Oscar Osburn Winther, *The Transportation Frontier: Trans-Mississippi West, 1865–1890*, p. 34.

3. David Nevin, *The Expressmen*, p. 68; R. D. Holt, "Old Texas Wagon Trains," *Frontier Times* 25 (September 1948): 264, 277–78; Winther, *The Transportation Frontier*, p. 34; Walker, *Wagonmaster*, p. 34.

4. Holt, "Old Texas Wagon Trains," p. 276.

5. Using a jerk line required the driver to ride the near (left) wheel-horse or mule and control the team by means of a line (leather strap or cotton rope) running to the near leader. To turn the team to the right, the rider gave the line a few quick jerks (hence the team *jerk line*). With a steady pull, the leader would turn the team left. The wheelhorse or mule was saddled with an English saddle or whatever was available. William E. Lass, *From the Missouri to the Great Salt Lake: An Account of Overland Freighting*, pp. 9–10.

6. J. J. Long, "My Indian Expeditions."

7. Walker, *Wagonmaster*, p. 70; Lass, *Overland Freighting*, p. 18; *Dodge City Times*, January 15, 1881. A skeleton found more than a year later a considerable distance from the trail was believed to be that of Reynolds. *Dodge City Times*, June 29, 1882.

8. *Dodge City Ford County Globe*, August 6, 1878; *Dodge City Times*, August 11, 1878; Carriker, *Fort Supply*, pp. 149–50; *Dodge City Ford County Globe*, April 2, August 17, 1879; *Dodge City Times*, August 11, 18, September 1, 1877.

9. For coverage of Lee's career in the Dodge City–Panhandle Region, see David F. Schofield, *W. M. D. Lee, Indian Trader*.

10. Holt, "Old Texas Wagon Trains," pp. 273–74; *Dodge City Ford County Globe*, January 8, May 4, 1878, June 14, August 6, September 16, October 21, 1879, November 3, 1885. Schofield lists these items among many in the partners' inventory: $845 worth of beads, 317 shovels, 44 vests, plus such personal-care items as toothbrushes and looking glasses, *W. M. D. Lee*, p. 20; *Dodge City Ford County Globe*, March 6, 1883. Other reported tonnage was equally impressive; in February 1879, Lee and Reynolds moved 485,575 pounds of stores for the army. *Ford County Globe*, February 17, 1879.

11. *Dodge City Times*, September 8, 1877. For discussion of Lee's attempt to monopolize trade, see Schofield, *W. M. D. Lee*, pp. 83 ff., and Rath, *Rath Trail*, p. 98.

12. Schofield, *W. M. D. Lee*, p. 107.

13. For an accounting of Charles Rath's life, see Rath, *Rath Trail*, and Ida Ellen Rath, *Early Ford County*.

14. David A. Dary, *The Buffalo Book: The Saga of an American Symbol*, p. 94.

15. Wright, *Dodge City*, p. 199.

16. Schofield, *W. M. D. Lee*, pp. 91–93; Naomi H. Kincaid, "Rath City," *West Texas Historical Association Year Book*, 24 (October 1948): 41–44; Bussell by Haley, July 19, 1926.

17. Wright, *Dodge City*, pp. 76–77; *Dodge City Times*, October 6, 1881; Holt, "Old Texas Wagon Trains," p. 273.

18. Wright, *Dodge City*, p. 140.

19. *Dodge City Ford County Globe*, January 2, 1883; Rath, *Rath Trail*, p. 183.

20. *Dodge City Ford County Globe*, March 20, May 4, August 3, September 7, 1880.

21. Ibid., October 4, 1881.

22. Rath, *Rath Trail*, p. 162.

23. Kansas State Census of 1885, Ford County; the *Dodge City Daily Globe*, August 24, 1936, at the time of Reighard's death, quoted an earlier interview.

24. *Dodge City Daily Globe*, August 26, 1936.

25. Ibid.

26. *Dodge City Ford County Globe*, June 22, 1880. "Old Clark County Ranch Figured in Early History," *Dodge City Daily Globe*, February 23, 1935.

27. Chrisman, *Lost Trails*, p. 105; *Dodge City Times*, April 13, 1878; De Arnent, *Bat Masterson*, p. 104; Earle R. Forest, "The Killing of Ed Masterson," *Brand Book of the Los Angeles Corral of Westerners* 2 (1949): 154–55.

28. "Old Clark County Ranch"; *Dodge City Ford County Globe*, June 22, 1880; Merritt Beeson Letters.

29. Merritt Beeson Letters; *Dodge City Ford County Globe*, October 7, 1879; *Dodge City Daily Globe*, August 24, 1936; "Old Clark County Ranch."

30. Dave Bowers, "Memoirs of Dave Bowers, Shamrock, Texas, July 15, 1940."

31. Loy to Haley, November 1, 1929; Jones to Sheffy, December 31, 1929; Romero, "Spanish Sheepmen," p. 63; William Curry Holden, *Alkali Trails or Social and Economic Movements of the Texas Frontier, 1846–1900*, p. 16.

32. *Texas Almanac*, p. 216; Young, *Dodge City*, p. 37; Vestal, *Queen of Cowtowns*, p. 68.

33. *Pioneer Stories of Meade County*, p. 238; Walker, *Wagonmaster*, p. 130.

34. For background on the Hutchinson family, see Chapter 9. Elijah Hutchinson to Martha Hutchinson, April 2, 1882. Bettie Hutchinson to Martha Haywood, July 24, 1899; *Fowler City Graphic*, April 14, June 23, November 18, 1887; *Dodge City Times*, February 26, 1885.

35. Bowers, "Memoirs," pp. 32, 119; "Freighting," p. 1; Burright, *Sun Rides High*, p. 73.

36. A. N. Howe quoted in *History of Beaver County* I: 443–44; William Curry Holden, "Robert Cypert Parrack, Buffalo Hunter and Fence Cutter," *West Texas Historical Association Year Book* 21 (October 1945): 38.

37. Romero, "Spanish Sheepman," pp. 56–57; Burright, *Sun Rides High*, p. 73.

38. "Freighting," p. 1.

39. Josiah Gregg, *The Commerce of the Prairies*, ed. Milo Milton Quaife, pp. 22–23; Newt F. Locke to J. Evetts Haley, July 16, 1926; Holt, "Old Texas Wagon Trains," p. 272.

40. Manning by Ranck, November 5, 1937; Interview, Arthur N. Howe by John L. McCarty; Loy to Haley, November 1, 1929.

41. Frank Collinson to Harold Bugbee, February 9, 1937; Haley, *Charles Goodnight*, p. 424; Winther, *Transportation Frontier*, p. 35.

42. Howe by McCarty; John Bratt, *Trails of Yesterday*, p. 177; Mooar to Haley, July 28, 1937; Lass, *Overland Freighting*, pp. 5–10.

43. "Freighting," p. 1.

44. Walker, *Wagonmaster*, pp. 97–99; Holden, "Robert Cypert Parrack," p. 38.

45. Holden, "Robert Cypert Parrack," p. 38; Cook, *Border and the Buffalo*, p. 218; Dennis Collins, *The Indians' Last Fight or The Dull Knife Raid*, pp. 14–15.

46. Romero, "Spanish Sheepmen on the Canadian," p. 63; Cook, *Border and the Buffalo*, p. 218; Holt, *Old Texas Wagon Trains*, p. 270.

47. Arthur N. Howe, "My Experience as a Pioneer"; Bowers, "Memoirs"; *Dodge City Times*, August 23, 1883; Oswald, "History of Fort Elliott," p. 28; Billy N. Pope, "The Freighter and Railroader in the Economic Pattern of Panhandle History," p. 34.

48. *Fort Griffin Echo*, September 17, 1881; *Dodge City Times*, September 1, 1881; *Dodge City Ford County Globe*, January 1, 1884.

Chapter 7. P. G. Reynolds, Mail Contractor

1. Schofield, *W. M. D. Lee*, p. 107.

2. Dyskstra, *Cattle Towns*, p. 94.

3. Colonel S. F. Tilghman, comp., "The Reynolds Family, 1530–1959"; Newsom, *Kicking Bird*, p. 8 ff.

4. Rex Reynolds to C. Robert Haywood, September 5, 1982; *Dodge City Kansas Cowboy*, November 1, 1884; *Dodge City Times*, July 19, 1888. The name Hard is frequently spelled Hart in newspaper accounts and even in official records.

5. The Reynolds-Quantrill relationship is based on family tradition and statements made in the press while P. G. was living and at the time of his death. *Dodge City Kansas Cowboy*, August 23, 1884; *Dodge City Times*, July 19, 1888. Quantrill did work with people helping fugitives to escape from Missouri, and as a double agent he stole Missouri-owned slaves on

some raids and returned fugitives to Missourians at other times. It is possible that he knew P. G. through the Underground Railroad.

6. Reynolds to Haywood, September 5, 1982; *Dodge City Kansas Cowboy*, August 23, 1884; Claims Settlements for Quantrill's Raid, Office of Audit of the State, September 19, 1887. The firm was recorded as Hart and Reynolds by the state audit. *Dodge City Times*, July 19, 1888.

7. *Lawrence Republican*, October 16, 1862.

8. *Dodge City Times*, July 19, 1888.

9. Reynolds to Haywood, October 16, 1982. P. G.'s son followed his father to Dodge "a few months later in 1875." Most sources agree on the 1875 date. Reynolds by Haley, July 18, 1934; Mrs. P. G. Reynolds' obituary, *Dodge City Kansas Journal*, August 26, 1910; P. G.'s obituary, *Dodge City Democrat*, July 21, 1888.

10. Young, *Dodge City*, p. 161; Charter of Incorporation of the Evangelical Christian Church, Dodge City, July 26, 1877.

11. *Dodge City Ford County Globe*, October 8, 1881; *Dodge City Globe Live Stock Journal*, October 8, 1885, March 9, May 18, 1886, June 7, 1887.

12. *Dodge City Ford County Globe*, October 21, 1879, April 22, July 8, 15, 22, 1884; *Dodge City Globe Live Stock Journal*, October 7, 1884, March 9, May 18, 1886; *Ashland Clark County Clipper*, February 5, 1885; *Dodge City Democrat*, October 11, 1884.

13. The pertinent letters, telegrams, ordinances, and newspaper comments concerning The War are reproduced in Miller and Snell, *Great Gunfighters*, pp. 369–413. De Arment, *Bat Masterson*, p. 253.

14. *Kansas City Evening Star*, May 9, 1883; *Dodge City Times*, May 3, 1883.

15. P. G. came to Webster's support later when he signed a petition urging him to run for mayor. Webster, with appropriate modesty, reported that the caliber of the "honored names on the petition" had persuaded him to accept the assignment. *Dodge City Globe Live Stock Journal*, March 9, 1886.

16. Quoted in Young, *Dodge City*, p. 124.

17. *Dodge City Times*, August 31, 1879.

18. Miller and Snell, *Great Gunfighters*, pp. 398 ff.

19. George R. Peck to M. W. Sutton, May 17, 1883.

20. *Dodge City Ford County Globe*, November 6, 1883; *Dodge City Times*, May 17, 1883; *Topeka Daily Commonwealth*, May 18, 1883.

21. *Dodge City Times*, May 17, 1883.

22. *Dodge City Ford County Globe*, August 18, 1880, August 16, 1883.

23. Ibid., August 30, 1883.

24. Klaine quoted in Young, *Dodge City*, p. 131; *Dodge City Kansas Cowboy*, November 7, 1885.

25. Newsom, *Kicking Bird*, p. 95; *Dodge City Times*, November 22, 1883.

26. *Dodge City Times*, September 1, 1877; *Dodge City Ford County Globe*, January 13, 1880. Reynolds to Haywood, September 5, 1982.

27. *Dodge City Journal*, April 4, 1940.

28. *Dodge City Daily Globe*, January 2, 1942.

29. *Dodge City Ford County Globe*, April 19, November 8, 1881, May 29, 1882, January 9, July 10, November 20, 1883; *Dodge City Globe Live Stock Journal*, December 29, 1885; *Dodge City Times*, November 27, 1883.

30. Wright, *Dodge City*, p. 204; *Dodge City Globe Live Stock Journal*, February 23, 1886; Charles C. Lowther, *Panhandle Parson*, p. 21.

31. Wright, *Dodge City*, p. 205.

32. Callison, *Bill Jones*, pp. 123–24.

33. Herron, *Owl Hoot Trail*, p. 16.

34. *Dodge City Times*, February 22, 1883; John Arnot, "A History of Tascosa."

35. Sullivan, *History of Meade County*, p. 105; *Dodge City Ford County Globe*, March 19, 1878, June 24, September 16, 1879; *Dodge City Times*, March 9, June 8, 1878.

36. *Dodge City Times*, April 6, 1878.

37. A. M. Gibson, *Report of the Attorney General on the Star Mail Service*, 47th Cong., 1st sess., 1881–82, p. 469; Winnie Davis Hale, "First Coach Made Appearance in 1887."

38. Gibson, *Report on the Star Mail Service*, p. 471; "Report of the Postmaster-General," *Annual Report*, 42d Cong., 2d sess., 1872, passim.

39. *Dodge City Globe Live Stock Journal*, January 31, 1888; Federal Census of 1880, Lawrence, Kansas; O. W. McAllaster, "My Experience in the Lawrence Raid," *Collections of the Kansas State Historical Society, 1911–1912* 12 (1912): 401; *Dodge City Kansas Cowboy*, November 22, 1884; *Offers for Carrying the Mail*, pp. 1302–45, 1483.

40. *Dodge City Globe Live Stock Journal*, May 11, 1886.

41. *Offers for Carrying the Mail*, pp. 1483–90.

42. James D. Norris and Arthur H. Shaffer, eds., *Politics and Patronage in the Gilded Age*, p. 294; George Frederick Howe, *Chester A. Arthur: A Quarter-Century of Machine Politics*, pp. 179–93; Louise Horton, "The Star Route Conspiracies," *Texana* 7 (1969): 220–33.

43. Tracy, "Personal Memoirs."

44. Interview, Dave R. McCormick by J. Evetts Haley, March 2, 1935.

45. Horton, "Star Route Conspiracies," p. 231; *Dodge City Times*, February 22, 1883.

46. *Dodge City Ford County Republican*, July 18, 1888.

47. Hayes by Haley, June 10, 1930.

48. O. P. Byers, "Personal Recollections of the Terrible Blizzard of 1886," *Collections of the Kansas State Historical Society, 1911–1912* 12 (1912): 109.

49. Tracy, "Personal Memoirs."
50. *Dodge City Times*, December 14, 1878.
51. *Dodge City Globe Live Stock Journal*, January 11, 1887; Ralph Moody, *Stagecoach West*, pp. 18–19.
52. *The Last Hook-Up*, a picture on a widely circulated postal card, was titled thus because it showed the last time a Reynolds coach was driven. The picture was taken in front of P. G.'s home at 801 Second Avenue. P. G.'s son George, the driver, is seated beside Tom Goodwin. Reynolds to Haywood, September 5, 1982. John Sullivan did the woodwork on Sughrue coaches and P. W. Beamer did the ironwork; both were Dodge City craftsmen. James R. Quinn in *History of Beaver County*, II, p. 15. *Dodge City Globe Live Stock Journal*, January 11, 1881.
53. *Dodge City Globe Live Stock Journal*, January 11, 1881.
54. *Dodge City Kansas Cowboy*, August 23, 1884; *Dodge City Globe Live Stock Journal*, July 3, 1883, January 31, 1888.
55. Reynolds to Haywood, September 5, 1982; Quinn in *History of Beaver County* II: 15; Moody, *Stagecoach West*, p. 20.
56. *Dodge City Ford County Globe*, August 6, 1878, September 30, 1874; Fire Insurance Maps of Dodge City, Sandborn-Perris Map Company, September, 1887; Interview, Willie Newberry Lewis by M. V. Sanders, August 26, 1935; *Dodge City Times*, March 9, 1878, November 23, 1882; *Wilburn Argus*, August 6, September 3, 1886; *Appleton Era*, January 7, 1886; *Dodge City Globe Live Stock Journal*, August 5, September 16, 1884.
57. *Dodge City Kansas Cowboy*, August 23, 1884; *Wilburn Argus*, July 6, 13, 1886.
58. *Dodge City Ford County Republican*, July 18, 1888.
59. Reynolds by Haley, July 18, 1934.
60. *Dodge City Times*, August 11, 1877, April 6, June 15, 1878; *Dodge City Globe Live Stock Journal*, January 6, 1886. P. G. may have kept the line to the military post open for passengers only. Sam Marshall was referred to as "the mail contractor for carrying mail from Dodge City to the post, Fort Supply" while Reynolds still had a coach line running. P. G. may have sublet from Marshall.
61. *Dodge City Globe Live Stock Journal*, March 19, 1878; *Dodge City Times*, March 8, September 14, 1878. The Reynolds letterhead carried this designation. P. G. Reynolds File, Boot Hill Museum Historical Library, Dodge City.
62. *Dodge City Ford County Globe*, September 16, 1879. This same item ran in a number of other papers; at least one, the *Clarendon News*, was not directly on the line.
63. *Dodge City Ford County Globe*, June 24, 1879, May 11, 1880, August 1, 1882; *Dodge City Times*, September 14, 1818, *Dodge City Globe Live Stock Journal*, March 17, 1885.

64. *Dodge City Times,* March 29, 1879, March 9, 1878; Reynolds by Haley, July 18, 1934; *Dodge City Globe Live Stock Journal,* May 25, July 13, 1880.

65. *Dodge City Globe Live Stock Journal,* March 2, July 6, 13, 1886, June 7, 1887; *Kinsley Mercury,* March 6, 1886.

66. *Appleton Era,* May 12, 1887.

67. Heine Schmidt, "Early Ford County Settler, Stage Driver," *Dodge City High Plains Journal,* September 4, 1952; *Dodge City Globe Live Stock Journal,* June 7, 1887; P. G. Reynolds File, Boot Hill Museum Research Library, Dodge City, Kansas.

68. *Dodge City Globe Live Stock Journal,* January 31, 1888; *Dodge City Times,* April 15, 1886. Apparently, Tisdale became sole owner soon after Reynolds' death and continued as superintendent of the line. *Harper Sentinel,* April 21, 1888.

69. *Ashland Clark County Clipper,* July 15, 1886.

70. *Dodge City Globe Live Stock Journal,* May 1, 1887; June 19, 1888; Newsom, *Kicking Bird,* p. 102; *Dodge City Democrat,* July 21, 1888.

Chapter 8. Stage Drivers

1. Moody, *Stagecoach West,* p. 17.

2. All pertinent newspaper accounts of Brown's career in Kansas are found in Miller and Snell, *Great Gunfighters,* pp. 47–64. For his fellow townsmen's evaluation of Brown, see the *Caldwell Commercial* of October 19, 1882 and the *Caldwell Journal* of May 8, 1884.

3. Tracy, "Personal Memoirs"; Nelson, *Cowman's Southwest,* pp. 265–66. On one visit the women were amazed to find Steed's language as pure as that "in the meetin' house." The stationkeeper explained to them that the Canadian River had a wonderful curative power for Steed, who understood God to be completely in control of all natural phenomena, including the weather and high water: "There's a storm up river, and whenever Steed expects high water the next day, he won't swear. When the Canadian is up, most people use good language till they get across."

4. Leo Oliva, *Fort Larned on the Santa Fe Trail,* p. 62. At Fort Elliott in 1875, teamsters received the same thirty-five dollars a month and laborers drew a dollar a day. Oswald, "History of Fort Elliott," p. 28.

5. Burright, *Sun Rides High,* p. 82.

6. *Dodge City Times,* July 19, 1888; *Dodge City Globe Live Stock Journal,* January 7, 1887; *Dodge City Ford County Globe,* May 25, 1880.

7. Nevin, *The Expressmen,* p. 176; Long, "My Indian Expeditions"; Schmidt, "Stage Driver"; Hayes by Haley, June 10, 1930.

8. Judge O. W. Williams, Miscellaneous Manuscripts; *Dodge City*

Times, November 12, 28, 1878; Bussell by Haley, July 19, 1926; Interview, P. T. Lieneman by Linnaeus B. Ranck, January 28, 1938.

9. *Dodge City Times,* September 20, 1879.

10. *Tascosa Pioneer,* June 26, 1886.

11. Ibid., November 28, 1878.

12. *Dodge City Kansas Cowboy,* June 6, 1885.

13. *Meade County Press-Democrat,* August 4, 1886.

14. Hale, "First Coach in 1887"; Haley, *Charles Goodnight,* p. 316. The *Dodge City Times* compared the 1878 figure of $1.20 per hundredweight for 100 miles with the 1879 cost of 86¢. Bob Cator found that goods could be shipped in from Colorado, but it would cost 5¢ a pound for the 150-mile trip. John M. Wilson to Robert Cator, April 18, 1879; Callison, *Bill Jones,* p. 92.

15. Mrs. Warren W. Wetsel, "The Life of Mrs. Warren W. Wetsel of Amarillo, Texas"; Interview, Mrs. B. W. Chamberlain by Willie Newberry Lewis, May 1, 1935; George M. Hoover, Saloon Account Books.

16. *Dodge City Globe Live Stock Journal,* November 16, 1886.

17. Hayes by Haley, June 10, 1930; the *Times* later identified the man as Joseph Lawrence, "a Bohemian." *Dodge City Times,* May 6, 20, 1877.

18. Nevin, *The Expressmen,* p. 122; Demas Barnes, *From the Atlantic to the Pacific Overland,* pp. 7–8.

19. Reynolds to Haywood, September 5, 1982; *Dodge City Ford County Globe,* January 13, 21, 1880; Schmidt, "Stage Driver."

20. Bussell by Haley, July 19, 1926; Marion Armstrong, "Memoirs."

21. Schmidt, "Stage Driver"; Reynolds to Haywood, September 5, 1982.

22. See the *Meade County Globe,* September 5, 1885. There was a sad sequel to the attempted robbery. A letter in Robbins' pocket told of the death of a brother in Colorado. Sheriff Pat Sughrue sent the letter to Robbins' mother, who requested that any valuables be sent to her as she needed "money very bad." Robbins had one nickel in his pocket; his personal belongings—saddle, horse, pistol—were sold to defray the expenses of burying him in potter's field. *Dodge City Kansas Cowboy,* September 19, October 3, 1885; *National Police Gazette,* October 3, 1885.

23. Nevin, *The Expressmen,* p. 32; Dobbs by McCarty, October 20, 1942.

24. *Dodge City Times,* January 15, 1881; Armstrong, "Memoirs."

25. *Dodge City Times,* February 5, 1881; McCarty, *Maverick Town,* pp. 68–70.

26. Byers, "Blizzard of 1886," p. 104.

27. Ibid., pp. 108–109; *Topeka Commonwealth,* January 13, 1885.

28. Schmidt, "Stage Driver."

29. J. Wright Mooar to J. Evetts Haley, April 11, 1936.

30. Judys by Haywood, July 6, 1982; Schmidt, "Stage Driver"; Bowers, "Memoirs"; *Dodge City Ford County Globe,* July 6, 1880.

31. Reginald Aldridge, *Life on a Ranch: Ranch Notes in Kansas, Colorado, the Indian Territory and Northern Texas*, pp. 178–80.

32. Schmidt, "Stage Driver."

33. Nevin, *The Expressmen*, p. 180; E. E. Carhart to J. Evetts Haley, July 20, 1926.

34. Burright, *Sun Rides High*, p. 82.

35. *Dodge City Ford County Globe*, September 9, 1879; Hayes by Haley, June 10, 1930; *Ashland Clark County Clipper*, February 26, 1885, June 23, 1887.

36. *Dodge City Globe Live Stock Journal*, September 29, 1885; *Dodge City Kansas Cowboy*, October 3, 1885; *Dodge City Democrat*, October 3, 1885; *Ashland Clark County Clipper*, February 26, 1885.

37. *Dodge City Times*, November 24, 1877.

38. David Norton, *Sketches of the Town of Old Town, Penobscot County, Maine*, p. 25.

39. Interview, Louis Haywood by C. Robert Haywood, November 5, 1974; Miscellaneous Plat Book, U.S. Land Office, Dodge City, Kansas.

40. *Dodge City Daily Globe*, November 29, 1918; *Fowler Gazette*, July 10, 1908, June 9, 1911; *Fowler News*, April 16, 1914.

41. *Fowler Gazette*, September 20, 1907.

42. C. Robert Haywood, "Uncle Ben's Grove," *Kansas Territorial* 1 (June–July 1981): 28–30.

43. *Dodge City Daily Globe*, December 2, 1918.

44. Marion Armstrong, Unpublished and Untitled Manuscript.

45. Ibid.

46. McCarty, *Old Tascosa*, pp. 96–99; Frederick R. Bechdolt, "Tascosa Clippings," p. 137; Laura V. Hamner, "Tales of Cape Willingham."

47. Ibid., p. 136; Armstrong, Unpublished and Untitled Manuscript; Olive K. Dixon, "A Long, Useful Life Ended," *Frontier Times* 3 (November 1925): 33.

48. R. G. Carter, *On the Border with Mackenzie*, p. 525.

49. Haley, *Buffalo War*, pp. 125 ff.

50. Rathjen, *Texas Panhandle Frontier*, pp. 206–10; J. J. Long to Raymond Bland, quoted in Riley, "History of Hemphill County," p. 25; Ernest R. Archambeau, "The Battle of Lyman's Wagon Train," *Panhandle-Plains Historical Review* 36 (1936): 90 ff; W. S. Nye, *Carbine and Lance: The Story of Old Fort Sill*, pp. 213 ff.

51. Long, "My Indian Expeditions"; J. T. Marshall, *The Miler Expedition of 1874–1875: An Eyewitness account of the Red River War*, p. 21.

52. Carter, *On the Border with Mackenzie*, p. 519.

53. Long, "My Indian Expeditions."

54. J. J. Long, "The Mail Line."

55. F. Newton Reynolds, "Pioneering The West: As Related to I. N.

Newt Bowers"; Lewis by Sanders, August 26, 1935; Robertson and Robertson, *Panhandle Pilgrimage*, p. 197; H. B. Bradford, "Wheeler County As I Knew It in the Early Days, as told to Dennis Reynolds"; Reynolds, "Pioneering in the West"; Dixon, "A Long Life Ended."

56. Reynolds, "Pioneering the West"; Dixon, "A Long Life Ended."

57. *Caldwell Commercial*, October 19, 1882; *Caldwell Journal*, May 8, 1884.

Chapter 9. Way Stations and the People Who Ran Them

1. To make a distinction between a cattle ranch and a station supplying food and forage to travelers, the latter was sometimes spelled with a final *e*: road ranche. It was an erratic practice, as much neglected by editors and settlers as used; therefore the spelling herein is simply *road ranch*.

2. Moody, *Stagecoach West*, pp. 87, 100; Nick Eggenhofer, *Wagons, Mules and Men*, pp. 151–57; Winther, *Transportation Frontier*, pp. 48–49; Donald F. Danker, "The Influence of Transportation Upon Nebraska Territory," *Nebraska History* 46 (June 1966): 194.

3. Winther, *Transportation Frontier*, pp. 67–68; *Dodge City Ford County Globe*, September 16, 1879.

4. Nevin, *The Expressmen*, p. 180.

5. Frank Dale Healy to Will G. Fields, May 15, 1940.

6. Burright, *Sun Rides High*, pp. 75–76.

7. Mrs. W. W. Owens, "Autobiography."

8. Tracy, "Personal Memoirs."

9. Nelson, *Cowman's Southwest*, p. 259.

10. William H. Perrin, *Kentucky: A History of the State*, pp. 696–97; M. H. Dunn, ed., *Early Lincoln County History*, p. 80; Federal Census of 1820, Kentucky.

11. *Pearlette Call*, January 17, 1880; *Fowler City Graphic*, October 29, 1887; 1820.

12. The road ranch was located on SE¼, SE¼, Sec. 20, Twp. 30, R. 26. *Fowler City Graphic*, November 19, 1885.

13. Elijah Hutchinson to Martha Hutchinson, April 2, 1882; *Fowler City Graphic*, October 29, 1887.

14. *Fowler City Graphic*, July 15, 1886; *Wilburn Argus*, April 6, 16, 1886. Netche and Jard also advertised their ranch on the Cimarron River in 1879. *Dodge City Ford County Globe*, February 28, 1879.

15. *Dodge City Globe Live Stock Journal*, April 20, 1886; *Wilburn Argus*, August 20, September 2, 24, 1886. See the Wilburn House advertisement in the *Fowler City Graphic*, January 20, 1887.

16. *Wilburn Argus*, August 6, 13, November 18, 1886.

17. Bernita McKissick to C. Robert Haywood, March 15, 1975; *Wilburn Argus*, July 16, August 6, 13, September 3, November 18, December 2, 1886, May 29, 1887; Corporation Charters, XXIV: 28; *Wilburn Argus*, June 23, 1887.

18. *Fowler Gazette*, September 15, 1911.

19. Miller and Snell, *Great Gunfighters*, p. 322; *Parsons Eclipse*, April 8, 1880; Interview, J. Phelps White by J. Evetts Haley, January 15, 1927.

20. Brown provided most of the details of his life in an article published in 1926. See "Life and Adventure of George W. Brown, Soldier, Pioneer, Scout, Plainsman and Buffalo Hunter," *Collections of the Kansas State Historical Society, 1926–1928* 17 (1928), pp. 98–134; Chrisman, *Lost Trails*, p. 23.

21. The Wells were artisian springs near Crooked Creek just east of present-day Meade, Kansas. The salt well appeared suddenly sometime between March 16, 1880, when a freighter passed over the Jones and Plummer Trail and found it normal, and March 18, when another freighter discovered that a sink hole about seventy-five feet in diameter had taken about half the trail. For several years commercial salt making by evaporation was carried on there. Sullivan, *History of Meade County*, pp. 96–101. Brown, "Life and Adventure," p. 130.

22. *Dodge City Ford County Globe*, December 23, 1879; *Pioneer Stories of Meade County*, p. 237.

23. *Dodge City Ford County Globe*, December 7, 1880.

24. George M. Hoover, Saloon Account Books, June 5, 1883 entries et seq.; McCarty, *Maverick Town*, p. 24; White by Haley, January 15, 1927; Boss Neff to His Grandson (Boss Neff, II).

25. Brown, "Life and Adventure," p. 134; Charles A. Siringo, *Riata and Spurs*, p. 59; *Fowler City Graphic*, September 3, 1885.

26. *Meade County Globe*, May 7, 1886; *Dodge City Times*, October 25, 1883; Brown, "Life and Adventure," pp. 132–33. Of the five children born to the Browns, only one survived to adulthood. Federal Census of 1900, Oklahoma, Canadian County, El Reno.

27. *Dodge City Times*, December 26, 1884; Chrisman, *Lost Trails*, pp. 24–25; *Kingfisher New World*, January 18, 1890.

28. Sullivan, *History of Meade County*, pp. 104–24; *Meade Press-Democrat*, March 11, May 6, 1886.

29. *Beaver City Pioneer*, June 19, 1886; *Meade Center Telegram*, July 29, 1886; Brown, "Life and Adventure," p. 132; *Meade County Press-Democrat*, August 4, 1886.

30. Brown, "Life and Adventure," p. 130; R. W. Griggs to George W. Brown, July 1, 1925; George W. Brown to William E. Connelley, February 13, March 1, 1926.

31. Springer leased his Ford County ranch or farm, then put it up for

sale in 1878. *Dodge City Times*, April 21, 1877; March 23, 1878. Jackson and Blau have the date of his settlement in the Panhandle as 1875; Cook places it in 1874, and Hayes remembered it as about "1876 or at least was there when we got to the Canadian in 1877." Berenice Lloyd Jackson and Max Blau, "The Tuttle Trail," *Chronicles of Oklahoma* 56 (Fall 1978): 315; Hayes by Haley, June 10, 1930; Cook, *Border and the Buffalo*, p. 137.

32. Cook, *Border and the Buffalo*, p. 137.

33. Carriker, *Fort Supply*, p. 151.

34. Callison, *Bill Jones*, p. 86.

35. *Dodge City Times*, March 23, 1878. His purchase of three hundred head of cattle from Dillard Fant, who was driving a herd through to Dodge City, is considered by some to be the first permanent herd in the Panhandle, but the date can be set back to 1874 when Springer arrived with cattle from his Kansas ranch. Hayes by Haley, June 10, 1930. Riley, "History of Hemphill County," p. 33.

36. *Dodge City Times*, November 23, 1878. A somewhat more elaborate story is given by Laura V. Hamner, who credits the killing to a plot by the soldiers to avenge their heavy losses at cards. Hamner, *Short Grass and Longhorns*, pp. 39–40; Bill Jones gave an account more nearly like that in the *Dodge City Times*. Callison, *Bill Jones*, p. 86. Cal Conatser told Glyndon M. Riley yet another version. All agree that gambling and Springer's personality were at the bottom of the trouble.

37. Jackson and Blau, "Tuttle Trail," p. 316.

38. Hamner, *Short Grass and Longhorns*, p. 41; Brainard by Haley, June 17, 1937; Hayes by Haley, June 10, 1930; Nelson, *Cowman's Southwest*, p. 278.

39. Brainard by Haley, June 17, 1937.

40. Ibid.; James R. Quinn, "Happenings of 1888 through 1890," in *History of Beaver County*, I: 15.

41. Callison, *Bill Jones*, pp. 53–54.

42. Ibid., pp. 54–56.

Chapter 10. End of the Trail

1. H. H. Halsell, *The Old Cimarron*, p. 152.

2. *Meade County Globe*, July 16, 1885, January 29, 1886; *Fowler City Graphic*, July 9, 23, 1885; Andrews, *History of Bloom*, p. 15; *Englewood Clark County Chief*, June 10, 1887.

3. *Meade County Press-Democrat*, March 4, 1886. In reality, Dodge merchants paid little attention to threats of other Kansas markets. In 1880 when the *Medicine Lodge Cresset* indicated that John Tuttle was preparing a new freighting trail from Springer Ranch to Medicine Lodge, the editor

of the *Dodge City Times* gave the rumor little credence. The existing trail to Dodge was "the most available route, being at all times passable and free from objections." Dodge City's Panhandle trade, the editor assured his readers, was secure. *Dodge City Times*, May 1, 1880.

4. *Ashland Clark County Clipper*, March 1, 1888; *Ashland Herald*, September 15, 1887.

5. For a discussion of the mutual contributions of railroad and wagon, see Pope, "Freighters and Railroader in this Economic Pattern of Panhandle History"; McCarty, *Maverick Town*, p. 253.

6. *Dodge City Kansas Cowboy*, October 24, 1885; *Bloom Weekly Telegram*, April 5, 1888; Young, *Dodge City*, p. 138, quoting the *Topeka Capital*.

7. Wright, *Dodge City*, p. 318.

8. Sullivan, *History of Meade County*, pp. 104–11; Owen D. Wiggans, "A History of Dodge City, Kansas."

9. Wright, *Dodge City*, p. 328; Hamner, "Free Grass," pp. 119–20.

10. Robert R. Dykstra, *The Cattle Towns*, p. 359; Reginald C. McGrane, *The Economic Development of the American Nation*, p. 44.

11. Zelinsky, *Cultural Geography*, pp. 13–14, 23.

12. *Wilburn Argus*, February 24, April 16, 1887.

13. Willa Cather, *My Ántonia*, p. 419.

Bibliography

MANUSCRIPTS AND PAPERS

Armstrong, Marion. "Memoirs." Tascosa and Related Materials, I, John L. McCarty Papers, Amarillo Public Library, Amarillo, Texas.
————. Unpublished and Untitled Manuscript. Earl Vandale Collection, Barker Library, University of Texas at Austin.
Arnot, John. "A History of Tascosa." Manuscript, Earl Vandale Collection, Barker Library, University of Texas at Austin.
————. "Tascosa Trail." Manuscript, Earl Vandale Collection, Barker Library, University of Texas at Austin.
Bair, Everett. "Echoes of Stage Lines in the Days of Custer and Sitting Bull." Manuscript, Early Day Stories File, John L. McCarty Papers, Amarillo Public Library, Amarillo, Texas.
Baird, Major George W. Papers. Microfilm, Manuscript Department, Kansas State Historical Society, Topeka.
Baldwin, Frank D. Diary. William Carey Brown Collection, University of Colorado, Boulder.
Bechdolt, Frederick R. "Tascosa Clippings." James H. East Papers, Barker Library, University of Texas at Austin.
Beeson, Merritt. Letters. George Reighard File, Boot Hill Museum Research Library, Dodge City, Kansas.
Black, Mrs. Hiram. "Lipscomb County History." Manuscript, Laura V. Hamner Collection, Barker Library, University of Texas at Austin.
Bowers, Dave. "Memoirs of Dave Bowers, Shamrock, Texas, July 15, 1940." Manuscript, Jesse J. Dyer Papers, Panhandle-Plains Historical Museum, Canyon, Texas.
Bradford, H. B. "Wheeler County As I Knew It in the Early Days, as told to Dennis Reynolds." Earl Vandale Collection, Barker Library, University of Texas at Austin.

Cator, James H. "Notes on the Life of James H. Cator." Manuscript, Panhandle-Plains Historical Museum, Canyon, Texas.

Cator Family Papers. Panhandle-Plains Historical Museum, Canyon, Texas.

Charter of Incorporation of the Evangelical Christian Church, Dodge City, July 26, 1877. W. S. Campbell Collection, Manuscript Department, Kansas State Historical Society, Topeka.

Comstock, Henry Griswold. "Henry Griswold Comstock's Return to Texas, January, 1872." Manuscript, J. R. Webb File, Texas Technical University, Lubbock.

Creaton, John. "An Autobiography, 1856–1932." Earl Vandale Collection, Barker Library, University of Texas at Austin.

Currie, Mrs. Tom (Daisy). "The Story of Her Life as Told to Me by Her." Manuscript, Mrs. Tom Currie File, Panhandle-Plains Historical Museum, Canyon, Texas.

Douglas, C. L. "Frontier Town: Tascosa, the Turbulent, Red, Raw, Liquor and Sudden Death." Manuscript, Tascosa, Texas File, Texas Collection, Baylor University, Waco, Texas.

"Fort Elliott, Texas," Records of the War Department, Office of the Quartermaster General, Reservation File, Indian-Pioneer History, Oklahoma Historical Society, Oklahoma City.

"Freighting." Manuscript, Tascosa and Related Materials, III, John L. McCarty Papers, Amarillo Public Library, Amarillo, Texas.

Gerlach, Capitola. "Gerlach's Store." WPA Writers Project, Panhandle Area, Box 2. Barker Library, University of Texas at Austin.

Hale, Winnie Davis. "First Coach Made Appearance in 1887." Manuscript, Tascosa and Related Material, I, John L. McCarty Papers, Amarillo Public Library, Amarillo, Texas.

Hamner, Laura V. "Free Grass." Manuscript, Earl Vandale Collection, University of Texas at Austin.

———. "Tales of Cape Willingham." Manuscript, Tascosa and Related Materials, VII, John L. McCarty Papers, Amarillo Public Library, Amarillo, Texas.

Hoover, George M. Saloon Account Books. Archives Department, Kansas State Historical Society, Topeka.

Howe, Arthur N. "My Experience as a Pioneer." Manuscript, Lipscomb County, Texas File 17, John L. McCarty Papers, Amarillo Public Library, Amarillo, Texas.

Hunnius, Carl Julius Adolph. "Survey of the Staked Plains and Headwaters of Red River." Manuscript, Hunnius File, Panhandle-Plains Historical Museum, Canyon, Texas.

"Kansas Post Offices." Manuscript Department, Kansas State Historical Society, Topeka.

Kirk, Margaret Locke. "The Story of a Gentle Lady Who Pioneered the Panhandle in 1882." Manuscript, Historical Materials File, John L. McCarty Papers, Amarillo Public Library, Amarillo, Texas.

Landis, Charles G. "Forty-seven years in Potter County." Manuscript, Earl Vandale Collection, Barker Library, University of Texas at Austin.

Long, J. J. "The Mail Line." J. J. Long Papers. Panhandle-Plains Historical Museum, Canyon, Texas.

————. "My Indian Expeditions." Manuscript, J. J. Long Papers, Panhandle-Plains Historical Museum, Canyon, Texas.

Loyd, O. H. "Oldham County, Texas: An Authentic Historical Brief of Old Tascosa and Oldham County." Manuscript, Tascosa and Related Materials, III, John L. McCarty Papers, Amarillo Public Library, Amarillo, Texas.

————. "Short Description of Oldham County, Texas." Manuscript, Earl Vandale Collection, Barker Library, University of Texas at Austin.

Lummus, Maud. "Pioneering: As Told to David Bowen." Manuscript, Panhandle-Plains Historical Museum, Canyon, Texas.

Notes on Early Clark County, Kansas. Compiled by the Clark County Chapter of the Kansas State Historical Society. 6 vols. Ashland, Kan., *Clark County Clipper*, 1939–70.

Owens, Mrs. W. W. "Autobiography." Manuscript, Panhandle-Plains Historical Museum, Canyon, Texas.

"Potter County's First Post Office." Manuscript, Panhandle Area, Box 2. Barker Library, University of Texas at Austin.

Rasch, Philip J. "Zulu in Hansford County." Manuscript, Philip J. Rasch File, Panhandle-Plains Historical Museum, Canyon, Texas.

Reeves, Frank. "Chuck Wagon Gossip." Manuscript, Folder 42, John L. McCarty Papers, Amarillo Public Library, Amarillo, Texas.

Reynolds, F. Newton. "Pioneering the West: As Related to I. N. Newt Bowers." Manuscript, Earl Vandale Collection, Barker Library, University of Texas at Austin.

Rye, Edgar. "Frontier Reminiscence." Manuscript, Carl Coke Rister Papers, Panhandle-Plains Historical Museum, Canyon, Texas.

Sieber, Coila. "Trail Maker." Manuscript in possession of Bill Jones, Anaheim, California.

"Story Telling Contest, February 18, 1927." Manuscript, Nita Stewart Haley Memorial Library, Midland, Texas.

Tilghman, Colonel S. F., comp. "The Reynolds Family, 1530–1959." Manuscript in possession of Rex Reynolds, Niles, Michigan.

Tracy, Fred Carter. "Personal Memoirs of Fred Carter Tracy, Beaver, Oklahoma." Manuscript, Oklahoma State Historical Society, Oklahoma City.

Wetsel, Mrs. Warren W. "The Life of Mrs. Warren W. Wetsel of Amarillo, Texas." Manuscript, Daisy Currie File, Panhandle-Plains Historical Museum, Canyon, Texas.

Williams, Judge O. W. Miscellaneous Manuscripts. Earl Vandale Collection, Barker Library, University of Texas at Austin.

Willingham, Cape. "History of the First Ranches." Manuscript, Nita Stewart Haley Memorial Library, Midland, Texas.

WPA Federal Writers Project, Manuscript, Panhandle Area, Box 2. Barker Library, University of Texas at Austin.

Wright, Beverley & Co. Business Records, 1879–1887. Boot Hill Museum Research Library, Dodge City, Kansas.

GOVERNMENT DOCUMENTS

Baldwin, Frank. "Baldwin's Report, August 20, 1874." Major George W. Baird Papers, Manuscript Department, Kansas State Historical Society, Topeka.

Claims Settlements for Quantrill's Raid. Office of Audit of the State, September 19, 1887. Archives Department, Kansas State Historical Society, Topeka.

Corporation Charters. Records Compiled by the Secretary of State, Kansas. 24 vols. Archives Department, Kansas State Historical Society, Topeka.

County Organization Census, Ford County, Kansas, October 21, 1872. Archives Department, Kansas State Historical Society, Topeka.

Deposition of James H. Cator, October 11, 1892. Indian Depredation Case No. 4601. Photocopy, Panhandle-Plains Historical Museum, Canyon, Texas.

Enlistment Record, Company Muster Rolls, and Medical Director's Office Records, Little Rock, Arkansas. National Archives, Washington, D.C.

Gould, Charles N. *The Geology and Water Resources of the Eastern Portion of the Panhandle of Texas.* U.S. Geological Survey, Water Supply and Irrigation Paper No. 154. Washington: Government Printing Office, 1906.

Kansas State Censuses of 1875, 1885, and 1895. Microfilm, Library, Kansas State Historical Society, Topeka.

Miscellaneous Plat Book, U.S. Land Office, Dodge City, Kansas. Archives Department, Kansas State Historical Society, Topeka.

Official Plat Records (Cadastral Survey), Office of the Bureau of Land Management. Microfilm, Archives Department, Kansas State Historical Society, Topeka.

U.S. Bureau of the Census. Census of 1880.

U.S. Congress. House. *Offers for Carrying the Mail*, 46th Cong., 2d sess., 1879–80. House Executive Documents.

U.S. Congress. House. "Report of the Postmaster-General," *Annual Report*, 42d Cong., 2d sess., 1872.

U.S. Congress. House. "Report of the Postmaster-General," *Annual Report*, 47th Cong., 2d sess., 1882.

U.S. Congress. House. A. M. Gibson, *Report of the Attorney General on the Star Mail Service*, 47th Cong., 1st sess., 1881–82.

U.S. Congress. Senate. "Report and Map of the Route from Fort Smith, Arkansas to Santa Fe, New Mexico, Made by Lieutenant Simpson." In *Report from the Secretary of War*. 31st Cong., 1st sess., 1850. S. Exec. Doc. 12.

INTERVIEWS

Anshutz, Mr. and Mrs. M. W., by J. Evetts Haley, June 16, 1937. Earl Vandale Collection, Barker Library, University of Texas at Austin.

Brainard, Ed, by J. Evetts Haley, June 17, 1937. Earl Vandale Collection, Barker Library, University of Texas at Austin.

Bussell, R. ("Dick"), by J. Evetts Haley, July 19, 1926, June 8, 1934. Nita Stewart Haley Memorial Library, Midland, Texas.

Chamberlain, Mrs. B. W., by Willie Newberry Lewis, May 1, 1935. Interview Files, Panhandle-Plains Historical Museum, Canyon, Texas.

Coffe, Woods, Jr., by C. Robert Haywood, July 20, 1983.

Dicken, John L., by Linnaeus B. Ranck, January 4, 1938. Indian-Pioneer History, Foreman Collection, XLV: 461–63, Oklahoma Historical Society, Oklahoma City.

Dobbs, Garrett H. ("Kid"), by John L. McCarty, October 20, 1942. John L. McCarty Papers, Amarillo Public Library, Amarillo, Texas.

Gerlach, George, by Olive K. Dixon, November 9, 1922. Interview File, Panhandle-Plains Historical Museum, Canyon, Texas.

Haile, Lew, by Boone McClure, March 11, 1959. Interview File, Panhandle-Plains Historical Museum, Canyon, Texas.

Harrison, Billy R., by C. Robert Haywood, June 11, 1982.

Hayes, Mose, by J. Evetts Haley, June 10, 1930. Earl Vandale Collection, Barker Library, University of Texas at Austin.

Haywood, Louis, by C. Robert Haywood, November 5, 1974.

Howe, Arthur N., by John L. McCarty. General West Panhandle File, John L. McCarty Papers, Amarillo Public Library, Amarillo, Texas.

Ingerton, Harry, by J. Evetts Haley, June 27, 1937. Nita Stewart Haley Memorial Library, Midland, Texas.

Jones, Alma, by J. Evetts Haley, December 13, 1936. Untranscribed notes, Nita Stewart Haley Memorial Library, Midland, Texas.

Judy, Mr. and Mrs. Tom A., by C. Robert Haywood, July 6, 1982.

Le Fors, R. A., by J. Evetts Haley, October 24, 1925. Panhandle Notes, II, Nita Stewart Haley Memorial Library, Midland, Texas.

Lewis, Willie Newberry, by M. V. Sanders, August 26, 1935. Panhandle-Plains Historical Museum, Canyon, Texas.

Lieneman, P. T., by Linnaeus B. Ranck, January 28, 1938. Indian-Pioneer History, Foreman Collection, Oklahoma Historical Society, Oklahoma City.

McClure, Boone, by Lew Haile, March 11, 1959. Interview File, Panhandle-Plains Historical Museum, Canyon, Texas.

McCormick, Dave R., by J. Evetts Haley, March 2, 1935. Earl Vandale Collection, Barker Library, University of Texas at Austin.

Manning, Sam, by Linnaeus B. Ranck, November 5, 1935. Indian-Pioneer History, Foreman Collection, CVIII: 62–65, Oklahoma Historical Society, Oklahoma City.

Mooar, J. Wright, by J. Evetts Haley, April 11, 1936, July 28, 1937. Nita Stewart Haley Memorial Library, Midland, Texas.

———, by J. Evetts Haley, March 2–4, 1939. W. S. Campbell Collection, Western History Collection, University of Oklahoma, Norman.

Reynolds, S. P., by J. Evetts Haley, July 18, 1934. Untranscribed Notes, Nita Stewart Haley Memorial Library, Midland, Texas.

Strickland, Mrs. I. T., by Herbert Rogers, September 13, 1937. Indian-Pioneer History, XLV: 467, Oklahoma Historical Society, Oklahoma City.

Webster, A. H., by J. Evetts Haley, April 9, 1927. Nita Stewart Haley Memorial Library, Midland, Texas.

White, J. Phelps, by J. Evetts Haley, January 15, 1927. Panhandle Notes, II, Nita Stewart Haley Memorial Library, Midland, Texas.

CORRESPONDENCE

Anshutz, M. W., to George Root, August 11, 1939. Anshutz Correspondence. Manuscript Department, Kansas State Historical Society, Topeka.

Archambeau, Ernest, to C. Robert Haywood, September 21, 1983.

Beeson, Merritt, to J. Evetts Haley, February 10, 1936. Nita Stewart Haley Memorial Library, Midland, Texas.

Brown, George W., to William E. Connelley, February 13, March 1, 1926. William E. Connelley Collection, Manuscript Department, Kansas State Historical Society, Topeka.

Carhart, E. E., to J. Evetts Haley, July 20, 1926. Panhandle Notes, I, Haley Collection, Nita Stewart Haley Memorial Library, Midland, Texas.

Collinson, Frank, to Harold Bugbee, February 9, 1937. Bugbee File, Panhandle-Plains Historical Museum, Canyon, Texas.

Griggs, R. W., to George W. Brown, July 1, 1925. William E. Connelley Collection, Manuscript Department, Kansas State Historical Society, Topeka.

Healy, Frank Dale, to Will G. Fields, May 15, 1940. Healy Collection in Western History Collection, University of Oklahoma, Norman.

Hoyt, Henry F., to Charles A. Siringo, June 9, 1921. Panhandle Notes, II, Nita Stewart Haley Memorial Library, Midland, Texas.

Hutchinson, Bettie, to Martha Haywood, July 24, 1899. Possession of Louis Haywood, Emporia, Kansas.

Hutchinson, Elijah, to Martha Hutchinson, April 2, 1882. Possession of C. Robert Haywood.

Jones, Bill, to William C. Griggs, April 9, 1981. Charles E. Jones Papers, Panhandle-Plains Historical Museum, Canyon, Texas.

———, to C. Robert Haywood, July 29, 1983.

Jones, C. E. ("Ed"), to L. F. Sheffy, December 31, 1929. Charles E. Jones Papers, Panhandle-Plains Historical Museum, Canyon, Texas.

Lafebre, E. C., to John D. Miles, June 14, 1874. Indian Archives, Oklahoma Historical Society, Oklahoma City.

Locke, Newt F., to J. Evetts Haley, July 16, 1926. Nita Stewart Haley Memorial Library, Midland, Texas.

Loy, M. H., to J. Evetts Haley, November 1, 1929. Nita Stewart Haley Memorial Library, Midland, Texas.

McCrea, Clayton, to Ernest Cator, Jr., May 16, 1932. Cator Family Papers, Panhandle-Plains Historical Museum, Canyon, Texas.

McKissick, Bernita, to C. Robert Haywood, March 15, 1975.

McMordie, O. R., to J. Evetts Haley, July 19, 1926. Nita Stewart Haley Memorial Library, Midland, Texas.

Mooar, J. Wright, to Andy Johnson, January 20, 1923. Andrew Johnson Papers, Historical Files, Boot Hill Museum Research Library, Dodge City, Kansas.

Munson, W. B., to Laura V. Hamner, June 29, 1921. Interview File, Panhandle-Plains Historical Museum, Canyon, Texas.

Neff, Boss, to His Grandson (Boss Neff II). Tascosa and Related Materials, V, John L. McCarty Papers, Amarillo Public Library, Amarillo, Texas.

Peck, George R., to M. W. Sutton, May 17, 1883. Governors' Correspondence, Archives Department, Kansas State Historical Society, Topeka.

Potter, Jack, to G. A. Root, March 19, 1926. Nita Stewart Haley Memorial Library, Midland, Texas.

Raymond, Henry, to Sadie Raymond, June 28, 1874. Major George W. Baird Papers, Manuscript Department, Kansas State Historical Society, Topeka.

Reynolds, P. G., to Robert Cator & Bro., December 10, 1881. Cator Family Papers, Panhandle-Plains Historical Museum, Canyon, Texas.

Reynolds, Rex, to C. Robert Haywood, September 5, October 16, 1982, September 8, 1984.

Squyres, Fred, to C. Robert Haywood, August 2, 1983.

Wilson, John M., to Robert Cator, April 18, 1879. Cator Family Papers, Panhandle-Plains Historical Museum, Canyon, Texas.

NEWSPAPERS

COLORADO
Trinidad Daily Advertiser
KANSAS
Appleton Era
Ashland Clark County Clipper
Bloom Weekly Telegram
Dodge City Daily Globe
Dodge City Democrat
Dodge City Ford County Globe
Dodge City Ford County Republican

Dodge City Globe Livestock Journal
Dodge City Globe-Republican
Dodge City High Plains Journal
Dodge City Journal
Dodge City Kansas Cowboy
Dodge City Kansas Journal
Dodge City Messenger
Dodge City Times
Englewood Clark County Chief
Fowler City Graphic

Fowler Gazette
Fowler News
Harper Sentinel
Kinsley Mercury
Kiowa Herald
Lawrence Daily Tribune
Lawrence Republican
Leavenworth Daily Commercial
Meade Center Telegram
Meade County Press-Democrat
Meade County Telegram
Meade Globe
Parsons Eclipse
Spearville News
Topeka Commonwealth
Topeka Daily Capital
Wilburn Argus

MISSOURI
Kansas City Evening Star
St. Louis Missouri Democrat

NEW YORK
National Police Gazette

OKLAHOMA
Beaver City Pioneer
Beaver Herald-Democrat
Kingfisher New World
Oklahoma City Daily Oklahoman
Woodward County Journal
Woodward Daily Press

TEXAS
Clarendon News
Fort Griffin Echo
Tascosa Pioneer

EARLY MAPS

Clark County, Kansas. Published by the *Ashland Clark County Clipper*, 1887. Manuscript Department, Kansas State Historical Society, Topeka.

Department of the Missouri, 1877. Sheet 2, New Edition. Lieutenant E. H. Ruffner, Chief Engineer. Panhandle-Plains Historical Museum, Canyon, Texas.

Early Routes and Trails. Delineator W. M. Hutchinson and Compiler G. A. Root. William Allen White Library, Emporia State University, Emporia, Kansas.

Fire Insurance Maps of Dodge City. Sandborn-Perris Map Company, September, 1887. Kansas Collection, Spencer Research Library, University of Kansas, Lawrence.

Free Homes in Kansas. Atchison, Topeka & Santa Fe Railroad, 1872. William Allen White Library, Emporia State University, Emporia, Kansas.

Hemphill County. State of Texas. Austin, Texas, July 1888. Texas State Archives, Austin.

Irrigator Print, Garden City, Kansas. Issued by L. G. Moore ca. 1885.

Kansas Collection, Spenser Research Library, University of Kansas, Lawrence.

Last Buffalo Hunt of Pawnees. Drawn by G. A. Kelly. Oklahoma Historical Society Library, Oklahoma City.

Meade County. Hand-drawn map by M. W. Anshutz, Ney, Kansas, to George A. Root, August 17, 1939. Manuscript Department, Kansas State Historical Society, Topeka.

Moore County, Texas. Trails and Drift Fence. Map in possession of Fred Squyres, Dumas, Texas.

The Official State Atlas of Kansas. Philadelphia: L. H. Everts & Co., 1887. Proposal for a New Road. Cator Family Papers, Panhandle-Plains Historical Museum, Canyon, Texas.

Standard Atlas of Ford County. Printed in Chicago, 1905–1906. Library, Kansas State Historical Society, Topeka.

Surveyor General's Township Maps. Kansas. Secretary of State's Office, Topeka.

Texas Panhandle, Hemphill County Along the Canadian River, 1890. Panhandle-Plains Historical Museum, Canyon, Texas.

THESES

Angell, Ruth Speer. "Background of Some Texas Cowboy Songs." M. A. thesis, Columbia University, 1937.

Gribble, Gerald. "George M. Hoover, Dodge City Pioneer." M. A. thesis, University of Wichita, 1940.

Hughes, William Hankins. "Old Fort Supply." M. A. thesis, Oklahoma Agricultural and Mechanical College, 1941.

Pope, Billy N. "The Freighter and Railroader in the Economic Pattern of Panhandle History." M. A. thesis, West Texas State College, 1956.

Riley, Glyndon M. "The History of Hemphill County." M. A. thesis, West Texas State Teachers College, 1939.

Wiggans, Owen D. "A History of Dodge City, Kansas." M. A. thesis, Colorado State College of Education, 1938.

ARTICLES

Archambeau, Ernest R. "The Battle of Lyman's Wagon Train." *Panhandle-Plains Historical Review* 36 (1936): 89–101.

Arnot, John. "My Recollections of Tascosa Before and After the Coming of Law." *Panhandle-Plains Historical Review* 6 (1933): 58–79.

Bennett, Addison. "Meade County in 1879, Personal Recollections, By A. Bennett, *For the Graphic.*" *Fowler City Graphic*, August 6, 27, September 3, 17, 1885.

Brown, George W. "Kansas Indian Wars." *Collections of the Kansas State Historical Society, 1926–1928* 17 (1928): 135–39.

————. "Life and Adventures of George W. Brown, Soldier, Pioneer, Scout, Plainsman and Buffalo Hunter." Ibid., 98–134.

Byers, O. P. "Personal Recollections of the Terrible Blizzard of 1886." *Collections of the Kansas State Historical Society, 1911–1912* 12 (1912): 99–121.

Cabe, Ernest, Jr. "A Sketch of the Life of James Hamilton Cator." *Panhandle-Plains Historical Review* 6 (1933): 13–23.

Crimmins, Colonel M. L. "Fort Elliott, Texas." *West Texas Historical Association Year Book* 23 (October 1947): 3–13.

Danker, Donald F. "The Influence of Transportation Upon Nebraska Territory." *Nebraska History* 46 (June 1966): 187–209.

Debo, Angie. "An English View of the Wild West." *Panhandle-Plains Historical Review* 6 (1933): 24–44.

Dixon, Olive K. "A Long, Useful Life Ended." *Frontier Times* 3 (November 1925): 33.

Forest, Earle R. "The Killing of Ed Masterson." *Brand Book of the Los Angeles Corral of Westerners* 2 (1949): 154–55.

Gard, Wayne. "The Mooar Brothers, Buffalo Hunters." *Southwest Historical Quarterly* 63 (July 1959): 31–46.

Garfield, Marvin. "Defense of Kansas Frontier, 1868–1869." *Kansas Historical Quarterly* 1 (November 1932): 451–74.

Haley, J. Evetts. "Texas Fever and the Winchester Quarantine." *Panhandle-Plains Historical Review* 8 (1935): 37–53.

Haywood, C. Robert. "Pearlette: A Mutual Aid Colony." *Kansas Historical Quarterly* 49 (Autumn 1976): 263–308.

————. "Uncle Ben's Grove." *Kansas Territorial* 1 (June–July, 1981): 28–30.

————. "The Dodge City War." *Kansas Territorial* 3 (May–June, 1983): 14–20.

Holden, William Curry. "Robert Cypert Parrack, Buffalo Hunter and Fence Cutter." *West Texas Historical Association Year Book* 21 (October 1945): 29–50.

Holt, R. D. "Old Texas Wagon Trains." *Frontier Times* 25 (September 1948): 269–78.

Horton, Louis. "The Star Route Conspiracies." *Texana* 7 (1969): 220–33.

Jackson, Berenice Loyd. "Jones and Plummer Cattle Trail." *Beaver Herald-Democrat* July 24, 1980.

———— and Max Blau. "The Tuttle Trail." *Chronicles of Oklahoma* 56 (Fall 1978): 315–21.

Jacobs, Richard T. "Military Reminiscences of Captain Richard T. Jacobs." *Chronicles of Oklahoma* 2 (March 1924): 9–36.

Kincaid, Naomi H. "Rath City." *West Texas Historical Association Year Book* 24 (October 1948): 40–44.

Kinchen, Oscar A. "The Squatters in No Man's Land." *Chronicles of Oklahoma* 26 (1948): 385–98.

McAllaster, O. W. "My Experience in the Lawrence Raid." *Collections of the Kansas State Historical Society, 1911–1912* 12 (1912): 401–04.

Mendenhall, Ella Wallingford. "Livery Barns." *Ashland Clark County Clipper*, July 2, 1942.

Mooar, J. Wright. "Buffalo Days as Told to James Winford Hunt." *Holland's: The Magazine of the South* 52 (January–September 1933): various paging.

"Old Clark County Ranch Figured in Early History." *Dodge City Daily Globe*, 23, 1935.

Oswald, James M. "History of Fort Elliott." *Panhandle-Plains Historical Review* 32 (1959): 1–59.

Platt, Jeremiah Evarts. "Circuit-Riding in Southwest Kansas in 1885 and 1886." Edited by Louise Barry. *Kansas Historical Quarterly* 12 (November 1943): 378–89.

Raymond, Henry H. "Diary of a Dodge City Buffalo Hunter, 1872–1873." Edited by Joseph W. Snell. *Kansas Historical Quarterly* 31 (Winter 1965): 345–96.

Ricker, Alvin. "Tascosa." *Oklahoma City Daily Oklahoman*, October 26, 1930.

Romero, José Ynocencio. "Spanish Sheepmen on the Canadian at Old Tascosa." Edited by Ernest R. Archambeau. *Panhandle-Plains Historical Review* 19 (1946): 45–72.

Runyon, A. L. "A. L. Runyon's Letters from the Nineteenth Kansas Regiment." *Kansas Historical Quarterly* 9 (February 1940): 58–76.

Schmidt, Heinie. "Early Ford County Settler, Stage Driver." *Dodge City High Plains Journal*, September 4, 1952.

"Seal of Cimarron Territory." *Chronicles of Oklahoma* 35 (Spring 1957): 2–11.

Sheffy, L. F. "Old Mobeetie: The Capital of the Panhandle." *West Texas Historical Association Year Book* 6 (June 1930): 3–16.

Simmons, India H. "Southwest History Corner." *Dodge City Daily Globe*, March 26, 1937.

Skaggs, Jimmy M. "The Route of the Great Western (Dodge City) Cattle Trail." *West Texas Historical Association Year Book* 41 (October 1965): 131–44.

Tennant, H. S. "The Two Cattle Trails." *Chronicles of Oklahoma* 14 (March 1936): 86–108.

Verhegen, Father Boniface, "A Missionary's Trip Through Southern Kansas in 1876." *The Abbey News* 13 (March 1940): 11–12.

Walden, John A. "Mosquitoes Got Scalps in Last Indian Scare," *Dodge City Daily Globe*, January 27, 1940.

———. "Pioneer Postoffices," *Ashland Clark County Clipper*, November 2, 1939.

Webb, J. R. "Chapters from the Frontier Life of Phin W. Reynolds." *West Texas Historical Association Year Book* 21 (October 1945): 110–44.

West, G. Derek. "The Battle of Adobe Walls (1874)." *Panhandle-Plains Historical Review* 26 (1963): 9–12.

Wright, Robert M. "Personal Reminiscences of Frontier Life in Southwest Kansas." *Collections of the Kansas Historical Society* 7 (1901–1902): 47–83.

BOOKS

Aldridge, Reginald. *Life on a Ranch: Ranch Notes in Kansas, Colorado, the Indian Territory and Northern Texas.* New York: D. Appleton, 1884.

Anderson, Charles G. *In Search of the Buffalo: The Story of J. Wright Mooar.* Seagraves, Texas: Pioneer Book Publishers, 1974.

Andrews, Jay S. *History of Bloom, Kansas.* Colby, Ks: Prairie Printers, 1963.

Atherton, Lewis. *The Cattle Kings.* Bloomington: Indiana University Press, 1961.

Barnes, Demas. *From the Atlantic to the Pacific Overland.* New York: D. Van Nostrand, 1866.

Baughman, Robert W. *Kansas Post Offices.* Topeka: Kansas State Historical Society, 1961.

Beggers, Don H. *Shackelford County Sketches.* Edited by Joan Farmer. Fort Griffin, Texas: Clear Fork Press, 1974.

Biddle, Ellen McGovrwan. *Reminiscences of a Soldier's Wife.* Philadelphia: J. B. Lippincott, 1907.

Bigger, Don H. *From Cattle Range to Cotton Patch.* Bandera, Texas: Frontier Times, 1944.

Bratt, John. *Trails of Yesterday.* Lincoln, Neb.: University Publishing, 1921.

Brayer, Garnett M., and Herbert O. Brayer. *American Cattle Trails: 1540–1900.* Bayside, N.Y.: American Pioneer Trails Association, 1952.

Brown, Dee. *Bury My Heart at Wounded Knee.* New York: Holt, Rinehart & Winston, 1970.

Brune, Gunnar. *Springs of Texas.* 2 vols. Fort Worth, Tex.: Branch-Smith, 1982.

Burright, Orrin Ulysses. *The Sun Rides High.* Quanah, Texas: Pioneer Woman Publishing, 1973.

Callison, John J. *Bill Jones of Paradise Valley, Oklahoma.* Chicago: M. A. Donahue, 1914.

Carriker, Robert C. *Fort Supply, Indian Territory: Frontier Outpost on the Plains.* Norman: University of Oklahoma Press, 1970.

Carter, Robert G. *On the Border with Mackenzie.* Washington, D.C.: Eynon Printing, 1935.

Cather, Willa. *My Ántonia.* Boston: Houghton Mifflin, 1918.

Chesley, Hervey E. *Trails Travelled; Tales Told.* Edited by Byron Price. Midland, Texas: Nita Stewart Haley Memorial Library, 1979.

Chrisman, Harry E. *Lost Trails of the Cimarron.* Denver: Swallow Press, 1961.

Collins, Dennis. *The Indians' Last Fight or The Dull Knife Raid.* Girard, Ks.: Press of the Appeal to Reason, ca. 1915.

Cook, John R. *The Border and the Buffalo: An Untold Story of the Southwest Plains.* Edited by Milo Milton Quaife. Chicago: Lakeside Press, 1938.

Custer, George Armstrong. *My Life on the Plains.* Norman: University of Oklahoma Press, 1962.

Dary, David A. *The Buffalo Book: The Saga of an American Symbol.* New York: Avon Books, 1975.

De Arment, Robert K. *Bat Masterson: The Man and the Legend.* Norman: University of Oklahoma Press, 1979.

Dixon, Olive K. *Life of "Billy" Dixon.* Dallas: Southwest Press, 1927.

Dunn, M. H., ed. *Early Lincoln County History*. Sanford, Ky.: Privately printed.

Dykstra, Robert R. *The Cattle Towns*. New York: Atheneum, 1979.

Eggenhofer, Nick. *Wagons, Mules and Men*. New York: Hastings House, 1961.

Einsel, Mary. *Kansas: The Priceless Prairie*. 1976.

Faulk, Odie B. *Dodge City: The Most Western Town of All*. New York: Oxford University Press, 1977.

Fife, Austin E., and Alta S. Fife. *Cowboy and Western Songs*. New York: Clarkson N. Potter, 1969.

Gard, Wayne. *The Chisholm Trail*. Norman: University of Oklahoma Press, 1954.

———. *The Great Buffalo Hunt*. New York: Alfred A. Knopf, 1959.

Gregg, Josiah. *The Commerce of the Prairies*. Edited by Milo Milton Quaife. Lincoln: University of Nebraska Press, 1967.

Haley, J. Evetts. *Charles Goodnight: Cowman and Plainsman*. Norman: University of Oklahoma Press, 1936.

———. *The XIT Ranch of Texas*. Norman: University of Oklahoma Press, 1967.

Haley, James L. *The Buffalo War*. Garden City, N.Y.: Doubleday, 1976.

Halsell, H. H. *The Old Cimarron*. Lubbock, Texas: Privately printed, 1944.

Hamner, Laura V. *Short Grass and Longhorns*. Norman: University of Oklahoma Press, 1943.

Hansford County Historical Commission, comp. *Hansford County Texas, 1876–1879*. Lubbock, Texas: Craftsman Printers, 1980.

Hecht, Arthur, comp. *Postal History in the Texas Panhandle*. Canyon, Texas: Panhandle-Plains Historical Society, 1960.

Herron, Jim. *Fifty Years on the Owl Hoot Trail*. Edited by Harry E. Chrisman. Chicago: Swallow Press, 1969.

A History of Beaver County, Cimarron Territory. 2 vols. Beaver, Ok.: Beaver County Historical Society, 1971.

A History of Lipscomb County. Compiled by Lipscomb County Historical Survey. 1976.

History of Miami and Roberts Counties. 1976.

Holden, William Curry. *Alkali Trails or Social and Economic Movements of the Texas Frontier, 1846–1900*. Dallas: Southwest Press, 1930.

Howe, George Frederick. *Chester A. Arthur: A Quarter-Century of Machine Politics*. New York: Dodd, Mead, 1934.

Hunter, J. Marvin, ed. *The Trail Drivers of Texas*. Comb. ed. Nashville: Cokesberry, 1925.

Jackson, W. Turrentine. *Wagon Roads West*. New Haven, Conn.: Yale University Press, 1952.

Jensen, Merrill, ed. *Regionalism in America*. Madison: University of Wisconsin Press, 1951.

Jones, Dotty. *A Search for Opportunity: A History of Hansford County*. Gruver, Texas: Privately printed, 1965.

Knaplund, Paul. *The British Empire, 1815–1939*. New York: Harper & Brothers, 1941.

Lass, William E. *From the Missouri to the Great Salt Lake: An Account of Overland Freighting*. Lincoln: Nebraska State Historical Society, 1972.

Lewis, Willie Newbury. *Between Sun and Sod*. Clarendon, Texas: Clarendon Press, 1938. Rev. ed. College Station: Texas A&M University Press, 1976.

Lowther, Charles C. *Panhandle Parson*. Nashville, Tenn.: Parthenon Press, 1942.

McCarty, John L. *Maverick Town: The Story of Old Tascosa*. Norman: University of Oklahoma Press, 1946.

McGinty, Billy. *The Old West*. Stillwater, Ok.: Ripley Review Publishers, 1936. Reprinted by Redlands Press, 1958.

McGrane, Reginald C. *The Economic Development of the American Nation*. Boston: Ginn and Company, 1950.

Marshall, J. T. *The Miles Expedition of 1874–1875: An Eyewitness Account of The Red River War*. Edited by Lonnie J. White. Austin, Texas: Encino Press, 1971.

Mayer, Frank H., and Charles B. Roth. *The Buffalo Harvest*. Denver: Sage Books, 1958.

Miller, Nyle H., and Joseph W. Snell. *Great Gunfighters of the Kansas Cowtowns, 1867–1886*. Lincoln: University of Nebraska Press, 1967.

Moody, Ralph. *Stagecoach West*. New York: Thomas Y. Crowell, 1967.

Nelson, Oliver. *The Cowman's Southwest*. Edited by Angie Debo. Glendale, Ca.: Arthur H. Clark, 1953.

Nevin, David. *The Expressmen*. New York: Time-Life Books, 1974.

Newsom, D. E. *Kicking Bird and the Birth of Oklahoma*. Perkins, Ok.: Evans Publications, 1983.

Norris, James D., and Arthur H. Shaffer, eds. *Politics and Patronage in the Gilded Age*. Madison: State Historical Society of Wisconsin, 1970.

Norton, David. *Sketches of the Town of Old Town, Penobscot County, Maine.* G. R. Robinson, 1881.

Nye, W. S. *Carbine and Lance: The Story of Old Fort Sill.* Norman: University of Oklahoma Press, 1983. First edition 1937.

Odum, Howard W., and Harry Estill Moore. *American Regionalism: A Cultural-Historical Approach to National Integration.* New York: Henry Holt, 1938.

Oliva, Leo. *Fort Larned on the Santa Fe Trail.* Topeka: Kansas State Historical Society, 1982.

O'Neal, Bill. *Henry Brown: The Outlaw-Marshal.* College Station, Texas: Creative Publishing, 1980.

Perrin, William H. *Kentucky: A History of the State.* Louisville, Ky.: F. A. Battey, 1886.

Pioneer Days in the Southwest: Thrilling Descriptions of Buffalo Hunting, Indian Fighting and Massacres, Cowboy Life and Home Building. Contribution by Charles Goodnight, Emanuel Dubbs, John A. Hart, and others. Guthrie, Ok.: State Capital Company, 1909.

Pioneer Stories of Meade County. Compiled by County Council of Womens Clubs, Meade County, Kansas. Second edition. 1965.

Potter, Jack. *Cattle Trails of the Old West.* Clayton, N.M.: Laura K. Krehbiel, 1935.

Pratt, Richard Henry. *Battlefield and Classroom.* Edited by Robert M. Utley. New Haven, Conn.: Yale University Press, 1964.

Rath, Ida Ellen. *The Rath Trail.* Wichita: McCormick-Armstrong, 1961.

———. *Early Ford County.* North Newton, Ks.: Mennonite Press, 1964.

Rathjen, Frederick W. *The Texas Panhandle Frontier.* Austin: University of Texas Press, 1975.

Richmond, Robert W. *Kansas: A Land of Contrast.* St. Louis: Forum Press, 1974.

Rister, Carl Coke. *Fort Griffin on the Texas Frontier.* Norman: University of Oklahoma Press, 1956.

Robertson, Pauline Durrett, and R. L. Robertson. *Panhandle Pilgrimage.* Amarillo, Texas: Paramount Publishing, 1976.

———. *Cowman's Country: Fifty Frontier Ranches in the Texas Panhandle, 1876–1887.* Amarillo, Texas: Paramount Publishing, 1981.

Roe, Frances Marie Antoinette. *Army Letters from an Officer's Wife, 1871–1888.* New York: D. Appleton, 1909.

Sandoz, Mari. *The Buffalo Hunters.* New York: Hastings House, 1954.

Schmidt, Heinie. *Ashes of My Campfire*. Dodge City, Kan.: Journal Inc., 1952.

Schofield, David F. *W. M. D. Lee, Indian Trader*. Published as Vol. 54 (1981) of *Panhandle-Plains Historical Review*.

Sinise, Jerry. *Pink Higgins, The Reluctant Gunfighter and Other Tales of the Panhandle*. Quanah, Texas: Nortex Press, 1973.

Siringo, Charles A. *Riata and Spurs*. Boston: Houghton Mifflin, 1927.

Skaggs, Jimmy M. *The Cattle-Trailing Industry*. Lawrence: University Press of Kansas, 1973.

Spratt, John Stricklin. *The Road to Spindletop: Economic Change in Texas, 1817–1901*. Austin: University of Texas Press, 1970.

Stanley, F. (Stanley Frances L. Crocchiola). *Rodeo Town: Canadian, Texas*. Denver: World Press, 1953.

Strate, David K. *Sentinel to the Cimarron: The Frontier Experience of Fort Dodge, Kansas*. Dodge City, Kan.: Cultural Heritage and Arts Center, 1970.

Sullivan, Dulcie. *The LS Brand: The Story of a Texas Panhandle Ranch*. Austin: University of Texas Press, 1968.

Sullivan, Frank S. *A History of Meade County, Kansas*. Topeka, Kan.: Crane & Company, 1916.

Texas Almanac. Galveston, Texas: W. Richardson, 1880.

Texas Business Directory for 1878–1889. Austin, Texas: Shaw and Blaylock, 1878.

Thomas, Myrna Tryon. *The Windswept Land: A History of Moore County, Texas*. Dumas, Texas: Privately printed, 1967.

Van Sickel, S. S. *A Story of Real Life on the Plains Written by Capt. S. S. Van Sickel*. Ca. 1890.

Vestal, Stanley. *Queen of Cowtowns: Dodge City*. Lincoln: University of Nebraska Press, 1952.

Walker, Henry Pickering. *The Wagonmaster: High Plains Freighting from the Earliest Days of the Santa Fe Trail to 1880*. Norman: University of Oklahoma Press, 1966.

Watkins, Ethel Etrick. *Annie: Child of the Prairie*. Lake Village, Ark.: Prairie Printers, 1975.

Webb, Walter Prescott. *The Great Plains*. New York: Grosset and Dunlap, 1931.

White, Lonnie J., ed. *Old Mobeetie, 1877–1885: Texas Panhandle News Items from the Dodge City Times*. Canyon, Texas: Panhandle-Plains Historical Society, 1967.

Winther, Oscar Osburn. *The Transportation Frontier: Trans-Mississippi West, 1865–1890*. New York: Holt, Rinehart and Winston, 1964.

Wright, Robert M. *Dodge City: The Cowboy Capital and the Great Southwest.* Wichita, Kan.: Eagle Press, 1913.

Young, Frederic R. *Dodge City: Up Through a Century in Story and Pictures.* Dodge City, Kan.: Boot Hill Museum, 1972.

Younger, Nettie M. *The History of My Pioneer Mother.* Privately printed, 1973.

Zelinsky, Wilbur. *The Cultural Geography of the United States.* Englewood Cliffs, N.J.: Prentice-Hall, 1973.

Index